Keep
the
Change

KEEP THE CHANGE

A Clueless Tipper's Quest to Become the Guru of the Gratuity

STEVE DUBLANICA

An Imprint of HarperCollinsPublishers

Author's note: I have changed the names of some establishments mentioned in this book. I have also changed the names of some individuals and modified identifying features, including physical descriptions, of other individuals to preserve their anonymity. In some cases, composite characters have been created and timelines have been compressed or altered to further preserve anonymity and to mantain narrative flow. The goal in all these cases was to protect people's privacy without damaging the integrity of the story.

HarperCollins books may be purchased for educational, business, or sales promotional use. For information, please write: Special Markets Department, HarperCollins Publishers, 10 East 53rd Street, New York, NY 10022.

FIRST EDITION

Library of Congress Cataloging-in-Publication Data has been applied for.

ISBN 978-0-06-178728-7

11 12 13 14 15 OV/RRD 10 9 8 7 6 5 4 3 2 1

TO ROBERT B. PARKER

"WE'D BE FOOLS NOT TO."

Contents

Keep the Change

'm sitting in a darkened corner of a Las Vegas strip club where a young woman is grinding her shapely rear end into my lap.

The girl is blond, beautiful, and, with the exception of her dental floss excuse for a G-string, completely naked. As she rubs against my crotch, the normal physiological reaction you'd expect to happen happens. Sensing the increase in vascular pressure, the girl arches her back, tilts her head rearward, and smiles.

"You like that, baby?" she purrs.

"Uh-huh," I reply, struggling to maintain cognition in the face of diverted blood flow.

"Where you from, baby?" the stripper says, her voice modulated in a good-girl-gone-bad falsetto.

"New York City," I lie.

"Ohhhhh, I love New York. I go there all the time."

"It's . . . a great town."

"Which part of New York do you live in?"

"The Lower East Side."

"I love the East Side," the girl says, twitching her hips from side to side. I have a funny feeling that if I had told this girl I was from Bayonne, I'd have gotten the same enthusiastic reaction.

"I go to the East Side whenever I'm in New York," she says. "It's my favorite part of town."

"Lots of good restaurants near Alphabet City."

A momentary shadow of confusion passes across the dancer's face. This girl's never heard of Alphabet City. The odds are good she's never even been to the Big Apple. But that doesn't surprise me. An exotic dancer once told me never to believe a word they say.

The girl hops off my lap, turns around, and straddles me. Leaning forward, she puts her arms around my neck and pulls my face to her chest. Her breasts smell like a mix of deodorant and baby powder.

"So, what brings you to Vegas, baby?" she asks. "Business or pleasure?"

"Business" is my muffled reply.

"But you're getting some pleasure in anyway," the stripper says. "You bad, bad boy."

"Ummmph!"

"What kind of work you do?"

"I'm"—can I really be saying this?—"I'm a writer."

"Really!" she says, her face registering surprise. "What do you write about?"

"Right now I'm writing a book about tipping."

The stripper laughs. For the first time I spot the real woman shrouded beneath the dim lights, makeup, and attitude. "My god," she says. "I should be in your book. I could tell you some stories."

"You *are* going to be in my book."

"Really?"

"Yep. It's about everybody who works for tips—you know, waiters, bartenders, bellhops, strippers . . ."

"How interesting," she says, undulating her body like a snake. "I think writers are sooo sexy."

"On behalf of my profession, I thank you."

"So, you're here doing research on little ol' me?" She starts to bounce up and down in my lap.

I tilt my head back against the wall and think it may be time to leave the stripper to perform her erotic ministrations.

"Yeah. You could say that."

I'm a stranger in a strange land doing strange things with strange people. It's my first visit to Las Vegas and the city's seductive undertow is tugging on my psyche. If you've got the money, Las Vegas offers you the chance to take a vacation from yourself and become an entirely different person. I've been here three days and I'm smoking cigars and drinking martinis at ten in the morning—stuff I never do at home. Since the moment I got off the plane, the town's marketing phrase—"What happens in Vegas stays in Vegas"—has been hissing in my ear like a sibilant entreaty from the serpent in the Garden of Eden. Those mystics from the Bible were right: you'll always find temptation in the desert.

As the strip club's high-wattage stereo system blasts music at levels guaranteed to induce hearing loss, the dancer, sensing I'm a derriere kind of guy, reverses position and recommences rubbing her bottom against my pants. Watching shadow and light play on the dragon tattoo running down the length of her spine, I feel my head start to spin. For the millionth time since I arrived in Sin City, I wonder, "How in the world did I end up here?"

The answer is simple. I'm on a journey to become a guru of the gratuity, a master of the art of the tip. My quest began on a sweltering day in August, months ago, when I accompanied my parents to a county fair in the hinterlands of Pennsylvania. After several hours of drinking beer, eating funnel cakes, and perusing prize-winning hogs and heifers, I had to take a leak. The fairground's bathroom was housed in a squat concrete building that looked like it could double as one of Saddam

Hussein's command bunkers. The interior was dark, hot, and filthy, and it reeked from the urine puddling on the floor. Holding my nose, I went in and relieved myself. Then, as I zipped up my fly, washed my hands, and turned to leave, I spotted an old man sitting in a folding chair and holding a plastic bucket. The crude cardboard sign at his feet read "TIPS APPRECIATED" in blocky Magic Marker letters.

I'd encountered bathroom attendants before, at nightclubs and high-end restaurants, but inside the restroom at a half-ass county fair? I had no idea what to give this man or even if I should give him anything. Overwhelmed by anxiety and embarrassment, I fished a dollar out of my pocket and dropped it into the old man's bucket.

"Thank you, sir," the man said, beaming. "You have yourself a lovely day."

"Um . . . you, too," I mumbled.

As I walked back out into the oppressive heat I shook my head. Why should I have left that guy a tip? What service did he provide that warranted a dollar from my pocket? He didn't offer me a towel, comb, condoms, or breath mints like restroom attendants do inside Manhattan's finer nightclubs. No service was provided that merited compensation, much less a gratuity. The more I thought about it, the more it bothered me.

Then I realized I was pissed because I hadn't known what to do. And that surprised me. You see, I wrote a book about waiting tables, called *Waiter Rant*, in which I complained that ordering from a waiter was one of the most taken-for-granted experiences in modern life. We do it so often that we often don't think about it. During my restaurant career I noticed that in those unguarded, autopilot moments when customers interacted with servers they often let their hidden prejudices, beliefs, and character flaws slip Freudianly to the surface. Here's a nifty example. One time a group of my friends came to have dinner at my restaurant while I was working. They're nice people— they're good to their children, arrange church bake sales, and call their mothers once a week. But the moment their butts hit the banquette I saw a side of them I had never seen before. Taking an almost perverse pleasure in seeing me in what they thought was a subservient role, they transformed into haughty, arrogant, demanding customers who ran me ragged the whole evening. For the duration of their meal I was just a functionary in the fulfillment of their gustatory desires. I had ceased to exist. That evening, I learned a lot about how my friends view the world. And that was the closest I ever came to hocking sputum into somebody's food.

Of course I had customers who behaved beautifully, too. Once, when a drunk was insulting my maternal lineage, a male patron offered to help me bodily eject the intoxicated miscreant from the premises. I declined his offer, but it was nice to know that he had my back. After I shut the drunk up by threatening him with a visit from the local constabulary, the male patron's wife congratulated me, saying, "Good for you. You shouldn't have to take that crap from people." That couple got free shit up the wazoo.

But the ultimate indicator of what customers thought about me came when it was time to leave the tip. That's right: The almighty gratuity, the big payoff. How I made my living. The reason I was *there*. Like the manner in which you order from a waiter, how you tip says a lot about who you are. It reveals your attitudes about money, how you spend it, your views on labor and class, whether you're generous or stingy, in the know or just plain ignorant. During my time as a waiter, I was always surprised how people tipped. Grouchy old slobs would leave me 30 percent, while well-dressed yuppie couples who sang my praises would leave a dollar. I took a crack at explaining how and why people tipped waiters in *Waiter Rant*, and it should come as no surprise that gratuities were one of the most controversial and talked-about parts of that book. (Well, the whole "dropping fart bombs on customers" thing raised a few eyebrows, too.)

After *Waiter Rant* hit bookstores and while the publicity tour was in full swing, I was interviewed by countless newspapers, radio shows, and television programs. Heck, I was even on *Oprah*. But no matter whom I talked to, the hottest topic always concerned tipping. And because of all that media exposure, people began to consider me an expert on the subject. One newspaper went as far as to call me a "tipping guru." All of this came back to me when I emerged from that sweltering bathroom in Pennsylvania. In that moment, I realized that I was nothing of the sort—that when it came to gratuities, I was in the dark. I might be called a tipping guru, but in my heart of hearts I knew I was as clueless about tipping as everyone else.

Gratuities in this country are a gigantic pain in the ass. A largely under-the-table, unregulated practice that accounts for a bit less than one half of 1 percent of America's GDP (approximately $66 billion!), tipping causes no end of confusion, anxiety, and anger for both the tipper and the tippee. Who gets a tip and who doesn't? How much should you leave? Can you break a twenty and ask for change? Should I tip the professional movers who lugged my new couch up the stairs, or just say thanks? How much should I tip the young delivery guy who brought my burrito or Pad Thai? Should I tip the gas station attendant pumping fuel into my car in the middle of an ice storm? What should I give my building's doormen at Christmas? Should the owner of the hair salon get a tip? And what should I tip the waiter if the service sucks?

Fear of what will happen if we're stingy with our tips stalks us throughout everyday life. Will the waiter I stiffed add a gob of spittle to my entrée? Will the doorman misplace my dry cleaning or discuss my love life on the Internet? Will the barber mess up my hair? Will I get whole milk instead of soy in my chai latte, or will my decaf lose the de-? Am I hurting people's feelings if I tip too little or too much? Do people who tip well get better treatment than those who don't? Is that fair? Or does tipping, as Eleanor Roosevelt once said, "add to the reputation Americans have for trying to buy their way into everything"?

With all the anxiety surrounding tipping, it's a miracle people leave their homes at all. When you think about it, tipping is a transaction within a transaction, an informal economy within a formal one. You're paying on top of something you've already paid for, almost like a *tax*. Who decided that, and why? Our country might have been founded on the principle of "no taxation without representation," but if Thomas Jefferson rose from the dead, bought a double mocha latte at Starbucks, and saw the tip jar, we might have another revolution.

Meanwhile, "tip creep," the solicitation of gratuities by professions that did not seek them before, is only fueling our social anxiety. Sure, there has always been a class of service workers who've received gratuities—bellhops, taxi drivers, porters, hairdressers, waiters, and so on. But now workers in professions that never sought tips before have their itching palms held out in record numbers. When I bought a hot dog near the Port Authority in Manhattan a few months ago, I was stunned to see a Styrofoam cup marked TIPS perched on top of the vendor's aluminum cart. Pizza parlors and ice-cream shops now sport guilt-inducing tip jars marked MONEY FOR COLLEGE, and gratuity receptacles are cropping up at the drive-thru windows of fast-food joints. And let's not even talk about the economic dissonance many of us experience when dropping that dollar into the jar at Starbucks. How did this come about? And how can people navigate the minefield that is tipping in this country and stay sane?

Standing outside that fetid bathroom in August, I decided to discover what tipping was all about. I'd explore the history of gratuities, examine their economic impact, explore what it was about tipping that made people anxious and pissed them off, and help them figure out how to tip with a clear and informed conscience. If people were calling me a tipping guru, I might as well earn the title. And if I really wanted to become the Jedi Master of the Tip, I knew I'd have to plunge headfirst into the devil's den itself: Las Vegas. Go figure: strippers work for tips, too.

*   *   *

Back in the strip club, I sip my fourth vodka martini of the evening and watch as the dancer's sinuous body writhes in the darkness. I'm three thousand miles from home, and nothing is familiar. I feel lonely. Sensing that something's amiss, the stripper turns around and gently brushes her breasts against my face. Even though I don't know this woman from Eve, I find her touch and smell very comforting. Of course I know her attentions are a purchased illusion, but, hell, I'll take it. It's only money.

Then I remember what brought me to Vegas in the first place. I'm on a quest. I lean back in my chair, focus my mind, and look into the stripper's eyes.

"So, honey," I say, "what do you think about tipping?"

"Oh, baby," she says, running a finger across my lips. "Do I have a story to tell you!"

CHAPTER 1

American Monster
A Brief History of Tipping

Before I get to the strippers, let's try to answer a basic question: Just how much of the American economy is tied up with tipping, and how did it get that way? Before I begin recounting my quest, you need to know how much cash we're talking about here.

So how much money do Americans plunk down in tips every year? It would be nice if I had a clear answer, but when I started delving into the numbers and statistics I got thoroughly confused. (I knew I should have paid attention in math class.) In desperation, I asked Michael Lynn, a professor at the Cornell University School of Hotel Administration, to help me out. He has been studying tipping for years and has written dozens of papers on the subject. He told me that no one really knows how much Americans spend on gratuities—probably because tipped workers have an unfortunate tendency to underreport their income to the IRS. No surprise there. I know several waiters who've had their paychecks garnisheed by the taxman. In fact, the only income that's more underreported than tips is money earned from illegal activities. I guess drug dealers, pimps, and crime syndicates don't know how to use Quicken software either. But Dr. Lynn gave me some guidance to help me formulate a halfway decent ballpark answer.

In 1982 the IRS commissioned the Survey Research Institute at the University of Illinois at Urbana-Champaign to study tipping. The study is a bit dated, but the most striking feature of that report is its conclusion: that waiters rake in 70 percent of *all* tips paid out in the United States. Using that 70 percent as a starting point, let's fast-forward to 2009 and extend the definition of "waiter" to include not only servers working in full-service eateries but also those employees in snack bars, coffee shops, bars, taverns, and hotel restaurants who also get tips. According to the National Restaurant Association, 2009 sales at these establishments totaled almost $248 billion.

If we multiply that $248 billion by the average tip percentage American waiters receive, we'll come up with a rough estimate of what they're tipped per year. Dr. Ofer Azar, an economics professor in Israel who's also written extensively about tipping, believes this average tip percentage to be 18.8. Dr. Lynn, citing research that shows people often tip a higher percentage on lower bills, thinks Azar's figure skews too high and suggests the tip percentage to be a more modest 15. Using both men's numbers to represent the lower and upper range, we can roughly estimate that American servers make between $37.2 and $46.6 billion a year in tips. And since the Survey Research Institute thinks American waiters get 70 percent of the American tip kitty, if we divide those figures by 0.7, we can estimate that all the tipped workers in the United States pull down somewhere between $53.1 and $66.6 *billion* a year in gratuities. Now, I'm not claiming these numbers are precise, but they give us a rough idea of the amount of money involved.

For the sake of argument, let's pick the larger of the two figures and say that American workers make about $66 billion a year in tips. That's almost one half of 1 percent of the U.S. gross domestic product. That doesn't sound like a lot until you realize that's as much scratch as Bill Gates and that rich Swede who owns IKEA have, *combined*. With that kind of money you could buy Uncle Sam fourteen Nimitz-class aircraft carriers *per year* and still have enough cash left over to buy a small island nation. Americans tip a lot of fucking money.

So how many Americans work for tips? Again, hard-and-fast figures are not easy to come by. But if you go to the Bureau of Labor Statistics website and add up all the occupations that receive gratuities as part of their compensation—waiter, hotel maid, food delivery person, etc.—you can estimate that roughly 5,021,890 workers are hustling for tips, give or take a few. That's more than 3 percent of the entire American workforce, more than twice the size of the entire U.S. military!

So tipping is a huge deal in the United States. But it wasn't always that way. True, records dating back to 1772 show that Thomas Jefferson tipped his slaves. And even George Washington, the guy whose face gets stuffed into millions of outstretched hands (and plenty of tight G-strings) every day, tipped his brother-in-law's servants in 1768. But in the average commercial life of the United States during the Revolutionary period, tipping was virtually unheard of. So how did tipping get so entrenched in American culture? Before setting out on my quest, my history teacher father advised me, "If you want to know where you're going, you have to know where you've been." That's right, everybody, it's time for a history lesson. Don't worry. I'll try to keep it short.

Some scholars argue that tipping originated in the Middle Ages. During feudal times, when lords and ladies traveled dirt roads frequented by wealth-redistribution advocates dressed in green tights and armed with longbows, they'd toss these guys a few coins to ensure their own safe passage. If you've ever ridden on the New York City subway and paid a bum to leave you alone, you know this dynamic is alive and well today. Other scholars believe that tipping began when those feudal lords started giving money to their subjects in recognition of good deeds, to tide them over during times of economic hardship, or as recompense for accidentally burning down their thatched-roof hovels. So tipping began as a type of charity. In fact, the Persian word *baksheesh*—which means to give alms, to express gratitude, to venerate, or to bribe—also means "to tip." Tipping today is all those things.

In the West, the earliest examples of tipping demonstrated a form of "trickle-down economics," with the aristocracy passing money down to the lower classes. And by the time Henry VIII was busy contracting syphilis in the 1530s, visitors to private homes in England had gotten into the habit of tipping their hosts' servants in exchange for services above and beyond their normal duties. Thus establishing, according to Kerry Segrave in his book *Tipping: An American Social History of Gratuities,* "the idea that a tip was given for something extra, either service or effort."

It wasn't long before this system of tipping the host's servants, a practice known as giving "vails," started to take on a life of its own. Much to the consternation of the upper classes, footmen, valets, and other household servants began to expect their vails as a matter of course, not as a reward for service beyond the call of duty. So when his lordship's guests were getting ready to leave after a week in the country, they'd find themselves surrounded by a cadre of servants with their hands out. And if you didn't pay, it wasn't uncommon for your horse to suddenly develop a sprain, your tapestries to go missing, or a footman to mutter he'd drop "gravy on your breeches." Seems like punishing bad tippers started at the tradition's inception. Scullery maids probably spat in their lordship's tankards of mead.

Things got so bad that the gentry whined that it was getting too expensive for them to visit their inbred brethren, and they lobbied to have vails abolished. Some of them even suggested that masters raise their servants' wages to make up for the shortfall. But these early attempts to corral tipping didn't go over well, even causing the servants to riot on occasion. Lest you think the vails benefited only the servants, it should be noted that noblemen scammed the system, too. Shifty aristocrats eager to make a buck started fleecing their royal brethren by throwing large parties, with cheap entertainment to keep the overhead down, and then profited by seizing a percentage of the vails their servants received. Though the giving of vails was controversial and often a target of reform, the tradition survived to varying degrees well into the twentieth century. And by the time the sun set on the British Empire, the descendants of these cranky dukes and earls discovered that if they wanted to hang on to their drafty manors, they'd have to open them up to the unwashed masses and sell tickets at the door. Now, that's ironic.

Tipping didn't stay down on his lordship's farm for long. As Europe began adopting a capitalist industrial economy, two things started happening: the number of common folk willing to be servants for the aristocracy decreased, and people flush with higher wages flocked to the cities, where they used restaurants, hotels, and mass transportation. It was then that the vail system mutated into the practice of tipping the help in restaurants and hotels. As more people became able to afford these new luxuries, they encountered more and more servants looking for tips. Whereas tipping was once an issue for wealthy people, the newly emergent middle class discovered that they now had to grease the palms of waiters, maids, and stablemen, just like their titled predecessors. Not everyone was happy with this development. After dining in a restaurant in the middle of the nineteenth century, the Scottish critic Thomas Carlyle wrote, "The dirty scrub of a waiter grumbled about his allowance, which I reckoned liberal. I added a sixpence to it, and [the waiter] produced a bow which I was near rewarding with a kick. Accursed be the race of flunkeys!" Did Carlyle have a bad attitude toward his waiter because he was an asshole? Because he was Scottish? No. He had a bad attitude because he was a snob.

The tasks people performed for their old bosses under the vail system—carrying bags, waiting tables, emptying chamber pots—were deemed menial labor and far below the dignity of the ruling class. So, when the gentry's former peons started having a few crowns in their pocket, they in turn began to view people who worked for tips in commercial settings as beneath them. This dynamic doesn't surprise me. Human beings have always had an innate need to feel like they're one rung above the next guy on the social ladder. When capitalism started making inroads and fewer people toiled inside castles, a void appeared and a new servant class had to be created to fill it. Aping their aristocratic forebears, the new middle class just had to have servants of their own. There's an old saying: "Somebody has to dig ditches." Well, someone always has to be the whipping boy; somebody always has to be the slave.

So from the very start of tipping, people viewed giving gratuities as an economic transaction that flowed from the socially superior downward. And if you don't think this attitude is still prevalent today, you're smoking crack.

So, just how did the word *tip* wiggle its way into our lexicon? One popular myth suggests it originated in the eighteenth century in a London coffee shop patronized by the writer and dictionary man Samuel Johnson. As the story goes, the Fleet Street shop's employees would put small bowls on the tables marked with the message, "To Insure Prompt Service," and the customers would periodically throw in a few coins to keep the java flowing. According to this etymological urban legend, people took the first letter of each word in the phrase and reduced it to the acronym TIPS.

The use of the word *tip* actually predates Samuel Johnson's coffee shop by at least a couple of centuries. As far back as 1509, Albrecht Dürer, the German painter and printer, wrote a letter asking one of his customers to give his apprentice a *trinkgeld*, or tip. And the *Oxford English Dictionary* gives four uses of the word *tip* prior to Johnson. The 1933 edition of the OED defines the verb *tip* as "to bestow a small present of money upon (an inferior), esp. upon a servant or employee of another, nominally in return for a service rendered or in order to obtain an extra

service," or as a slang term that originated among thieves meaning to "pass from one to another," like a stock tip or a racing tip.
So, sorry folks, you can't lay blame for the word *tip* at the feet
of those proto-baristas.

I think the word *tip* got its start in bars. Feeling guilty that
some poor bar wench was working while they were having fun,
patrons would assuage their conscience by tossing her a few
coins so she could buy herself a drink after work. Don't we
often tell modern bartenders, "Hey, have a drink on me"? And
the fact that the word *tip* is associated with boozing it up in
so many languages seems to support this theory. The French
word for tip is *pourboire*, from *pour boire*, or "for drinking."
The Spanish counterpart, *propina*, comes from *propinar*, or
"invite to drink," and the German *trinkgeld* and the Danish
drikkepenge translate into "drink money." If that's not enough
to convince you, the word *tip* translates into "drink money" or
its near equivalent also in Bosnia, Croatia, the Czech Republic,
Finland, Iceland, Israel, Kazakhstan, Latvia, Sweden, and even
Vietnam. The word *tip* could also be the short form of the word
tipple, which means to drink—often to excess. And if you saw
how waiters use their tips to get hammered after a shift, you'd
probably lean toward this explanation of the word's origins.

So, if tipping started in the Old World, how did it end up
in the New? It certainly didn't come over on the *Mayflower*,
if that's what you're thinking. Prior to the Civil War, tipping
was rare in America, a fact that caused no small amount of
amazement to European travel writers of the day. Ofer Azar
suggests that this might have been because America did not yet
have a large servant class, and waiters and coachmen considered
themselves employees and so were not interested in tips. But
when newly rich Americans started traveling to Europe in ear-
nest after the Civil War, they brought the practice back home to
show their friends how cosmopolitan and au courant they were.
But we also have to remember that post–Civil War America rapidly became a major industrial and economic world power. And

as its citizens began earning higher wages, just like their European counterparts, they suddenly had more discretionary income to spend at hotels, in restaurants, and in the new railroad system crisscrossing the United States. But it was when employers discovered that they could use gratuities to pay their workers lower or even no wages at all that tipping really took off.

The company that may have been most responsible for the ubiquity of tipping in America is the Pullman Palace Car Company. Founded by George Pullman in 1867, the company built and staffed luxurious sleeping cars that enabled passengers to ride the country's expanding railroad system in comfort and style. To cater to these passengers in the decades after Emancipation, the company hired thousands of ex-slaves to work as porters. By the early 1900s, Pullman was the largest employer of black people in America. But George Pullman wasn't exactly a civil rights leader, mind you. Always seeking to bolster his bottom line, he paid his workers low wages and forced them to rely on tips to survive. And if a porter complained about his compensation, he could quickly find himself out of a job. After the Financial Panic of 1893, a time when many businesses found themselves unwilling to pay any semblance of a living wage, and cut jobs and salaries to keep profits as high as possible, the Pullman Company led the way in 1894 by slashing its employees' wages by 30 percent. Eventually Pullman's workers went on strike, and, with support from the American Railway Union, led by Eugene Debs, paralyzed the nation's railways. This caused President Grover Cleveland to send in the army to bust the union, resulting in the deaths of thirteen strikers. After George Pullman died in 1897, the new president of the company was even more antilabor and wage-stingy than his predecessor. The Pullman Company is one of the earliest examples of a large American company using gratuities to subsidize its workforce olster its bottom line. In 1915 the Pullman Company em- 500 porters, who made $27.50 a month in wages—bad back then. If the porters hadn't received tips, the company would've had to increase their wages to $60 a month just to keep them above subsistence level—which would have added $2,535,000 a year to Pullman's payroll costs. There wasn't a snowball's chance in hell of that ever happening. And even with their tips, Pullman's porters never came close to making $60 a month.

The Pullman Company shafted their porters because they were poor, black, and easy to exploit. If you think I'm exaggerating about this racist attitude, just read what a Pullman executive said when asked why his company exclusively hired blacks from the South: "The southern Negro is more pleasing to the traveling public," he said. "He is more adapted to wait on people and serve with a smile." And if that wasn't bad enough, the company cynically made sure its passengers knew the porters were underpaid and depended on tips to survive. This led the *St. Louis Republic* to editorialize, "Other corporations before now have underpaid their employees . . . but it remained for the Pullman Company to discover how to work the sympathies of the public in such a manner as to induce the public to make up, by gratuities, for its failure to pay its employees a living wage." The editorial concluded, "It was the Pullman Company which fastened the tipping habit on the American People and they used the Negro as the instrument to do it." And can you guess the name of the guy who succeeded Pullman and continued to slavishly force thousands of African American men to rely on tips? Robert Todd Lincoln, the son of the Great Emancipator himself, Honest Abe. You can't make this stuff up.

Since we're on the subject of Abe Lincoln, let me put forth a pet theory of mine. Prior to the signing of the Emancipation Proclamation, tipping was rare in this country. But a scant fifty years after the Thirteenth Amendment was enacted, five million American workers were making between $200 million and $500 million in tips. In other words, it took centuries for tipping to develop in Europe, but when it got to America it exploded

Ebola virus. Why did that happen? Azar, the economics ssor, is somewhat incorrect in his suggestion that America didn't have a large servant class prior to the Civil War. Sure we did—we had slaves. But after they were freed there was suddenly a dearth of cheap labor, and something had to fill the vacuum. And that something was tipping. So when the traveling upper classes imported this nouveau riche habit from Europe, employers such as Pullman were quick to realize they could play on public sympathy to use gratuities to shift part of their payroll burden onto the backs of the American consumer. And since the public had already been conditioned by centuries of slavery to having low-cost servants in their midst, the stage was set for tipping to take hold. It should come as no surprise that the first workers forced to depend on gratuities were ex-slaves. And when millions of immigrants began crashing onto America's shores in the late 1800s—becoming waiters, barbers, bellhops, and the like—the new system of tipping was in place to exploit them.

Equating the sudden rise of tipping with the end of slavery may sound controversial, but I'm not the only one who sees this correlation. In 1916 William Rufus Scott, in his antitipping book *The Itching Palm*, wrote, "If it seems astounding that this aristocratic practice should reach such stupendous proportions in a republic, we must remember that the same republic allowed slavery to reach stupendous proportions." Bill and I are on the same page here. "Whereas the form of servitude is different," Scott goes on to write, "the slavery is none the less real in the case of the tip taker."

Still, tipping wasn't exactly welcomed with open arms. Believing this aristocratic practice was antithetical to the egalitarian ideals of our Founding Fathers (conveniently forgetting that they not only owned slaves, but tipped them!), some do-gooders openly agitated against the practice. In the late nineteenth and early twentieth century, antitipping leagues with names like the Society for the Prevention of Useless Giving, the Anti-Tipping Society of America, and the Commercial Travelers National

League, called upon hotel owners and restaurateurs to end this "pernicious practice" and start paying their workers a living wage. And while some establishments experimented with service charges and "tipless" restaurants and hotels, they were not exactly keen on the idea. "Please do not tip unless you feel like it," one such "reforming" hotelier wrote in a circular he gave out to his guests. "But, if you do tip, let your tipping be yielding to a genuine desire—not conforming to an outrageous custom." Sounds kind of wishy-washy to me.

To be fair, I'm sure some of those owners were genuine in their high-minded ideals—but I suspect most of the others were not. Tipping was popular not just because it allowed operators to lower labor costs, but also because it gave them an opportunity to line their own pockets! Remember how those dukes and earls in Europe stole vails from their servants? The same thing started happening the moment tipping appeared in America. Take bellhops in New York City hotels in the early 1900s, for example. Back then most hotels didn't keep bellhops on the payroll to take care of the guests' luggage; they outsourced the work to a private contractor, a head porter, who supplied all the baggage carts and hired the personnel. So the bellhops worked for the head porter, not for the hotel. The head porter paid the bellhops a measly twenty-five dollars a month to work twelve-hour days and provided them meals from the hotel restaurant. In return, however, the bellhops were forced to give the head porter *all* the tips they received from guests—even though the guests operated under the assumption that the bellhops kept the money. If a bellhop kept a tip or committed the faux pas of handing a tip to the head porter in front of a guest, he could be fired. This cozy arrangement allowed the head porter to make scads of money while his workers toiled for less than a dollar a day. Eventually the bellhops got sick of this system, unionized, went on strike, and forced hotels to put them on the payroll and let them keep their own tips.

Another tip-stealing scam occurred in hotel coatrooms. In

1906, outside concessions would pay hotels more than $300 a month to check guests' hats and coats, and in return, the concessionaire got to keep all the tips the checkers collected. Again, guests tipped a coat-check girl assuming she would keep the gratuity. But just like those head porters, the concession owners were keeping all the tips for themselves and paying the girls a pittance. As Segrave notes, in order to make sure they Hoovered up every last nickel, it was a common practice for owners to give an appointed "head" a leather pouch in which he or she would deposit all the gratuities received for checking coats and hats. This head also spied on the coatroom workers to ensure that every dime they got in tips went into the pouch. Nice, huh? What would they have thought about video cameras? And if this wasn't enough, they issued the girls uniforms with no pockets so there was no chance they could squirrel away a tip. I hope some of them stuck coins in their bras.

The same greedy shenanigans occurred in restaurants. In the 1920s, waitresses at Alice Foote's McDougall Coffee Shop in New York not only received no wages, but they had to pay the establishment ten dollars a week for the privilege of working there, and subsist on tips alone. By the time they paid out their weekly bribe, they had little left for themselves. Some restaurateurs helped themselves to all the waiters' tips and paid them back a fraction of what the customers gave them. The practice became so pervasive that in 1939 the state of Nevada passed a law requiring employers who took tips given to workers to publicly post signs to that effect.

While modern labor laws are a bit fuzzy, it's generally illegal for tips to be diverted from workers who earn them to pay the wages of those who don't. For example, in many states it's verboten for a restaurant to use a portion of their servers' tips to pay individuals not directly involved with waiting tables. But it happens all the time! I know a restaurant in New Jersey where the owner uses the threat of termination to force his waiters to kick back a percentage of their gratuities to the kitchen staff. And I know another well-regarded restaurant just outside New York City where the owner paid his brother's managerial salary by giving him a full cut from the waiters' tip pool. Both of these owners flagrantly violated their states' labor laws. The practice of tipping gives unscrupulous owners the chance to "double-dip." Not only are their labor costs reduced, but some owners have come to regard tips as their own personal revenue stream. Starting with felonious nobility in the Middle Ages to restaurants today, wherever you find gratuities you'll find criminality. This reality led antitipping crusader William Rufus Scott to write, "Tipping is the training school of graft."

Realizing they weren't going to make any inroads with hotel and restaurant owners, the antitipping wonks did what any self-respecting fringe group does: they used the political system. At first they had some success. Political figures such as President William Howard Taft became the "patron saint" of the antitipping crusade, and before long the states of Arkansas, Iowa, Mississippi, South Carolina, Tennessee, and Washington had all passed laws prohibiting employees from accepting or soliciting gratuities. In some localities it was illegal for a customer even to try *giving* a tip. If you tipped a waiter in Tennessee in 1915 you could be fined twenty-five dollars! But the business owners bitched and lobbied their representatives, and by the late 1920s all these laws were off the books. They would never return. And the antitipping leagues? They faded into obscurity.

It is no surprise that many tipped workers weren't keen on surviving on tips. In 1909 unionized waiters in New York decided to fight the practice of tipping by refusing gratuities and insisting on being paid a minimum wage of $2.50 a day. And in 1911 the International Hotel Workers Union went on record demanding "higher wages and no necessity of depending on tips." Of course all this talk meant management would have to pay their employees more money, which, not surprisingly, they were unwilling to do. They had gotten used to the free lunch and

/eren't budging. So the waiters were caught between a rock and a hard place. If they didn't accept tips out of pride but weren't paid a living wage, they'd go hungry. So, economic pressure forced them to accept gratuities. "The tip makes of you a malicious, envious hateful creature," one agitated waiter remarked. "But we cannot do away with it just yet." Samuel Gompers, the legendary union leader, applauded these servers' efforts, claiming that waiters who still wanted to work for tips had the moral makeup of "pirates."

I think early efforts to curtail tipping failed for two reasons. For one thing, many customers *liked* giving tips. America has always deluded itself into believing it is a classless society. Not so. The nation may have outlawed royal titles at its founding, but we quickly replaced titled peerages with the aristocracy of wealth. Remember, tipping began its rise during the Gilded Age, a time when men like John D. Rockefeller, Andrew Carnegie, Andrew Mellon, and John Pierpont Morgan were treated like rock stars—the Bill Gateses and Warren Buffets of their day. (In fact, if you adjust for inflation, they had even more money than Bill and Warren!) Americans were in love with money. And just like our celebrity-crazed culture today, people back then, even if they didn't have the resources of a Morgan or Rockefeller, wanted to lead rock-star lives. Tipping can give people the momentary illusion that they belong to a higher class of people. This drove William Rufus Scott *crazy*. "Tipping, and the aristocratic idea it exemplifies," he wrote, "is what we left Europe to escape." He added: "In a republic where all men were supposed to be equal, some cannot be superior until they grind other men into dust. Tipping comes into a democracy to provide that relation."

The other reasons the effort to curtail tipping failed is much simpler: fear and sympathy. Revenge against bad tippers didn't end with footmen spraining horses or dripping gravy on some wigged fop's breeches. Early waiters were quick to develop the time-honored practices that modern servers still use to admonish parsimonious customers today—insolence, bad service, seating people by the toilet, losing reservations, and throwing bad tips back at them. By 1918, Chicago waiters had gotten into the habit of slipping "Mickey Finns," composed of antimony and potassium tartrate, into the food and drink of bad tippers, a concoction that caused headaches, nausea, dizziness, depression, vomiting, and, in at least three cases, death! The mere suggestion of vengeance is the waiter's personal nuclear option. Fear keeps the masses in line and paying up.

Also, Americans are a generous people. And when they realized that workers depended on tips to survive, this was a direct challenge to their sense of generosity. Many people tip out of sympathy for the workingman, and companies such as Pullman exploited that sense of compassion. As giving gratuities became an established custom, customers—whether they liked tipping or not—wanted to avoid appearing mean-spirited and cheap, so they ponied up.

So, snobbery, fear, and sympathy burned tipping into the American psyche as a social norm a century ago. And publishers of the era printed countless etiquette books and tipping guides, further fixing the practice in the public's mind.

Still, despite tipping's widespread acceptance, Americans have always been ambivalent about it. Even after antitipping laws and organizations got tossed onto the dust heap of history, media outlets continued to rail against the giving of gratuities. In 1925 the *New York Times* wrote that "a stranger coming to New York on business considers life here to be one tip after another," and declared that hoteliers and restaurateurs had no one to blame but themselves, as it was "they who have helped build up the tipping idea." And in 1946, *Life* magazine editorialized, "The old thin dime isn't what it used to be. A national nuisance should be eliminated." Calling tipping a modern evil, the editorial stated that tipping "tends to stratify the social structure. It places a price tag on servility—or scurrility." "A worse indictment of tipping," the editorial went on to say, "is the fact it causes living standards of large and important groups of workers to reflect with immediate and often acute sensitiveness every fluctuation in the state of business. One day waiters and redcaps, barbers and bellboys are princes—the next, paupers." Oh, man, I know that dynamic well.

Tipping aggravates people like nobody's business, and it sells papers. This frenzy has taken on a whole new life with the Internet. And while countless websites have been created by servers to promote good tipping habits, there are just as many websites and blog posts that slam the practice. Just look at this random posting from 2009:

> I hate tipping . . . Tipping is stupid. Think about it.
> Restaurant employees get paid a b.s. salary because
> the employers expect them to make up the remainder
> of their salary based on tips. That is ridiculous. How
> about Applebees or whatever mom-and-pop eatery you
> go to pay its employees a full wage be it the minimum or
> higher that's their business, and stop expecting ME to
> pay their employees' salaries.

The sentiments expressed in that post echo the opinions penned by those old newspapermen in the first half of the twentieth century. Like bell-bottoms and platform shoes, anger over tipping has become fashionable again.

Ambivalence about tipping was present at the start and is still very much with us today. Many of us who say we're good tippers secretly loathe those tip jars. And the same old games are still being played. Tipped workers are still getting ripped off, and just like Carlyle back in the 1800s, many people look upon tipped workers as inferior beings. Whether it's emptying chamber pots or waiting tables today, nothing much has really changed.

Today, tipping is a multibillion-dollar monster with millions of people in its clutches. Taking root in the post-slavery economy of the Gilded Age, it was fertilized by exploitation, confusion, resentment, and avarice, and it spread like a virulent weed in less than fifty years. We took an Old World tradition and turned it into something bigger and badder than our European cousins could ever have imagined. Now tipping is a huge part of the American economy—but we still view it with deep ambivalence. That's not surprising: we started out as an ambivalent country. At our founding we declared that "all men are created equal," but we still kept other people as property. Today we have a black president, but about 24 percent of African Americans still live below the poverty line. We have always been good about having two minds about something and living with the tension that creates. The same applies to tipping.

As I start my journey toward tipping guruhood I feel like I'm standing on the edge of a dark and dangerous wood. Tipping is an undiscovered country, a frontier poorly understood and barely mapped out. What will I find? Will I like what I see? Will people really tell me what they think about tipping? I can't shake the feeling that a creature of unimaginable power lies in wait to devour me. Taking a deep breath, I strap on my sword and, like Beowulf, Frodo, or Luke Skywalker before me, leap headfirst into the cloud of unknowing.

CHAPTER 2

The Crucible
Waiters, Waitresses, and Maître d's

"Tipping is an interesting behavior," Michael Lynn has written, "because tips are voluntary payments given after services have been rendered. Consumers rarely pay more than necessary for goods and services. Tipping represents a multibillion-dollar exception to this general rule. It is an exception that raises questions about why people tip."

Dr. Lynn is right: tipping is a weird economic transaction. How many of us walk into a department store and say, "Hey! I'll pay you twenty percent extra for that coat!" If anything, we try to pay less. We wait for sales, haggle and use coupons, but normally we'll never pay a penny over retail. And why should we? But that's what we do every time we leave a tip on a restaurant table or in a tip jar. We pay *extra*.

So why do we pay extra? Why do we tip? I was a waiter for almost nine years and, to be honest, I haven't got a clue. But after slaving in the restaurant trenches there's one thing I do know: *quality of service has almost nothing to do with the tip a server receives*. Any waiter whose IQ hasn't been lowered by alcohol and Quaaludes will tell you that there's no rhyme or reason as to why some customers tip and others don't. I could give one patron incredible service and get two pennies, while with another, I could get his order wrong, insult his heritage, leer at his wife, make fun of his kids, and *still* get 20 percent. Customers who looked like they had scads of money used to stiff me, while people with dirt under their fingernails and bad manners would give me the best tip of the night. If tips were based solely on the quality of service, waiters would have gone extinct long ago.

According to a Zagat survey, 80 percent of Americans prefer leaving a voluntary gratuity instead of paying a fixed service charge because they believe tipping offers an incentive for waiters to provide good service. They believe that "extra" they're paying rewards the quality of the service they receive. But that's not actually the case. There is a correlation between service quality and tip, but that correlation is very small. How small? After studying customers' tipping behaviors extensively, Dr. Lynn came up with this statistical gem. "If zero means no relationship and one means a perfect relationship," he said, "then the correlation between service and tips is 0.2. A lot closer to zero than to one." Having flunked statistics in college, I asked Lynn to dumb it down for me. "Put another way," Lynn said, "service has no more effect on the tip than how sunny it is outside."

I know, I know. Right now you're shaking your head and saying, "If the service is good, I tip. If the service sucks, I don't." But that's not what happens. In 1997 two researchers named Bodvarsson and Gibson surveyed five restaurants to see how service quality affected tips. After they crunched the numbers, they noted that the customers who ranked the service highest increased their tips by only a measly 0.44 percent of the bill. When you're a waiter, that's chump change. And it tells servers that no matter how hard they hustle, their service has a negligible effect on their tip.

Of course some studies argue that good service increases tips. In one 2003 study, researchers asked customers to rate servers on a service scale of 1 to 5. They found that each point on this service scale increased a waiter's tip by 1.49 percent of the bill size. Restaurant patrons used this scale to score servers in five areas: appearance, knowledge, friendliness, speed of service, and attentiveness. Speed and friendliness added to a waiter's tip percentage, but appearance and attentiveness had no statistically significant effect. And a server's knowledge actually *reduced* his tip, causing Israeli economist Ofer Azar to note in his paper "The Social Norm of Tipping: A Review," "The latter result is surprising, as it suggests that diners tip less when they consider their waiter more knowledgeable."

I think Azar is on the money here. Despite the fact that I knew my restaurant's menu like the back of my hand, many of my customers got annoyed when they realized I knew more about the food than they did. And whenever I gently corrected a customer when he or she mispronounced a menu item, my tip was sure to go south. I guess some people want their waiters speedy and friendly but distracted and stupid. I attribute this aggravating effect to the thousands of "foodies" spawned by that marketing colossus called the Food Network. After watching chefs such as Bobby Flay, Mario Batali, and Emeril Lagasse work their considerable magic on the boob tube, these culinary geeks automatically assume they're culinary experts.

If you ask restaurant patrons why they've left a bad tip, they will almost always say, "Because the service was bad." But social scientists will tell you that people are piss-poor when it comes to identifying the causes of their own behavior. When customers say they gave a bad tip because of poor service there might be just a little bit of self-justification going on. It's much easier and less embarrassing to lay blame for bad tipping at the waiter's feet than to admit, "I didn't tip because I was broke," ". . . I got into a fight with my boyfriend," ". . . the server didn't give me her phone number," or ". . . I'm a raging asshole."

When Zagat stated that 80 percent of Americans believe service quality affects their tip, you have to remember that these people weren't asked that question with a waiter hovering over them, check in hand. It was asked as a hypothetical question, safe from a server's malevolent gaze. But when people are faced with the actual reality of leaving a tip, their behavior is quite different. An online poll at the website Tipping.org posed this question: "Do you feel pressured to tip at a restaurant even if you feel you received bad service?" Seventy percent of the 3,332 respondents answered yes. And since people hate feeling pressured and embarrassed, you'd better believe they cave and leave a tip despite getting bad service. So, there's a chasm between what people think about gratuities and what they actually tip. And in all my years as a server, no patron ever told me, "I'm giving you a bad tip because your service sucked." Most customers just don't have the balls.

That's why restaurant customers get so agitated at tip time. If tipping were something as straightforward as rewarding or punishing service quality, it'd be a no-brainer. There'd be no cognitive dissonance. There'd be no worrying. You'd put as much thought into the tip as you would paying a highway toll. Tipping should be easy, but it's not. Why people tip the way they do is a question that has bedeviled researchers for years. But when waiters are getting shitfaced at the local watering hole after work, they love to postulate their own alcohol-and-benzodiazepine-infused theories.

PEOPLE TIP BECAUSE THEY HAVE TO

Tipping a waiter in the United States is a social norm. Okay, this isn't some alcoholic waiter theory. In fact, many social scientists think this is a big reason why people tip. In case you forgot Sociology 101, social norms are the rules for how people should act in a given group or society. These norms are either internalized, so you obey them without regard to reward or punishment, or they're enforced by positive or negative sanctions from without. For example, unless you're a U.S. senator, striking up a conversation with a guy taking a dump in the public bathroom stall next to yours is considered a no-no. American society has been saying that waiters should get tips for well over a hundred years. It's a social contract. When you don't tip, you run the risk of social opprobrium (your waiter gobbing in your food; your date thinking you're a cheap bastard) or inner guilt and shame. Since most of us like to go along to get along, we leave a tip—even when the waiter sucks.

PEOPLE TIP TO REDUCE SERVER ENVY

You're enjoying yourself while the waiter's working. You don't want the server to be envious, so you tip him, in effect saying, "I'm having a good time and you're not. Here's some money so you can do what I'm doing later." Remember how *tip* in most languages translates into "drink money"? Trust me, after dealing with the dining public, a waiter requires vast quantities of mind-numbing alcohol.

PEOPLE TIP TO AVOID JUDGING

After a hard day's work you don't want to deal with troubling issues like evaluating the quality of a waiter's service. You're in a restaurant to enjoy some down time, not act like a judge on *American Idol*. Many restaurant patrons are Paula Abdul types who exclaim, "I love you! You're wonderful!" no matter how much the service stinks. But then there's always the occasional prick who thinks he's Simon Cowell.

PEOPLE TIP BECAUSE THEY'VE "BEEN THERE"

You know what it's like to work for a living. You know waiters make less than minimum wage, and so you tip accordingly, even extra. In my experience, bartenders, waiters, taxi drivers, beauticians, construction workers, self-made millionaires, and Mafia guys are the best tippers.

PEOPLE TIP TO FEEL GENEROUS
Let's face it: most of us like to be perceived as generous. It's a pleasant feeling. And human beings often repeat behaviors that make them feel good. So, yes, I'm saying generosity is a bit like crack.

PEOPLE TIP BECAUSE THEY FEEL GUILTY
A waiter is your temporary servant. Many customers, usually whiny, neurotic liberals, are uneasy with this perceived power differential and they tip to make themselves feel better out of bourgeois guilt.

PEOPLE TIP TO GAIN THE WAITER'S APPROVAL
This amazes people, but it's true. When I was a waiter, my MO was to treat customers with a delicate blend of polite indifference and friendly arrogance. People like to be liked, so when a waiter plays hard to get, that often increases a customer's desire to win his approval. Waiting tables can be a real mind game, and servers aren't above engaging in psychological warfare.

PEOPLE TIP TO SHOW OFF
Some people tip to impress their friends, get laid, assert their social status, or proclaim what a big set of balls they have. That's not surprising—in this age of reality television, many people like to act as if they're rock stars. The entire cast of *Jersey Shore* is indicative of this phenomenon.

PEOPLE TIP BECAUSE THEY'RE SMART
Dr. Lynn may have stated that service quality affects tips only 2 percent of the time. But tips affect a waiter's

perception of the patron *100 percent* of the time. Good
tippers get extra attention, the best seat in the house,
and loads of free shit. Bad tippers get seated next to
the toilets, find themselves shut out on Valentine's Day,
never get anything gratis, and are left wondering why
the waiters sneer at them.

Interestingly enough, Dr. Lynn stated that tipping is found
in countries with high levels of extroversion and neuroses. And
guess which nation ranks number one in both categories? The
good ol' USA.

The fact that service has such a small effect on tipping has serious implications for the restaurant industry. Very often waiters and restaurant managers will look at tip percentages as an
evaluation of performance. If a waiter's tips hover near 20 percent, he must be doing something right. But if he has a low tip
percentage, he must be a fuckup. Many waiters and managers
fall into this mode of thinking, but they're operating from a
false premise. I can't tell you how many times I've seen excellent
servers go home at the end of the night with no money in their
pocket while some cocaine-snorting, unhygienic, socially inept
server rakes in all the cash. Waiters love to crow about how
much money they make, thinking it's a testament to their professionalism. It isn't. Very often it's merely the luck of the draw.

Basically a waiter's compensation depends on unseen mental
processes going on inside the customer's head. And like ancient
cave dwellers who didn't understand that the sun is a gigantic fusion reactor ninety-three million miles away, and instead
turned it into a deity worthy of human sacrifice, waiters have
tried wrapping their heads around the mystery of tipping by
cooking up some pretty interesting metaphysical systems.

Just like our god-fearing Stone Age forebears, servers can be
a pretty superstitious lot. For example, it's taboo for a waiter to

remark, "We're going to be busy tonight," because his fellow servers will then say, "Thanks a lot, asshole. Now the restaurant will be dead." Waiters believe that statements like that are akin to telling an actor "Good luck" instead of "Break a leg." Another example of this irrationality is the old waiter axiom "You can never make good tips two nights in row." In an effort to protect themselves emotionally from the vagaries of tipping, waiters will often turn to concepts like karma, or regard tipping as some kind of deity. I've heard waiters blame the "table gods" after a crappy shift or pray to Lady Luck, the God of Tipping, or the Lord of the Gratuity to get them through their shift. And there were quite a few times I saw servers ready to ritually sacrifice a busboy so they could make the rent.

A smart restaurateur knows that tips aren't a reliable indicator of a server's prowess. A savvy operator evaluates his waiters by a different set of criteria. First off, does the server embody the owner's philosophy? Danny Meyer runs a topflight chain of restaurants and his mantra is to create a warm, inviting, and hospitable environment for all his guests. You might be an über-tip-making machine, but if you violate Danny's tenets you'll be out of a job. Another sign of a good waiter is that she establishes relationships with her customers and creates a stable of regulars—people who specifically ask for that server whenever they come in to dine. And the biggest determinant of a good waiter is how much product he sells. Tips don't go into honest owners' pockets, but the profits from the sale of food and wine do. So the best way to evaluate a waiter's performance is from his sales figures—not his tips.

Many restaurant owners, however, are dysfunctional idiots. Sadly many have ulterior motives regarding servers' tips because they're stealing them! Tip theft is *rampant* in the restaurant industry. In New York State it's illegal for a restaurant operator to divert tip money to individuals who do not directly work with the tables. You know, people such as mistresses, bookies, and drug dealers. In 2009, for example, the *New York Post* reported that Sparks Steak House in Manhattan paid $3.15 million to settle a class-action lawsuit that charged that the restaurant "illegally deducted money from the 'tip pool' which was supposed to be shared among about 60 waiters to pay other workers, including bartenders, the pastry chef, the wine-cellar master and banquet manager." That's a no-no. As Lou Pechman, the attorney who filed the Sparks lawsuit, told me, tip and wage theft is so prevalent in New York City that the town has become "one giant piñata" for lawyers like him.

Some restaurateurs have tried to remove the uncertain customer variable by instituting a service charge. On the surface it sounds like a good idea. Just slap an automatic 18 to 20 percent charge on every check and give that money to the waiters. Thomas Keller instituted this system in his restaurants, and it has worked very well. But that's because Keller operates a first-class business that charges very high menu prices, has good quality control, and is able to give servers goodies like salaries, health benefits, and sick and vacation days. Most restaurants are small operations that can't hope to compete with a restaurant in Keller's class.

You'd think waiters would like the security a service charge might bring to their income, but you'd be wrong. Waiters are like gamblers. They love holding out for a windfall: the chance that some amazing customer will drop a $500 tip in their lap. They're also keenly aware that some restaurateurs will keep part of the "service charge" to pad their profits and then stiff the servers. But the greatest reason servers don't like service charges? Taxes.

Waiters have to pay taxes only on the tips they report, and when you're dealing with cash, it's very easy to hide what you actually make. I know servers who have reported $26,000 a year in tipped income when they actually raked in $50,000. This makes sense, because the IRS believes that less than half of all tip income is actually reported. That's billions in tax revenue lost every year! And if a restaurant goes over to a service charge, then Uncle Sam will scrutinize every penny of a waiter's income. For most waiters, the less the IRS knows, the better. Tipping helps facilitate income tax evasion. Hey, it's not just for rich guys with bank accounts in the Cayman Islands.

In any case, most waiters don't keep all the tips they receive. Tip pooling, in which waiters throw all the tips they earn into a kitty and divide them up evenly at the end of the night, is common throughout the restaurant industry. It bugs the hell out of me. When you bust your butt and earn $300 in a night and have to share it with some lazy-ass who generated only $75 in gratuities, you can understand some waiters' displeasure. So-called pool houses work only when they are well-run restaurants employing careful supervision to ensure that all the servers are pulling their own weight. But in a restaurant where the manager is extorting bribes, the owner is banging the hostess, the chef is snorting coke, and the prep cooks are throwing thousands of dollars of produce into the backs of their cars, it should come as no surprise that the level of supervision that makes a pool house work is conspicuously absent. I much prefer the system in which a waiter "eats what he kills," keeping the tips he personally makes from his tables.

According to that University of Illinois study, waiters make 70 percent of all the tips paid out in America. So when you think about it, restaurants are the crucible of tipping, the place where most people are first exposed to the practice. But since Americans are a neurotic lot, it's no surprise that we're thoroughly confused about how to tip. And this confusion causes servers to suffer from a psychiatric malady called "waiter nightmares."

Anyone who's ever waited tables has suffered from this condition. Whether you work in a restaurant today or slaved in some country club twenty years ago to pay for college, the odds are good you've suffered from this malady. Like a Jungian archetype, most waiter dreams usually share the same characteristics—the restaurant is immense, the menu is in Cyrillic, and no matter how fast you work you are always hopelessly behind—in a situation waiters call "being in the weeds." At best you wake up from these night terrors mildly annoyed. At worst, you jump out of bed with heart palpitations, a cold sweat, and an impending sense of doom. It's small wonder so many waiters have Xanax in their medicine cabinets.

I think this condition is caused by the fact that a waiter's compensation is at the mercy of those mysterious mental processes that go through a customer's head at tip time. And this sense of not knowing whether you'll make the rent implants a constant feeling of anxiety into a waiter's subconscious, leading to bad dreams. I once had a real doozy, all about customers asking me how they should tip. . . .

It's Saturday night and I'm working in a restaurant the size of Arkansas. Instead of the fine Italian food we normally serve, the bill of fare has shifted to some kind of Ethiopian/Aboriginal fusion cuisine and the chef's special is baked monkey heads with an elephant drool reduction. After somehow managing to feed the thousands of customers the cracked-out hostess seated in my section, I start handing out the checks. And it's then that the customers reveal their ignorance about tipping.

"Here you are, my good man," a customer says, tipping me all of five cents. "Thank you very much indeed."

"Five fucking cents!" I scream. "Where the hell are you from? England?"

"How did you know?" the man says. "Was it my accent?"

"No. It's because you know shit about tipping."

"Now, see here."

I pull a gun out from under my apron and press it against the hapless Brit's head.

"Listen here, asshole," I say. "Unlike your country, waiters in the USA are not paid a salary. We get like four bucks an hour. So if you don't tip me, I don't eat."

"I . . . I . . ." the man says, his sweat dripping on the cold steel of the gun barrel. "I didn't know."

"You're supposed to tip me fifteen to twenty percent of the bill, punk," I say in my best Dirty Harry voice. "And I want it *now*."

After the terrified Englishman forks over my tip, I go to a table of old ladies who are paying with a gift certificate. God, how I hate those things.

"Thank you, waiter," one of the ancient harridans says, handing me some money. "We're all settled up."

I look at the bill. The total was one hundred dollars. They had a gift certificate for fifty bucks, probably given to them by their guilt-ridden offspring. And they've tipped me only $7.50.

"Listen here, Grandma," I say. "When you pay with a gift certificate you're supposed to tip on the whole check—not what's left over afterward."

"You're not a very nice man," she says.

"I'm a waiter, lady. I'm not working here for my health."

"Well, if you think I'm tipping you fifteen dollars, you're insane."

"Fork it over, lady," I say, wondering what the prison term for strangling an old lady would be.

Of course the old ladies complain to the manager on their way out. He pulls me aside to give me a reprimand. But since he's dressed like a demented clown, I run away from him. I hate clowns.

The next table to pay their bill is a four-top of oenophiles who drank $400 worth of wine and ate $60 worth of food. I can tell these people are going to be trouble because they brought in their own set of Riedel wineglasses in those pretentious wicker baskets. And when I see my tip my suspicions are confirmed.

"You tipped me nine bucks on a four-hundred-and-sixty-dollar check! What's the matter with you people?"

"We don't tip on wine, waiter," says the host, a black-turtleneck-

and-Birkenstock-wearing hippie/yuppie hybrid. "How hard is it to open a bottle of wine?"

I take the empty bottle of Barolo and smash it over the man's head, rendering him unconscious. "You're always supposed to tip on wine and booze," I shout at his terrified companions. "Always! If your party was six or more we would've slapped on the gratuity and you would've had to tip on the wine. Why's it different when there's only four of you?" Then I reach into the knocked-out patron's pocket, grab his wallet, and steal the tip he was supposed to have given me—ninety-two dollars. Yeah, I gave myself 20 percent. But it's my dream.

After I deliver a hundred martinis to a table of nuns, a young couple with a little girl waves me over.

"We're all paid up, waiter," the father says. "Thank you."

"I certainly hope you enjoyed everything," I say, observing the mess the girl made at the table. I don't know about you, but I get worried when little kids draw crayon pictures of people stabbing each other all over the tablecloth.

"Yes, everything was excellent," the father says, handing me the bill. "You're the *best* waiter we've ever had."

I groan loudly and flip open the leather-bound check holder. The bill was seventy-five dollars and that's what I got—exactly seventy-five dollars. The dreaded verbal tip has struck again.

"Where's my tip?"

"But we said you're the best waiter we ever had," the mother says indignantly.

"Lady, do you think I can pay my rent by telling my landlord, 'Gee, you're the best landlord I ever had'?"

"Well, I never . . ." the father sputters.

"That's okay," I say, pointing to the parents' demented little girl as she chants, "Redrum! Redrum!" "How much for the little girl?"

"What?" the father shouts.

"How much for the women?" I say, channeling John Belushi.

"Your women. I want to buy your women. The little girl, your daughter . . . sell her to me. Sell me your children!"

The parents hand over the possessed little girl and run out of the restaurant. I give her to the chef and ask him to cook up something special. Yum Yum.

"You can't do that," the crazed-looking clown manager says as he's snorting a line of coke while smoking a joint at the same time. "If you don't watch your step you're gonna get canned."

Beads of nervous sweat run down my back. I need this job. If I lose it I won't be able to pursue my dream of becoming an East German porn star. "Yes, sir," I say humbly. "It won't happen again."

After I deliver four platters of roasted elephant trunk to table 4,034,582, a man wearing a Viking helmet and hosting a party of twelve people signals that he's ready to pay the check. So I go to the register, tack on the 18 percent service charge, and hand him the bill.

"What the hell?" the man shouts. "Why'd you give yourself an eighteen percent tip?"

I explain to the man that because large parties take so long to eat I can't turn his table over to make more in tips. And since his party's been here ten hours, if I get stiffed I'll have worked for free.

"Well, I'm not paying it," Hagar the Horrible growls. "*You're not worth eighteen percent.*"

"Sir," I explain, "legally you don't have to pay a gratuity. But since the menu reads, 'A service charge of eighteen percent will be levied on parties of six or more,' you have to pay it."

"Bullshit!"

"If the bill read 'gratuity,' sir," I explain calmly, "then you'd be within your rights not to pay it. But since we call it a 'service charge,' it's part of the bill. If you don't pay it it's considered theft of service."

"Whatcha gonna do," Hagar says, "take the money from me?"

"Heavens no, sir. That's what the police are for."

Suddenly a heavily armed SWAT team rappels down from the ceiling, hogties all the customers, and hurls them into the paddy wagon waiting outside.

"While you're at it," I say to one of the balaclava-covered troopers. "I'd check out the guy dressed in the clown suit. He's got weed! He's got weed!"

"Thanks, man," the officer says, racking his shotgun. "We'll get him." Ah, problem solved.

As I run through the restaurant, I'm assaulted with questions from the guests. "Do I have to tip on top of the tax?" No, you don't. But I'll love you if you do.

"Waiter," a woman wearing pearls whines, "should I tip you in cash or on my maxed out credit card?"

"All waiters prefer to be tipped in cash, madam. That way the owner can't steal my tips, and what the IRS doesn't know won't hurt them."

"*I'm* an IRS agent," the woman says calmly. "Didn't you fail to file a return in 1988?"

"Meal's on the house, lady."

Later, as I'm delivering a tray of lizard blood cocktails to a table, a bunch of Arab sheiks eating eel and caribou sashimi wave me over.

"Excuse me, sir," one of the sheiks says. "But how do you tip on sushi?"

"Easy. Tip twenty percent. Leave fifteen percent for the waiter and put five percent in the sushi chef's jar."

"Excellent advice," the sheik says, handing me an emerald the size of my fist. "Thank you very much."

Suddenly a greedy-looking busboy comes running over to me. "I saw that! I saw that! You have to tip out on that!"

The busboy's right. Waiters don't get to keep all the tips they make. We have to tip out busboys, bartenders, hostesses, corrupt managers, and the owner's mistress. I'm lucky if I keep 70 to 80 percent of what I make. But I want to get it on with Ilsa under the klieg lights.

"Oh, yeah?" I say to the busboy, dialing my cell phone. "You have two seconds to forget about what you saw before I call Immigration."

"*La Migra*!" he shouts. "*La Migra*!" causing all the busboys to run out the back door. Shit, now I have to clear all four thousand tables by myself.

As I race through the restaurant I drop a check at a table of four middle-aged women who've been sitting for four days drinking water and lemon, and who shared one small chicken Caesar salad and asked for endless pots of hot water to brew tea bags they'd brought from home. Their check is ten bucks. The tip's a buck-fifty.

"Listen, you cows," I say. "You've been here for four days talking about 'your lives as women.' You know what we call you people! Grazers! Stop chewing your cud and tip me extra for taking up valuable real estate."

Suddenly one of the women morphs into a bovine and says, "Moo."

As the rest of the night rolls on, I answer question after question. Yes, if the owner comps you the bill or another table picks up the check, and if I'm not taken care of, you have to tip me. Takeout? Tip 10 percent. Tipping on a buffet? Well, someone has to clear your dishes and refill your sodas. Fork over 15 percent. Should I grease the maître d's palm to get a good table? That makes you look like a poseur. Most high-class joints know where they're going to plant your ass long before you ever arrive. Do you honestly think they're going to rearrange their carefully crafted seating plan just because you slipped them an Andy Jackson? Get real. And if they skip over people who've made reservations weeks in advance, who else are they screwing?

Finally I get to my last table of the night. It's a redheaded vixen wearing a bikini. "Listen, waiter," she says. "I don't have enough money to leave you a tip. Can we barter or something?"

"What do you have in mind?"

The woman searches through her purse and offers me Valium, marijuana, tickets to a Barry Manilow concert, a purple dildo, and a copy of *Swank* magazine.

"No dice, sister. You can't barter for a tip. I can't pay off my gambling debts with Barry singing 'Copacabana.' "

"How about I give you a blow job?"

"Now we're talking." Hey, I've been known to compromise my principles from time to time.

But just before she can get started, I remember in horror that I forgot to refill the sodas on table seventeen. "You're outta here!" the redhead says, suddenly transforming into my John Wayne Gacy–esque clown manager. "You're fired."

Waking up covered in hives and screaming, I run to the bathroom to upchuck my dinner. Waiter nightmares can be intense.

Later, as I'm pressing my head against the cold porcelain bowl, I think about my dream and wonder why some people tip and some don't. And as the nightmare clears from my head, I realize something more is going on than half-ass theories, casual observations, or science. Something big. Something powerful. Working in a restaurant didn't teach me why people tip, but, unbeknownst to me, all those years taking orders, dealing with customers, and writing about it laid the groundwork for my quest to become a tipping guru. And if tipping is truly a god, just like the Prophet Jacob, he's been speaking to me through visions.

But something tells me Jacob never got cheated out of a wet dream.

CHAPTER 3

House Dick
Doormen, Bellhops, Maids, and Concierges

I love fancy hotels. Holing up in a sexy deluxe suite with one-thousand-thread-count Egyptian cotton sheets, a plasma TV, and a waterfall shower and subsisting on room service is my idea of a good time. Freed from the protean drudgery of making my bed, doing laundry, and scrubbing the toilet, I have more time on my hands—time in which I can liberate those overpriced candies and Lilliputian bottles of booze from my suite's minibar. In a hotel your wish is the staff's command. Want steak and lobster tail at three in the morning? It's there. Need your clothes dry-cleaned? Shoes shined? A shirt mended? Just call the front desk and someone will race upstairs and take care of it for you. All this and tasty little mints on my pillow at bedtime. Being cocooned in the discreet luxury of a fine hotel helps me relax and unwind. It makes me feel like a better person. If I were rich beyond the dreams of avarice I'd book myself into the Waldorf-Astoria and never leave. Some people prefer visiting bucolic bed-and-breakfasts or crashing on friends' couches. Me? I'm a fancy-hotel man. Always have been. Always will be.

There's one thing about a hotel, however, that makes me anxious: tipping. Faced with doormen, bellhops, valets, maids, and mysterious concierges, it can feel like you've wandered onto a tipping minefield, where the slightest misstep will trigger an explosion of awkwardness, bad service, embarrassment, and shame. With all the anxiety the situation can cause, it's surprising maids don't substitute industrial-strength Valium for those nightly mints. Staying in a hotel, even a fancy one, can be anything but relaxing. Happily, all this suffering is unnecessary. If you just take the time to learn the hows and whys of hotel tipping, you'll sleep more soundly in your rented bed.

In my quest to understand all things tipping, I decided to become a house dick. Get your mind out of the gutter, people. We're not talking about penises here. In the 1930s, before the word became associated with genitalia, *dick* was slang for "detective." In the time of Sam Spade and Philip Marlowe, every self-respecting hotel had a "house man," or hotel detective, to provide security. In the hard-boiled parlance of the day, these men were called "house dicks." So, breaking out my trench coat and fedora, I hit the streets and talked up hotel workers at lodgings great and small to find out how to tip whether you're staying at the Trump Plaza International or the Red Roof Inn.

The first person you encounter upon arriving at a fancy hotel is the doorman. Tracing back their lineage to the *iânitors* of ancient Rome, doormen are members of an ancient profession. In fact, up until the early 1970s the position of porter, also known as an *ostiarius*, or ostiary, was the lowest of the four minor clerical orders of the Catholic Church. Today the position is far from religious, but its role remains the same: to man the gate.

"We're the first face you see," Charles, a doorman working at a New York hotel, says to me. "So it's our job to be the friendly, welcoming face of the establishment. We have to make a good impression."

"Do you expect a tip every time you open a door for someone?" I ask.

"Of course not, that's my job. If you want to give me a buck, I'll take it. But it's not expected."

A tall, cheerful-looking fellow with a ready smile, Charles is pursuing a degree in hotel management at night. "I actually prefer working days," he says. "That way I can go to school, and people tend to be better tippers when they check in."

"Why's that?"

"When people are checking in they are usually more generous," he explains, adjusting the brim of his red hat. "Their trip is just starting, they've got cash in their pockets, and they're happy. But when they check out they've just paid a big bill, so they're less likely to tip. I don't like to be here on checkout days, like Sunday. The guests are less likely to be in a giving mood. They're grouchy; they've got to return to reality."

Tipping a hotel doorman is a pretty straightforward affair: just about everything calls for a simple single or two. He's got the big whistle, so if he hails you a cab, slip him one or two bucks. If he takes your bags out of your car and puts them on the luggage cart, tip him a dollar a bag. If you saddle him with a heavy steamer trunk packed for an African safari, however, tip him extra. If there's no bellhop and he runs the bags up to your room, slip him one or two dollars per bag.

"Doormen are also tuned into the local scene," Charles says. "If you want to go to a gentlemen's club, I'll hook you up. I know where all the good bars, nightclubs, and local hangouts are. Just ask me." For this kind of service, Charles tells me, the normal tip is two or three dollars.

"So how do you do here," I ask, "moneywise?" Charles suddenly looks suspicious. I can't blame him. It's not polite to ask people what they make.

"I do okay," he replies. I mentally kick myself. I pushed Charles too fast and he closed down. Bogie wouldn't have been pleased with me. But while my investigative manner leaves much to be desired, I know why Charles had reason to be secretive.

According to Payscale, an online salary database, the average pay for a hotel doorman nationwide is $10.42 per hour. In addition to base salary and benefits, they usually average $5.00

in tips per hour. But the reality is that many doorman make a lot of money off the books. What Charles doesn't know is that I'm wised up to the doorman racket. Some of these guys make a killing.

If you're a doorman at the right hotel, all those dollar bills can really add up. At some high-profile hotels a doorman can clear $80,000 to $100,000 a year. In fact, some front doors in big cities can be so lucrative that when they retire, doormen aren't above selling their positions. And the bidding wars that erupt can be intense. I can understand why people would compete for these seemingly lowly jobs. A guy working a hotel door near Columbus Circle told me he takes home $500 in cash on a good night. "Three hundred on a bad one," he said. Hey, for $300 a night, tax-free, I'll stand out in the freezing cold.

Some doormen augment their income through kickback schemes. "We control the taxis," Ephraim, a doorman at a premier L.A. hotel told me. "We control which taxi gets what passenger. If you want to go ten blocks we'll just hail any old cab cruising by. But if you're going to the airport, we'll put you in a cab we've got an arrangement with."

Many taxi drivers hate wasting time waiting in cab lines only to deliver some lazy-ass passenger ten blocks away. Some would rather make a few lucrative airport runs and long hauls than spend valuable time doing little drives across the city. So to get an edge on the cutthroat competition, some hacks give hotel doormen kickbacks in return for big fares, a practice known as "buying the door." In November 2009, the *Miami Herald* reported that the going kickback rates that Miami hacks doled out to doormen were "eight dollars to Miami International Airport, fifteen to Fort Lauderdale Airport, and three dollars to the Port of Miami." Shocked? You shouldn't be. Money makes the world go round. In his book *Hotel Secrets from the Travel Detective*, Peter Greenberg illustrates how to spot a New York hotel doorman indulging in this practice. Whenever you ask a doorman for a cab, he'll first ask you where you want to go. If it's a short hop, he'll hail a passing cab. But if you want to go to the airport, he'll signal to his buddies waiting in the cab line. If he raises an index finger, that means he's signaling that the fare wants to go to Kennedy. Two fingers means LaGuardia, and three means a nice fat fare to Newark. And the doorman gets a cut, usually five to ten bucks.

Intrigued, I went undercover to see if Greenberg's assertion was true. I waltzed into a Midtown hotel, made chitchat with the front desk, then walked back outside and asked the doorman to hail me a cab. Several taxis were idling in the cab line.

"Where are you going, sir?" the doorman asked.

"Port Authority," I replied, feeling like Serpico.

Just like Greenberg said he would, the doorman stepped into the street and flagged down a passing cab. I tipped the doorman a dollar and went on my merry way. Later that evening, when a different doorman was on duty, I repeated the process. Only, this time, I asked for a cab to Newark Airport. Sure enough, the doorman waved three fingers, and a cab waiting near the entrance slid forward to pick me up. I tipped the doorman and got into the car—and that's when the fun started.

After explaining to the cabbie who I was and what kind of book I was writing, I asked him, "So, how much did you kick back to get this fare?"

"I don't know what you're talking about," the cabbie said in broken English.

"Don't worry," I replied. "I'm not with the Taxi and Limousine Commission. But you bought the door. What's the kickback?"

The driver slowed his rig to the curb and shouted, "Get out of my cab!"

"I'm just trying to . . ."

"GET OUT!" the cabbie thundered, a homicidal gleam forming in his eye. Sigh. I kind of figured that would happen. Maybe

Philip Marlowe would have done a better job. So, the next time you're in a New York hotel, see if the doorman pulls this routine. If he does, it probably means he's in on this little scam.

Not all doormen participate in these shenanigans. In many localities, buying the door is illegal, and if hotel management catches a doorman doing it, he can be fired. But while many doormen are content with picking up honest tips all day, some of their brethren aren't above a little chicanery. So when you see one of those fur-capped hotel doormen shivering on the street, don't get too broken up. The guy might make more than you.

The next employee you encounter at a fine hotel is the parking valet. I'll cover these guys in more detail in a later chapter, but with regard to valets at a hotel, suffice it to say, money talks—if you don't want your car buried in the bowels of the parking garage, where it'll take half an hour of automotive Rubik's Cubeing to extricate it, slip the valet a ten spot. When I was staying in an L.A. hotel, I knew I'd be constantly using my car, so when I arrived I gave the valet a crisp twenty. The result? Whenever I called for my car it was waiting for me in five minutes flat with the motor running. Now, we all know hotel parking lot fees are usurious—often accounting for 25 percent of the hotel bill. Well, some doormen and valets might be inclined to park your car on the street for twenty bucks. That way you save some green, and the doorman or valet makes out. "We'd have guests with really expensive cars," Robin, a concierge at a Chicago hotel, told me. "They didn't want the car in the garage, so they'd give the doorman twenty bucks to leave it in the driveway and watch over it. Management looked the other way because having Aston Martins and Bentleys in front of the place made us look more upscale." But is it a win-win situation? Remember, if your car is not in the garage and it gets stolen or damaged, there won't be any hotel insurance funds to fix it. So, indulge in this practice at your own risk.

After your car has been parked, your next stop is the front desk. Normally you don't have to tip these employees. But if you and your honey want some extra time rolling between those one-thousand-thread-count sheets, a five-dollar tip for early or late checkout is the way to go. And if the hotel is at max capacity and you hear, "I'm sorry, but we need the room," bump it up to an Andy Jackson and you may find they don't need the room *that* badly.

After you check in, the next hotel employee you'll encounter is the one who often causes the most tipping anxiety: the bellhop. How many movies and TV shows have depicted a clueless guest staring at a smarmy bellhop with his hand stuck out? Whatever you do, don't give the bellhop a quarter. The standard tip for a bellhop is one or two dollars per bag when you check in and when you check out. If you've got more than two bags, an even ten dollars is fine. But be sure to tip him *after* he takes your bags up to the room. Sometimes a bellhop will take your bags to the front desk and just drop them there, leaving you to do the heavy lifting. That doesn't deserve a tip no matter how down with the workingman you are. And if you tip prematurely you risk having someone other than the porter you greased carrying up your bags. Many bellhops pool their tips, but not all. And since hotels don't post their tipping policies in black and white, you don't want to get stuck awkwardly explaining to the guy who carried your luggage that you already tipped the guy downstairs.

Tip delivery is all-important when it comes to bellhops. But don't make a big deal about it. With minimal eye contact, discreetly slip him (or her) the cash with a brief thank-you. Just channel the spirit of Cary Grant. And don't ask the bellhop if he can break a twenty so you can give him two measly dollars. That's déclassé. When you go to a hotel, it's your responsibility to have tipping cash on hand. Bellhops don't take debit cards.

Gratuities can turn what's usually a minimum-wage job into something workers can support their family on. "I can make two hundred dollars on a good day," Alan, a bellhop who works at the same Manhattan hotel as Charles, tells me. "But some days? Shit, I make nothing."

"What percentage of guests tip?"

"Not enough," Alan says with a snort. "The business travelers? They're usually cool. It's the tourists who usually never stay in hotels who screw you."

As Alan and I talk, I discover that "tip avoidance" is big in hotels. "Many people are just cheap," Alan says. "When you offer to take their bags, they'll look at you like you're trying to rob them. I had one lady scream, 'Don't touch my stuff!' Almost got me in trouble."

"They don't want you to carry the bags because then they'll have to tip you?"

"Listen," Alan says. "If all you've got is a carry-on, I understand. But we get guests coming in here with ten suitcases. They'll make two or three trips up and down the elevator to get all their stuff. Why bother going to a hotel? That's what I'm here for!"

"Ever get revenge on bad tippers?"

"Oh," Alan says, "bags have been known to get thrown in the wrong cab from time to time. If you've lost your claim check we'll pretend we can't find the luggage. Stuff like that."

That guests insist on carrying their own bags is no surprise. Many hotel guests will go to great lengths to avoid paying gratuities. When ordering room service, for example, they'll ask the waiter to slip the check under the door for them to sign and to leave the food outside. And when a hotel worker brings up dry cleaning, shined shoes, or some other item, the customer will let them in and then mysteriously disappear into the bathroom. "I've seen guests avoid the door the doorman's opened for them just because they don't want to tip," Alan said. "They can get obnoxious sometimes."

Remember how those guys from antitipping organizations like the Commercial Travelers National League agitated for the establishment of "tipless hotels"? Well, sometime back in the early part of the twentieth century, hotels like the Fort Shelby in Detroit and the Statler Hotel in Boston installed "servidors"— panels in each guestroom door that allowed workers to deliver laundry and other items without "disturbing the guests." But the real reason for servidors was to limit embarrassing human- to-human interaction whereby guests might feel guilt-tripped into tipping. Today the Boston Park Plaza Hotel, the newest incarnation of the old Statler, still has the old servidors, though they're no longer used. But the desire to dodge tips in hotels is still alive and well.

According to the latest figures, there are 433,000 hotel house- keepers in the United States. Paid anywhere between minimum wage and ten bucks an hour, they earn average salaries be- tween $17,000 and $19,000 a year. That's not a lot of money. And maids complain that tipping is a foreign concept for many guests. On average, maids make only 7 percent of their income from tips. American hotel guests are notoriously cheap in this regard.

"You're lucky if you ever get tipped," Andrea, a motel house- keeper in Arizona tells me. "Most guests leave us nothing."

"But what do you consider a good tip?"

"Two or three bucks," Andrea says. "But if you leave a big mess, you should tip more." When I informally surveyed some of my friends about tipping hotel maids they stared at me blankly and said, "I didn't know you had to tip them!" Luckily, I always knew this was the case. When I was a boy vacationing with my parents, my mother always made sure to leave some money for the motel maid. I guess you could say Mom gave me my first les- sons about tipping, planting the seeds for my eventual quest to become the Jedi Master of Gratuities. (Thanks, Mom!) Folks, you *have* to tip hotel maids. In fact, a good rule of thumb for housekeeping staff is two to three dollars for a day in a motel and five dollars a day if you stay at a fancy-schmancy place. And if you're a slob, ten dollars a day is considered appropriate. Maids have a very labor-intensive job. Andrea tells me that she works from 8:30 a.m. until 2:00 p.m. and is responsible for cleaning ten rooms a day. Assigned rooms at random via a computer print-out, she races through the motel to perform her housecleaning chores within the time allotted. "Stayovers are always the easiest," she explains. "You make the beds, empty the garbage, and just make sure everything's neat. It's a light turnover. But check-outs are much more work."

After you've checked out, maids often have only half an hour to prepare the room for the next guest. Think of how fast you clean your apartment before a hot date shows up and multiply that by a factor of three. Within this strict time limit a house-keeper has to strip the linens, vacuum, dust, clean the bath-room, empty the garbage, wash the windows, make sure you've left nothing behind, and chase out lingering bad odors with air freshener.

"So when people are piglets," Andrea explains, "I could spend an hour cleaning their room and fall behind. That sucks."

And what guests do to hotel rooms borders on the obscene. Maids have told me they've found semen stains on the walls, drug paraphernalia on top of the TV set, marijuana seeds in the bed, used sex toys in dresser drawers, boogers on bathroom walls, rotting food, dog shit, human shit, vomit, menstrual blood on the sheets, dirty diapers on the floor, and, my personal favorite, chocolate pudding all over the walls. "I thought a shit bomb had exploded in the room," Andrea tells me. "But when I noticed all the little brown handprints I realized someone had just let their little brat smear pudding all over the walls." So a note to parents out there: if someone else has to clean up after your little darlings, tip heavy.

During a phone interview with Rebecca, a maid at an extended-stay hotel near Scranton, Pennsylvania, she had even more horror stories for me. "There was a man," she said. "I don't know where he was bleeding from, but we'd find these big bandages in the bathroom garbage. And there was blood all over his sheets. We had to put them in biohazard bags."

"Sounds like a criminal on the lam nursing a gunshot wound," I replied. "Did he tip at least?"

"Him? No way," she said. If I had to clean up a wounded bank robber's bloody mess and he didn't tip, I'd call the cops on his ass.

"We also had these people who stayed with us for two years," Rebecca said. "They were dirty, nasty hippie types. Their room smelled so bad—like armpits and buttholes rubbed all over the room. They used to leave turds floating in the toilet, and the guy would cut his hair and leave it all over the sink. Whenever I cleaned their tub it always had this nasty blue ring around it. I never figured out what caused it.

"At one point we actually had to stop going to that room because they'd talk up the staff to the point where they'd keep us there for two hours. Then the kookiness started. 'You look tired,' they'd say. 'Why don't you lie down on the bed and we'll rub your shoulders?' Ugh."

"Blue rings and creepiness," I said. "Sound like dream guests."

"And they'd never tip us," Rebecca said. "And then you get the people who try tipping you with stuff—joints, cocaine, and beer . . ."

"Beer doesn't help you with your car payment, does it?"

"No," Rebecca sighed. "But you can take it home and feel better about not making your car payment."

Just like bellhops, how you deliver a tip to a hotel housekeeper makes all the difference. "I had one guy," Rebecca said. "He'd dump a pile of change on the bed with a Post-it note saying, 'This is for you!' Not the right way to do it."

When you tip a hotel maid, you should place the money in an envelope marked "For Housekeeping" and leave it in a conspicuous place, like the desk or the bathroom counter. If you just leave loose bills lying around, the maid is going to think you've left money behind and she won't want to risk being accused of stealing it. Some guests like to leave one large tip at the end of their stay. That's wrong. You should leave a small tip each day of your stay. In many hotels, housekeeping assignments are generated randomly, so when you leave a gratuity every day, you ensure that the actual person cleaning your room gets paid. You could leave your maid fifty dollars at the end of the week only to have a maid just coming back from vacation putting it in her pocket. Rebecca from Scranton also told me that leaving a daily tip is important for another reason: it reduces the odds that management will steal the money.

"I had a manager named Dan who'd show up half an hour earlier than everyone else," Rebecca told me. "Then he'd go around to the checkouts that were already gone and steal the tips." Sounds like some restaurant managers I know.

"Well, you don't take my money from me," Rebecca said. "So I went into a room that wasn't checked out when the cleaning assignments were printed, but who left shortly after I got there. I snuck in and found the tip—a five and two ones—and drew a star on the five with a teal marker. Then I went up to Dan and said, 'Gee, I haven't been to room two-sixteen yet. I don't think they've left. Could you check for me?' After Dan checks he comes back and says, 'It's okay. They're gone. You can turn it over now.' Of course when I went back to the room, the tip was gone.

"So I went down to the front desk and had Dan paged," Rebecca said, delighting in telling me how she laid a trap for her sketchy manager. "Then I went into the GM's office and told him, 'Larry, I need your help. I think Dan's taking our money. I know you've had complaints in the past.' Larry said, 'Let me take care of it.' So when Dan came to the office Larry made him empty his pockets. Sure enough, he had the marked five."

"Busted," I said.

"Big time."

"Did he get fired?"

"No," Rebecca said. "He was good at his job and had been there a long time. But Larry forced him to clean up the dirty, nasty hippies' room after that. Dan never stole from us again." Karma is indeed a bitch. I hope Dan likes back rubs.

"How does it make you feel when guests leave bad tips and big messes?" I asked. "That must get to you."

"It's a mixture of rage and disgust," Rebecca said. "The rage was 'It's going to take a long time to clean this room.' The disgust came from knowing I have to clean up."

"Are there ways to get revenge on customers who are rude or bad tippers?"

"Oh, I'll do a half-ass job," Rebecca said. "Every day you're supposed to get new sheets. If my guests are jerks I'll just sticky-roll their sheets [i.e., swipe them with an adhesive lint remover that looks like a paint roller] and say, 'The hell with 'em. No clean sheets for you!' Or I'll push the dirt around with a wet rag, never disinfect anything—it'd look clean, but it really isn't."

A hotel maid can really screw you if you're a bad-tipping smoker. When management discovers you've been lighting up in a nonsmoking room a $250 fine can be slapped on to your bill. If you're a decent guest and the maid finds a cigarette butt floating in the bowl, she might look the other way. But if you're a skinflint she might report you to the manager, and suddenly your stay will have become much more expensive.

Not all revenge tactics are so subtle. A concierge who used to work at a five-star hotel in Napa Valley told me how her frustrated male staff would ejaculate onto guests' sheets.

"Spooging the sheets," I said. "Primitive. Angry. I like it. But what made the staff so furious that they'd want to do that?"

The Napa concierge explained that two kinds of customers stayed at her $1,000-a-night-and-up hotel: rich people who could easily afford the room and poseurs who would scrape together enough cash to stay one or two nights. The poseurs thought they were entitled to luxury on a daily basis, but they actually couldn't afford it. Obnoxious name-dropping people who'd maxed out their credit cards, were behind on their Lexus payments, and were living beyond their means would run the staff ragged trying to squeeze every last dime out of their experience. "These are the kind of people who never tip and who nitpick over every little thing," the concierge explained. "They were more about being seen in our hotel than enjoying it. They'd seem like nice people, but they weren't decent people. They'd treat the staff like crap and then turn around and steal the towels. Sometimes people just snapped."

So, here's a lesson for you. If you want to avoid having dirty, DNA-daubed sheets, behave yourself when you're in a hotel. As all the maids told me: you're a guest, so act like one. If you were staying at a friend's house would you inseminate their walls or leave floaters in the toilet? Would you order your host around and treat him like shit? Because housekeepers are anonymous servants, many guests think this gives them license to treat the room like it's their own personal pigsty. Hotel maids are professionals: treat them that way.

Other, ancillary services in hotels involve tipping. Room service is an easy one. The workers who wheel those covered trays up to your room aren't usually paid like waiters. They receive a regular wage, and a service charge of 15 to 20 percent is normally tacked on to every check. So, just as you would tip a waiter in Europe, all you have to do is give them a couple of dollars on top of the service charge, as a thank-you. In the rare case where no service charge is added, tip them as you would a regular waiter. But don't end up double-tipping them 30 percent! With other hotel services—dry cleaning, shoeshines, extra pillows—tip the person who provides the service a couple of bucks. They're making your life easier, so you should do the same in return.

Nothing exemplifies the ethos "you scratch my back I'll scratch yours" like the hotel concierge. In the 1993 movie *For Love or Money*, Michael J. Fox plays a hard-hustling concierge at a five-star New York hotel. "Don't confuse yourself with all these small denominations," he tells a guest who tries to give him five dollars in gratitude for a big favor. "You wait until I feel like the best friend you ever had. Then you give me a tip so big it feels like passing a kidney stone."

When I heard that line it scared the shit out of me. Like most people, I think of concierges as shadowy über-beings who exist to make the impossible possible. Need caviar from the Caspian? A concierge will get it FedEx'd overnight. Want to take a bath in water drawn from Icelandic springs? He'll rustle up fifty gallons of it for you. Want a helicopter ride to view a property in the country? Done. Need a tailor to fit you for a suit at three in the morning? He's on his way. Restaurant reservations and theater tickets out of the reach of mere mortals? With a concierge, they're always available. And in addition to working their acts of consumerist legerdemain, concierges also help guests fly under the radar. A prime example of this service is when they help celebrities check in under assumed names. Ozzy Osborne has gone by the name Harry Bollocks, the late Michael Jackson was Sir William Marshall, and Tiger Woods's nom d'amour was B. Simpson.

Now, I like hotels, but my budget is more Motel 6 than Mandarin Oriental. So, I've had little experience with concierges. And, quite frankly, after hearing Michael J. Fox's concierge's crack about the kidney stone, I was scared I could never afford using one. And that opinion only got reinforced when I tried interviewing concierges at some snotty L.A. and New York hotels. Most of my overtures were rejected. Phone calls went unreturned, and the one member of that clan I did finally manage to talk to, a thin, dapper man named Louis, was guarded and evasive. He was painfully polite, though.

I know hotels can be dens of iniquity. Hotel workers have told me the reason you sometimes can't get an early check-in is because the general manager is banging the hotel cocktail waitress in room 313 or the bartender is using the room to rendezvous with a bored housewife while her husband is playing golf. But according to Louis, everything at his hotel was excellent, above-board, antiseptic, and boring. His doormen never got kickbacks from cabbies, management was the soul of propriety, the guests were always perfect, and their ejaculate never made it onto the sheets, let alone the walls. Something told me Louis was full of shit. So I did a bit more digging and found out how the concierge thing really works.

What I discovered surprised me. Concierges don't really depend on your tips to make money. "We have arrangements with all sorts of providers," Lexi, a former concierge at a five-star Houston hotel told me. "We've got deals with florists, massage therapists, gentlemen's clubs, limo drivers, restaurants, ticket vendors, nightclubs, shoemakers, makeup artists, doctors, tailors—whatever. If you need something, we know who to call."

And as with doormen and cabbies, part of this "arrangement" is the almighty kickback. "I had a lady whose makeup artist was a no-show the day of her wedding," Lexi told me. "So I got her one in a pinch. She was so grateful she tipped me a hundred bucks. But what she didn't know was the makeup artist also gave me a percentage of the sale. So I got paid coming and going.

"But the biggest bang for your buck was limousines," Lexi said. "If a guest needed a limo, we'd set him up with a company we had a deal with. It was a win-win situation. The guest got a rate that was cheaper than if he'd called himself, the livery service got business, and we'd get a kickback at the end of the month in our paycheck."

If you've ever wondered how concierges are able to make the impossible possible, wonder no more: it's all about money. They throw business to preferred providers and then get greased in return. In many ways they're like salesmen operating on a commission basis. Some hotels have even institutionalized the practice, turning their concierges into a glorified sales staff. "Say you use a concierge to order flowers, get a limo, or have a personal masseuse come to your room," Lexi told me. "At my hotel, [these services were] added to your bill and at the end of the month the hotel gave us a percentage of the sale in our paychecks on top of our base pay. We used to keep the entire commission, but after a while the hotel started taking ten percent." I guess management always gets their cut.

Not all hotels work this way. Some establishments don't care what kinds of deals their concierges make, as long as the guests are kept happy. In these hotels, kickbacks are paid out the old-fashioned way: in envelopes stuffed with cash. "We had arrangements with the tour guide operators," Robin from Chicago told me. "If I arranged a tour, you'd leave me a deposit and I'd ensure you got a spot on the tour. Then when you got to the bus or the boat, you'd pay the balance to the operator. What the guests don't know is the deposit goes into my pocket. You're paying the same price either way, but that's how the tour guides kick back to us. And every month, the limo company I dealt with would give me an envelope stuffed with cash."

I had always thought concierges were highly paid professionals. But the reality is, for the amount of work they do, they aren't. Some concierges, such as those who belong to Les Clefs d'Or—a professional society of concierges distinguished by the crossed golden keys they wear on their uniform lapels—usually command higher salaries. But they are a rarity, and are normally found in management positions. For the average concierge, the pay can vary wildly, between $20,000 and $50,000 a year, depending on the hotel. Most of the workers I spoke with pulled down $12 to $16 an hour. So it comes as no surprise that concierges hustle to make extra money. "I'd say the arrangements account for at least half my income," Lexi told me. "I made twenty thousand dollars from my ticket vendor during the Super Bowl," he said. Arrangements, tips, and "freebies" can make up 50 to 70 percent of a concierge's income. "Because I recommend restaurants to guests," Robin said, "I get free meals wherever I go. That's a sort of compensation in itself."

Some concierges operate a pool house. "All the arrangements

were pooled," Lexi from Houston said, "put in our paychecks, and taxed. But any cash-in-hand tips or private arrangements I kept for myself." Other concierges, like an independent contractor waiter, keep only the tips from the arrangements they personally make for a customer. "I once set up a magic weekend for a guy to propose to his fiancée," Robin said. "I set up restaurant reservations, carriage rides, the works. Luckily the girl said yes, and the guy tipped me a hundred and seventy dollars at the end of their stay. That was all mine."

Many hotels frown upon kickbacks, and in some cities it can be a violation of business law. In 2008, attorneys for the city of San Diego sent a letter to hotels in the city stating, "Concierges at your hotel may be in violation of Business and Professions Code section 17200. Such violations 'may occur where a concierge makes referrals to a restaurant or business without disclosing to the hotel patron that gratuities, gifts or other items of value have been provided by the restaurant or business for the referral.'" Some concierges such as Louis say they never get kickbacks from referrals, contenting themselves with the tips guests give them. When I talked to Lexi, however, she said any concierge who claims not to have arrangements with providers is "lying." "Kickbacks are endemic in the hotel industry," said Anthony Lassman, the publisher of the luxury travel guidebook *Nota Bene*. "You have to go a long way to find a concierge who isn't on the take."

Hotel guests have complained that they've been victims of the hard sell by concierges hustling for commissions. "That's where you have to be careful," Robin told me. "You have to give the customer what *they* want. If you can set up something for a guest with a provider who kicks back, great. But if you can't, you have to give the customer what they're asking for." Some concierges are very ethical in this regard and some are not.

I know I've made hotels sound like hustler central. But is that surprising? Just look at how doctors used to accept free trips to the Bahamas and lavish dinners from pharmaceutical firms for prescribing one drug over another. Kickbacks are an integral part of capitalism, so, to paraphrase Captain Renault from *Casablanca*, we shouldn't say, "I am shocked, shocked to find out kickbacks are going on in this hotel!" Still, you should make use of concierges whenever you can. "Concierges are a dying breed," Lexi told me. "And that's a shame. We can make your stay a wonderful experience and give you access to services you wouldn't expect a hotel to provide." That's true. As I visited hotels around the country I discovered that concierges could be the traveler's best friends. They helped me find good places to eat, mailed packages for me, assisted me with car rentals, changed my flight times, made reservations at other hotels, and, when I was doubled over in pain from gastritis, they rustled up some Prilosec from an all-night pharmacy at 3:00 a.m. When you're a traveler far from home, the concierge—in fact all the staff at a hotel—can be like a surrogate family.

When I was staying at a hotel in L.A., I smoked cigars and shot the breeze with the staff on the patio, learned all about their lives, and made quite a few friends. So when I head back there, I know I'll be staying with them again. They made me feel warm, welcome, and safe. And a good concierge can turn your trip into something really special. Say you're taking your wife or husband on a romantic vacation to a city you know nothing about. A good concierge can set you up with an itinerary, direct you to all the cool places, and turn a ho-hum trip into a vacation you'll never forget. All you have to do is ask him for help. And the tips expected are quite reasonable, so you don't have to feel like you're passing a kidney stone. If a concierge gets you into a popular restaurant or secures hard-to-find tickets for a Broadway show, a twenty will suffice.

As Lexi told me, some concierges can set you up with escorts, but usually you go to doormen for that kind of stuff. "They always have a 'friend' or a number you can call," Lexi said. While some concierges are in on that action, they all have a reputation for discretion they must adhere to. And sometimes they blow it.

"I had a good regular who always came in with this particular lady friend," Lexi told me. "Well, he comes in one day, his lady friend's not with him, and he gives me a Tiffany necklace to put in the safe. It was worth, like, two grand. Well, I don't see the man and his lady friend for the rest of his stay. So a couple of weeks later he comes back with his regular girl and stops at the front desk to get something. So I asked the lady, 'So, how'd you like the necklace?' "

"Uh-oh." I can see where this is going.

"You got it," Lexi said. "The necklace wasn't for *that* lady friend. So the guy had to smooth-talk his way out of it and shell out two thousand dollars for another necklace. He stopped being a regular after that." Oops.

Most of us don't get to stay in fancy hotels very often. But even if you stay at a motel or a Holiday Inn, places where they don't have specialized staff, the principle is still the same. In this age of cost cutting, many hotels don't have concierges anymore, so the front desk is expected to fill that role. Depending on the hotel, this can be a hit-or-miss proposition, like asking for directions at a gas station. But if they help make your stay more comfortable, tip them as you would a concierge.

Tipping at a hotel is easy and can turn an average stay into an extraordinary one. And it helps build nice rapport with the staff, so return trips are more pleasant. Just as in restaurants, hotel staff will bend over backward for decent people who tip well. So bring some tipping cash, behave yourself, don't be a piggy, and you won't need Valium to get you through your stay. And don't be a dick.

CHAPTER 4

The Thirteen-Dollar Miracle
Auto Mechanics, Parking Valets, and Car Wash Attendants

According to a 2009 Arbitron survey, Americans spend an average of two hours a day in cars as either a driver or a passenger. If you do a little figuring, that comes out to about thirty days a year. And if you drive from the time you get your learner's permit until your statistical drop-dead age of seventy-eight, you'll spend *five years* behind the wheel. No wonder Preparation H is such a perennial bestseller. And tipping is a big part of our automotive existence. Don't think so? Read on.

A few months into my guru quest I decided to take a break and drive to a late-night rendezvous with a young woman. But just as I eased my car onto the highway I heard an ominous bang from the front driver's-side tire. Being the cautious type, I pulled into a rest stop to inspect the damage. After checking all the tires and finding nothing amiss, I got back into my car and continued my journey toward martinis and possible nookie. Big mistake.

In order to save time, I decided to take a shortcut through a really bad New Jersey neighborhood. Just as I was driving past a warren of burnt-out crack houses I heard the unmistakable *thud, thud, thud* of a flat tire. Seized with a sense of dread, I realized I must have gotten a slow leak a few miles back and *now* the tire had decided to fail. Talk about bad luck. I thought about pulling over and slapping on the donut, but a *Death Wish II* montage of street-roaming criminals flickered though the cinema of my mind. With my luck, some Bloods or Crips would offer to help me with my problem, resulting in my car up on blocks and me bleeding in the street deprived of my wallet. I told myself that I was making a stereotypical evaluation of a rough neighborhood. "Good people live here," the voice in my cerebral cortex said soothingly. "You're just as likely to get mugged in your own town. You can't drive on a flat. Pull over and fix the problem." But my primitive lizard brain screamed, "Get the fuck outta here!" Guess which side won.

I put the pedal to the metal and drove through the danger zone in search of a haven. That's one of the interesting things about living in New Jersey—affluent burgs routinely border some of the most crime-ridden cities in the state. I knew that if I could just go *one* more mile I'd find sanctuary. So with my car sounding like a live cat being chewed up in a blender, I blew through four red lights and found a safe side street in a tony residential neighborhood. But when I got out to inspect the damage, my heart sank. My front tire was not only flat and shredded, but also smoking. And to make matters worse, it was ten degrees outside and the leather coat I was wearing, while great for bar-hopping, was inadequate insulation against arctic temperatures. With my libido as deflated as my tire, I made the survival decision to abandon my car and get it fixed the next morning. Somehow I managed to get home before I froze solid.

I had somewhere to be the next day, and not being mobile was going to put a crimp in my plans. So after a friend took me to retrieve my stricken vehicle, I navigated my limping car to my regular mechanic. When I pulled into the station's lot I noticed a huge line of cars waiting to be fixed. I wasn't worried. I had an ace in the hole.

Gasmar, my Armenian mechanic, came out of the service bay covered in grease. I explained what had happened. "I need a new tire, but I'm pretty sure I fucked up something. Any chance you can take care of it now? I've got to be somewhere later."

"No problem," Gasmar said. "I'll take your car just as soon as I'm done doing this oil change."

Why did Gasmar bump me to the head of the line? Why did he bypass all the customers who had gone to the trouble of making an appointment? Simple: I tip him. For the past several years I've slipped Gasmar a ten spot every time he's done something for my car. And every Christmas he gets a greeting card and twenty bucks. Over the course of a year, I probably give him seventy to eighty dollars in gratuities. Now, since car repairs are expensive, you might think I'm being a tad excessive. I'm not. For me, tipping Gasmar is a form of insurance. In addition to rewarding his honest and efficient service, my money is buying me something else: preferential treatment.

Remember how the old Persian word *baksheesh* can mean almsgiving, or a bribe or tip? As Israeli economist Ofer Azar outlined in his paper "Why Pay Extra? Tipping and the Importance of Social Norms and Feelings in Economic Theory," tipping comes in all shapes and sizes. The good professor breaks tips down into six categories.

REWARD TIP
A tip given after a service is rendered to reward good service, such as that given to a waiter after the meal is finished.

PRICE TIP
A tip given after a service is rendered as the price of the service, such as a tip to a skycap and other baggage handlers.

ADVANCE TIP

A tip given before a service is rendered to induce good service. Slipping a twenty into a waiter's hand and saying, "I'll take good care of you, you take good care of me," is a perfect example.

BRIBE

A tip given before a service is rendered, such as that used to grease a maître d' to give you the best table in a restaurant when you don't have a reservation.

GIFT TIP

A cash or a nonmonetary gift meant to say, "Thank you."

HOLIDAY TIP

A tip given once a year to workers who serve the consumer during the year and are not normally tipped.

I guess my tips to Gasmar are an "advance bribe" hybrid. When I entered the station's waiting room to grab some coffee, I found a hard-charging salesman type flipping through an out-of-date issue of *Road and Track* and berating his subordinates on his cell phone.

"Say," he said hotly, once he'd ended his call and noticed that Gasmar was putting my car on the lift, "why's he taking your car ahead of mine?"

"Because I had an appointment," I lied, not wanting to make trouble for Gasmar. I got the sense the man knew he was getting the shaft, but I didn't care. My investment in Gasmar was paying off. Besides, by the way the man had been yelling at his coworkers on the phone, I pegged him as a bad tipper.

Some of you may think, "That's not fair! You should have to wait like everyone else!" Give me a break. Look around you: people use money to jump ahead of each other every day.

Pay extra for that ticket at Disneyworld and you'll leap over sweaty tourists with wailing children and get first crack at the best rides. Fly first class and in addition to the privilege of getting killed right after the pilot in the event of a crash, you get on and off the plane first. When I go to my doctor, I have to wait forty-five minutes for a triple-booked fifteen-minute slot that had to be arranged weeks in advance. But if I shelled out a couple of thousand dollars a year to belong to a concierge medical practice, they'd take me that same day. And if you're a good tipper you'll always get a reservation in a restaurant ahead of a bad one.

When it comes to cars and tipping, nowhere is the capitalistic ethos "money talks and bullshit walks" more evident than with car valets and parking attendants.

Full disclosure: I suffer from a condition called "parking rage." Akin to road rage, this mental illness arises when there are too many cars and not enough spots to park them. Hunting for parking causes an edgy, nasty, territorial ogre to overwhelm my normal laid-back self. How bad can I get? My friends, I'll swipe a parking spot from a nun. When I see someone whose only apparent condition is obesity slide into a handicapped spot, I want to blow up their car with an antitank rocket. And those "pregnant women only" spots at the mall? When the going gets tough, I'll snake one of those spots in a heartbeat. When it comes to parking, I'm a real asshole—but an asshole in recovery. After a girlfriend told me, "I think you have issues," I decided to get a handle on my problem before I inadvertently ended up on an episode of *Cops*. Barefoot, shirtless, and crazed on national television is not a good look for me.

It wasn't cognitive therapy, relaxation techniques, yoga, or heavy-duty medication that helped me tame the beast. It was the simple realization that parking follows the law of supply and demand. Too many cars and not enough spots means the price to park your car goes up. Most people in Manhattan try to find cheap or free street parking because they're sick of feeding the meter every two hours or they can't stand usurious garage fees. But looking for that free parking consumes another kind of capital: time. And because I'm going to spend a total of five years in my car as it is, I came to the conclusion that temporal waste was the source of my anger. So I changed my behavior. Now I use public transportation whenever I go into the city. Not because I'm green or any of that self-aggrandizing hippie horseshit—but because I don't want to stress out! And on the rare occasion I do drive in, if I can't find a spot in fifteen minutes, I pay to put my car in a garage. Same thing when I go to a restaurant or the mall. If the free spots are full and valet services are offered, I'll gladly hand over my keys. Sure, that can get pricey, but keeping the ogre at bay is worth every penny. Car valets and parking lot attendants are to me what an AA sponsor is to an alcoholic. They keep me on the straight and narrow. And tips help keep me sober.

A while back, I was meeting a friend playing league softball in a park on the Upper West Side of Manhattan. I thought I'd catch the last inning of the game before driving downtown for dinner and drinks. But since finding street parking on the West Side is like finding a virgin in a whorehouse, I pulled into a nearby garage.

"Sorry," the attendant said. "Lot's full."

I pressed a twenty-dollar bill into the attendant's hand. "Listen, man," I said. "I only need half an hour. Will this cut it?"

"No problem, sir," the attendant said, pocketing the money. He didn't even give me a claim ticket. And when I returned a half hour later, my car was parked right by the cashier's booth. No muss, no fuss, and my inner ogre was held in check. Another example of how passing around a little green can make your life easier.

With garage fees in urban areas as high as they are, I can understand why people don't tip parking lot attendants. But since the median salary for an attendant is a shade over $18,000 a year, believe me, gratuities are appreciated. Two bucks is a good tip: a dollar when the attendant takes your car and a dollar when he returns it. And if you're a regular at a parking garage, residential or commercial, tipping becomes even more important. If you're a bad tipper or a general pain in the ass, the attendant will bury your car so deep in the bowels of the garage that it'll take eons to retrieve it. I've heard people complain that they call the garage an hour ahead of time and their car still isn't ready when they get there. Hmm . . . I wonder why? If you're in a hurry that can really suck. So, what if you're a regular but short on dough? I knew one cash-strapped girl who tried tipping her Latino lot attendant in Spanish ham and cookies. That's sweet, but if you don't happen to have *real* money in your pocket, be sure to thank the attendant and tell him you'll catch him the next time.

Parking valets at hotels, restaurants, and nightclubs don't want to be tipped in porcine currency. Unlike attendants in commercial parking garages, many car valets are paid below minimum wage, with the expectation that tips will make up the difference. Pork and cookies don't cut it.

"I recently got promoted to supervisor, so I get six-fifteen an hour," Jake, a car valet at a Boca Raton hotel told me. "A normal line valet makes four-fifteen an hour. I think it went up to four-nineteen with the minimum wage hikes which just happened. An extra four cents an hour—very helpful."

"What can a valet pull down in tips?"

"The tips can range from forty dollars on a bad day to a hundred and twenty on a good day," Jake said. "A really good day is a hundred and sixty."

"And that's per valet?"

"Yeah, each guy. When I first got there in 2005 the money was ridiculous. Because we were understaffed, we were pulling in anywhere from a hundred and seventy five to two hundred and eighty a day, every day. We made so much money . . . But that was when times were flush. The recession's affecting us. I get my thirty-six hours a week so I keep my health insurance. Most people have been cut back to two or three shifts a week. So we're down twenty bucks a shift."

I wince. That's a $400 monthly shortfall—an amount that would cover my car payment and my cable bill.

Jake explains that staffing levels are very important for car valets. Too many valets, and the tips are diluted. But since the garage at Jake's hotel holds close to five hundred cars, if they have too few workers the job is well nigh impossible. "You really need one valet for every thirty-six to forty cars, depending on the group and how much activity there is," Jake said. "And that keeps the guys happy. They're busy that way and we're not overstaffed." Funny, that's the same way staffing in a restaurant works.

As we talk, I learn Jake's got an interesting story. Twenty-nine years old and originally from Ohio, he's been a car valet for nine years. After earning a degree in exercise physiology and a personal training certificate from the American College of Sports Medicine, he used to run fitness programs for a corporate exercise outfit in Columbus. "I was absolutely miserable," he said. "I was in an office all day long, doing paperwork, fixing all the equipment, and I had seven bosses who at any given time could give me something to do. And the pay was miserable. I was getting ten dollars and fifty cents an hour in 2004. And this is with a college degree."

Jake wasn't just sick of being a low-paid corporate fitness drone, he was also sick of life in the Buckeye State. "I don't know if you've ever been to Ohio," he said, "but the sun doesn't really shine. It kind of glows nine months out of the year. In the summer you see the sun a little bit. It's like a fluorescent lightbulb." Jake's deliverance from monetary and vitamin D deficiency came from a most unlikely source: a severed hand.

When he started as a car valet in Columbus he became good friends with a guy named Mike. "He went down to Florida to do hurricane cleanup," Jake said. "But then he got a job at a bleach bottle factory and got injured that year on Halloween. His hand got cut off."

"Awwww!" I howled. "At a bleach bottle factory?" Turns out the machine that trimmed the edges off the plastic bottles severed Mike's hand.

"They reattached it," Jake said. "But there was a problem with his workman's comp, so he went broke. So now Mike's living poor as dirt in an apartment with a bad hand, his roommate bailed, he wasn't taking care of himself and I wanted to make a move. And since this guy is like a brother to me, I went down to take care of him.

"But when I got to his apartment Mike didn't have a job yet. The only furniture he had was an old hospital door he got from hurricane cleanup on top of four boxes, a TV, a lawn chair, and a single mattress. There was no food in the kitchen. I think there were some pickles. Since I had no car I had to walk a mile and a half to a 7-Eleven for a Snickers and Coke gourmet breakfast. 'My god,' I thought to myself, 'we got to get some groceries and something to sit on!' I slept on the dog bed the first night I was there."

Despite the inauspicious start, moving to sunny Florida turned out to be a good thing for Jake. After several surgeries, Mike eventually regained most of the use of his hand, and he and Jake landed jobs valeting cars at an upscale hotel in Boca. And it was at that hotel that Jake met the girl he would marry.

"Linda worked guest services at the hotel," Jake said "I literally would drive in front of her, and she'd be by the bell stand. I remember the first day I saw her. I gave her a balloon that some kid gave me as a tip."

"A kid gave you a balloon as a tip?"

"It was a Mercury Villager I pulled up for a family," Jake said. "The dad gave me two bucks. The kid came up. The dad explained tipping to him, so the kid gave me his balloon. It was very sweet."

"So a tip led to you getting married?"

"Yep."

Jake has some very definite ideas about tipping a car valet. One of those is that you should tip a valet when you *drop off* your car, not when you pick it up.

"It's something I've never really understood," Jake says. "You hand over your keys to the second most valuable possession in your life, next to your home—at *minimum*, it's worth five grand. So wouldn't you want to tip me up front to take care of it?" And what constitutes a good tip? Jake explains that a two-dollar gratuity when you drop off or pick up your car is acceptable. "Two bucks will get you full standard service and I don't have any feeling of ill will toward you at all."

"And if I give you a five?"

"I will remember your face and your last name. And I'll probably remember your ticket number and where you're parked," Jake said.

"But if I want extra service, like keeping an eye on my car and having it ready at a moment's notice. How much for that?"

"Twenty talks, man," Jake said. "If I see a twenty, we are in business."

"Money does talk," Adriana, a car valet in California, agreed. "If we've got a few people in line and some guy's in a hurry? He wants out and gives you his ticket and a twenty-dollar bill? Trust me, that man is *next*. But then you'll get people trying to jump the line, yelling, 'I want my car and I want it now!' but not offering you any money. Do you think I'm going to bend backward for you? If you want to jump ahead in line, the tip's got to be up front." Adriana believes five bucks is a good tip for standard valet service. "Twenties are wonderful, but we're realistic," she said. "But the dollars are hard to take."

Being a valet is such a physical job, they *earn* their money. "It's all about hustle," Jake said. "We *run*. When we're busy, we run four or five hours a shift. We had a guy wear a pedometer for a week once. And when we were slammed he was averaging seven miles a shift running."

"You guys must all be skinny."

"Anybody who lasts is skinny," Jake said. "And you have to remember in Florida the summer is when we're busy. And it's ninety-four degrees; with the humidity it feels like a hundred and three or four. So it's an extremely tough job to have. You've got to run for all these cars in this crazy heat and smile and be nice, soaked in sweat. And then you get stiffed on three or four cars in a row and you're just like, 'Dammit! Just gotta keep smiling.' "

"Who are the worst tippers?"

"Lexus drivers," Jake said, without skipping a beat. "In fact we have something at the hotel that we call the 'Lexus dollar.' That's because a Lexus driver will usually give you nothing or just a dollar. And if a Lexus driver gives you a five? We call that a 'Lexus Twenty.' "

When I asked Jake why he thought Lexus drivers were bad tippers, he said, "It's something about the car. I think it's because a Lexus is just over the cusp of affordable luxury. It's just past the edge of Toyota. So people who buy them are stretching themselves a little bit, you know? Also people who buy the cheapest Mercedes, the C-Class 230—it's about the same price as a Toyota Avalon . . . Those people are the same way. They're stretching it. They really want a Mercedes, but they probably shouldn't have bought one. So they don't tip very well."

Jake's description of Lexus owners reminds me of what the hotel concierge in Napa Valley told me about guests who could technically afford the outrageous rates but "were stretching themselves a little bit." They were all about appearance, running the staff ragged and squeezing every last dime out of their "experience."

To be fair, I posed the same question to readers on my website: When you think of cheap tippers, what brand of car comes to mind? Other carmakers got whacked, too. But I'd like to make Lexus the official car of cheap tippers because, quite simply, I'm prejudiced. Now, before you send hate mail my way, let me say that I'm sure many Lexus owners are kind and decent people. But I've always hated those pretentious commercials Lexus puts out every Christmas. You know, the ones where J. Crew–catalog husbands give their perky 3-percent-body-fat wives a $60,000 car topped with a red bow while that smug announcer's condescending, snobby voice makes you feel suicidally inadequate because all you gave your wife was a pair of slippers. I'd love to see *SNL* make a mock commercial where Bloods and Crips surprise our overconsumptively blissed-out couple in the middle of their driveway, hogtie them with that stupid bow, put their Lexus up on blocks, strip it in two minutes and then torch its eviscerated shell while Buffy and Tyler watch, horrified, from their perfectly snow-covered lawn. And then, as the gangbangers pull away, the ringleader shouts, "Now *that's* a December to remember, bitches!"

Okay, so maybe that's an example of my automotive issues busting out.

After nine years parking cars, Jake has broken down the characteristics of good and bad tippers a little better for me. Businessmen, it seems, are the best when it comes to gratuities. "They take their luggage out quick, we write them a ticket, and if they've got money they'll give us a five. The minimum is two dollars."

Rich people tend to be lousy tippers. "Sometimes they don't tip at all," Jake said. "I had a woman come in with a Rolls-Royce Phantom, a four-hundred-and-fifty-thousand-dollar-plus car that makes you feel like you're driving a cloud. It's a huge car and it just kind of floats. When you put it in gear, the selector is so smooth you don't even hear it click. It just says, 'Okay, you can drive now. Enjoy.' And this lady would never tip, ever. And I can't figure it out." Now, I know not all rich people are bad tippers, because I got plenty of good tips from wealthy customers when I was a waiter. There are two common explanations service people give as to why the upper classes are parsimonious with tips: either they don't know what it's like to work for a living or they can afford their luxuries precisely because they've hung on to every nickel they've ever made. Insensitive to the economic realities common folk face, they're cheap toward others but often generous to themselves. That's an affliction that strikes rich and poor alike, but let's face it—it's easier when you're loaded.

"We also have something we call the BTT," Jake said. "The Big Truck Tip. Guys who drive big trucks tend to tip very well. Big Ford pickup trucks: F-350s, F-250s, the big Chevys, the 2500 and 3500, the GMCs, Hummers, Sequoias. They tend to tip very well."

It is often said that your car is a reflection of your personality. If your car is always clean, it might signal that you're a highly organized individual or anal-retentive and vain. And if you're car is always dirty? Well, you could be just too busy to clean it, have kids, not care what people think, or suffer from major depression. What a car valet finds in your car can also tell them a lot about you. Over the course of Jake's career he's found drugs, guns, and dirty diapers stuffed underneath the seats. It must be nice to know some of your customers are heavily armed speed freaks who live in filth.

"What's the weirdest thing you've ever found in a car?"

"A naked man masturbating," Jake said.

"You're kidding me."

"It happened when I was valeting in the gay district in Columbus," Jake said. "I found a guy in a red Mercedes SLK convertible rubbing one out. And when I confronted him he got mad at me! I'm like, 'Dude, you're out of your mind. You're the one naked and masturbating in somebody else's car!' Turned out he was some guy's boyfriend and he was all messed up on drugs. The boyfriend intervened, no charges were filed, and I got tipped ten dollars for my trouble." Personally, I think Jake sold out. If I caught a guy spooging on the dashboard of a car, I'd want a Ben Franklin to ensure my silence.

"Is there any way car valets can get revenge on their customers?" I asked.

"There's a maneuver I learned in Ohio," Jake said, "and it's been passed down through the valet chain of life. It's called the 'DBS.' That's short for the 'dirt butt scoot.' A valet runs all day long and sweats, you know? When you sit down and get up all day long your butt takes a beating. So let's say we have a guest come in and he's just a total asshole. He wants everything now, is completely inconsiderate, and pulls up talking on his cell phone to boot. That really pisses me off. Man, you're in a place of business. The valet's standing there trying to help you, and you're on the phone? And on top of that, if the guy's mean, nasty, doesn't tip, and expects the world—well, if the valet snaps there's a good chance you're gonna get a DBS. And the way that that happens is the valet will take your car down into the garage, open the passenger door, pull his pants down, and rub his bare, sweaty ass all over the seats."

Turns out this maneuver works better when the car's upholstery is fabric. Kind of gives the term *skid marks* a whole new meaning.

"There are other things we can do that'll fuck up your car," Dmitri, a parking lot attendant in Washington, D.C., told me. "If you're a tool, we'll burn the e-brake completely out of your car. Jam the emergency brake up or down and just murder it so you don't have an e-brake anymore."

"Wow," I said. "Now, that's angry."

"That's nothing," Dmitri said. "We can do things to your car that you won't notice right away. Depending on the model of the car, we can turn the distributor cap and mess up the timing. That might not cause a problem that day, but eventually you'll have issues. And . . . we can . . . turn the steering wheel all the way to the left or right, press the front tire against a column and pull the alignment out of whack. You might not notice it when you leave, but as soon as you get on the highway you'll be like, 'Why is my car skewing to the left?' "

"But what happens when a customer does notice it?"

"By the time they discover the problem they're off the

grounds," Dmitri said. "And by then it's too late. When you leave the lot, our insurance can't be held liable for the damage. So you want a word of advice for your readers? Always inspect your car before you leave!"

I guess the lesson you can take away from all this is always tip the guy who parks your cars. As Jake said, he's handling one of the most expensive items you own.

Back at the service station, Gasmar had finished work on my car. "You were very lucky," he said, handing me the bill. Turns out my little sojourn in the 'hood had cost me only a new tire, and there was no extensive damage. Slipping Gasmar a twenty for his troubles, I pulled out of the station and headed over to the car wash. After her traumatizing evening my baby needed a bath.

It was winter, and everyone's car was dusted with road salt, so the car wash was crazy busy. Since bribery wouldn't help me jump this line, I used the time out to collect all the detritus that had been compressing into sedimentary layers inside my Chevy Malibu—candy wrappers, paper coffee cups, fast-food cartons, a pizza crust, used straws, napkins, a cigar butt—and tossed them into the trash. Being the kind of guy who keeps a clean apartment but a dirty car, I remembered Jake's admonition about stinky automobiles. Man, if I pulled into a hotel with my car in that condition, the valets would be none too happy with me.

The car wash is another place where tipping intersects the automotive world. But when I tried delving into this sudsy world I ran into a brick wall. Nobody, and I mean nobody, would give me the time of day.

Whether they're food delivery people, bathroom attendants, or waiters, tipped workers get exploited every day. Unscrupulous companies are quick to siphon off their workers' tips in order to lower overhead, increase profits, and line their own pockets. Wage theft is rampant, and some companies are cynically throwing their workers to the wolves. And it's tough for people to complain about their working conditions when they're trying to put food on the table. It's easy to be a Cesar Chavez when times are flush, but when your children are hungry, concepts like fairness and justice often have to take a backseat to reality. Some cynical employers are counting on this fact to stick it to the American workers even harder. How many times, even if you have a cushy white-collar job, have you had to tolerate insane bosses, "do more with less," and juggle impossible workloads because resisting might mean missing your next mortgage payment? Now imagine you're a poor immigrant with no education, few prospects, and are working for a petty tyrant. That's what many car wash attendants are dealing with daily.

While most car wash operators are honest, honorable people, some have acted like opportunistic dirtbags. In Tennessee, one car wash had to pay 120 of its former and current employees a $130,000 settlement for violating wage and hour practices. In California, the owners of a car wash in Hollywood had to shell out $450,000 to settle a complaint. In almost all cases, the victims of these scams were poor, illegal Latino immigrants. And in all the car washes in my neighborhood, guess who washes the cars? Mexicans. No wonder no one wanted to talk to me.

Eventually I got lucky and one car wash operator invited me to take a peek inside his operation. Because he was so skittish about being identified, I agreed not to give the slightest indication where his business was located. Due to liability issues, I was not allowed to work at the car wash, only observe. And the first thing I observed was that there weren't any Mexicans.

"You noticed that, huh?" Artie, the owner's son told me. "That's because we don't hire illegal immigrants. We're aboveboard here. Everyone's paid the full minimum wage for every hour they're on the premises, and they get to keep all their tips."

"You mean there are car washes where workers don't even get to keep their tips?"

"There are places," Artie said, "where the owners will take the tip bucket in the back, count it, take what they want, and then give what's left over to the workers." A familiar line from the Gospel of Matthew floats into my head: "Even the little that he has will be taken away."

Artie gives me a tour of the facility, and I'm immediately impressed with how orderly, clean, and well maintained the car wash is. But I'm also stunned by how much all the equipment costs. The water softener system costs $92,000. Water recycler: $60,000. Conveyor belt: another $60,000. Grille brushes: $15,000. Towel dryers: $23,000. Those big spinning brushes: $28,000 apiece. Even the computer system costs $40,000. When you factor in water, taxes, salaries, and electricity, it quickly becomes apparent that the overhead at a car wash is very high. "To start a car wash from the ground up," Artie tells me, "would cost you about $3.2 million. And that's why some car washes cut corners when it comes to paying their guys. It allows them to undercut honest operators like us. If you ever see a car wash whose prices are drastically lower than everybody else's, be suspicious."

Artie is a squared-away guy with short-clipped hair and a no-nonsense attitude. The car wash has been in the family for years, and he and his younger brother have every intention of running it as efficiently as their father does. And the key to efficiency is to monitor staffing.

"On a bright, sunny day we'll have fourteen guys working here," Artie said. "But if it's a slow day or it rains, we'll cut them to reduce payroll."

"So the guys here don't know if they're going to work a full day," I said.

"That's true," Artie admitted. "But when we cut them they're free to leave. Those Mexican guys you see at other car washes? They'll hang out there all day."

The car wash's hours are from 7:45 a.m. until 5:30 p.m. Unlike car washes where a bunch of guys will work on your car and pool the tips, this place has one guy who takes your car off the conveyer belt and does all the buffing and drying. Just like a restaurant where the waiters are independent contractors, a good hustler can rake in a lot of tips. In fact, some regular customers request attendants by name.

"What about the guys in the front? The guys who vacuum the car and put it on the belt. Do they get tips?"

"Not as much as the guys on the back end," Artie said. "But to make up for that, on top of their base pay we'll give each front guy ten cents per car. So if they do two hundred and fifty cars in a day they'll see an extra twenty-five dollars in their paycheck.

"But the real profit in a car wash comes from all the extras," Artie told me. "When you ask for RainEx that costs us five cents an application. But we charge you a buck fifty." I smile to myself. What machine soft drinks are to a restaurant owner, RainEx is to a car wash guy. Fountain drinks cost the restaurant pennies, but some places charge you two bucks or more for a Coke. *Kaching!*

After the tour, I start talking to the workers. They're mostly young college guys trying to cover the rent, plus a few pros and one or two functioning alcoholics. Timmy is the newest member of the team. A tall, impossibly young kid with red hair, big ears, and freckles, he reminds me of a childhood buddy of mine who joined the army after high school and fought in the first Gulf War. Suddenly I feel old.

"So how do you like it here?"

"It's great," Timmy said, enthusiastically. "I can make seventy dollars in tips a day. Sometimes even a hundred."

"What's considered a good tip?"

"About three or four dollars a car. A five is nice." Even if every customer tipped Timmy five bucks, to break a hundred he'd have to work on twenty cars. Oh man, my knees would blow out by that point.

"Hard work, though, isn't it?"

"Yes, sir."

I moved on to Will, a laid-off finance guy in his late twenties working at the car wash to pay the bills. I asked him the same question I'd asked Timmy.

"I can make seventy a day," Will said, shrugging. "Sometimes a hundred. It's okay." Funny how ten years can change your perspective. "But I've got other things going on," he said haltingly, handing me a business card. "I do consulting and stuff on the side."

For Timmy, the car wash is a summer frolic; for Will, it's a punishment. I try to imagine myself here washing cars at age forty-two and having a former girlfriend see me doing it. The thought pains me. I wonder what it's doing to Will.

It takes me only a few minutes to find Paul, the car wash's alpha male. A wiry guy with a loping stride and a slightly bemused look on his face, when I cornered him he launched into a description of the travails of a car wash attendant.

"The best kind of customer," he said, "is the regular customer. Their cars are usually clean, so there's not a lot of work to be done, and they're good tippers."

"Who are the bad tippers?"

"Cops are bad," Paul said. "They come here with their patrol cars and seldom tip. Limo drivers are even worse. But I'll tell ya, those Mini Cooper owners are really weird."

"How are Lexus owners?" I asked, hoping my suspicions would be confirmed.

"They're okay," Paul said. "The real pains are the SUVs. More surface area, more nooks and crannies to clean. People should tip more if they have an SUV. Then we have the pointers."

"Pointers," Paul explained, are overanxious customers who hover over car wash attendants and point out every speck of dirt on their car. "These people are expecting a thirteen-dollar miracle. They want a hundred-and-twenty-dollar detail job but don't want to pay for it."

Paul rakes in more money than most of the other guys, often $600 to $750 over a forty-hour week. Customers ask for him by name, and he's got a stable of regulars who supply him with a steady income. "I've got a guy who comes in here with what we call a 'trophy car,' a Mercedes SL-550. He tips me sixty bucks every Wednesday."

When I was a waiter I had a stable of regulars, too. They would request to sit in my section and they tipped well. One couple, the Mickelsons, tipped me thirty dollars a week, every week without fail. Eventually I reached a stage in my waiter evolution where I classified tippers by which of my bills they paid. The Mickelsons were my cable bill, the Levis covered my car payment, and the Robertses didn't even cover my monthly outlay for gum. But then again, they were teachers.

Because Paul hustles products like RainEx and tire treatments to his patrons, he's a profit center for the car wash. "Paul can basically do whatever he wants around here," Artie told me later. "And he often does." I smile when I hear that. Paul's like the headwaiter in a restaurant—the big swinging dick who makes the lion's share of the money.

Back in Jersey it's finally my car's turn to go through the wash. I'm getting the sixteen-dollar "deluxe service," which I hope will detoxify my car. As I step out of the driver's seat, I hand two dollars to the guy with the vacuum. "Sorry about the dirt."

"No problem."

When my car emerges from the wash, Latino workers descend on it like a pack of wolves, furiously shining and buffing. The car is ready in ten minutes.

"New car smell?" one of the attendants asks, holding a bottle.

"Yes, thank you," I say, handing him a five-dollar bill. I never put the tip in the can, because I want to make sure the workers get it.

As my car is being perfumed, I notice a frail old woman with a bad perm job hectoring a worker with a bandanna wrapped around his head. "You missed a spot," she screeches, pointing to a damp patch on her car's bumper. "I paid thirteen dollars! I want it done right!"

I shake my head. People who want thirteen-dollar miracles are everywhere. They're the prix-fixers in every restaurant, the hotel guest strivers, the car valet stiffers, and the "pointers" at car washes. They're the worst of the worst. Cheap people who expect the world but have no idea how to pay for it. If you want preferential treatment you have to pay for it up front. Money talks and bullshit walks. That's the American way.

All told, I tipped the car wash guys almost 50 percent, and my car was immaculate. Now, you don't have to tip that large; three to five bucks is the standard gratuity, a bit more if you're driving an SUV. But if you're like me and hate to clean your car, the extra service and convenience a tip buys are worth it. Besides, if you're going to spend five years in a car you might as well be comfortable being there.

As I drive away, the red-haired lady is still pestering her attendant, gunning for her thirteen-dollar miracle. When I see her car, I smile. It's a Lexus. Where are the Bloods and Crips when you need them?

CHAPTER 5

Jars and Bars

Baristas, Bartenders, and Tattoo Artists

Twenty years ago you would have been hard-pressed to find a tip jar anywhere. Now they're *everywhere*: in fast-food joints and pizzerias, at hot-dog stands, in convenience stores, even at gas stations. These little jars are the best example of "tip creep": the expansion of the tip into every nook and cranny of American life. Who gave birth to this phenomenon, or at least midwifed it? Why, Starbucks of course! Just look at the timeline. In the early 1990s, Starbucks grew from a small group of Seattle coffee shops into the behemoth we know and love (and love to hate) today. Soon after it became a nationwide company, other businesses started imitating its tip jars, and before you could say, "White Chocolate Mocha," the things started showing up all over the place. The irony in all this? *There's no such thing as a tip jar in Starbucks.* Now, before you think the cigars I've been smoking are laced with PCP, hear me out. I didn't say people don't leave gratuities at the corporate titan of java joints; there just aren't any tip jars, at least officially.

"If you look in any Starbucks," Chris, the manager of one of the company's South Carolina stores, tells me, "you'll never see the words *tip jar* on the tip jars. That's a violation of company policy."

"So, what can you put on there?"

"Nothing whatsoever. You are forbidden to put the words *tips* or *tip jar* on the tip jar. You can decorate it any way you want, as long as the words *tips* or *tip jar* are not referred to in any way."

That's a far cry from what a barista in an independent shop told me. "On our tip jar we wrote, 'Tipping. A nice thing people do for one another. Like not peeing in a public pool when you really have to go.'" I wonder how the CEO of Starbucks would react if one of his baristas did that! Then again, associating coffee with urination is probably not a good business plan.

"So why don't they allow you to write 'tip jar' on the tip jar?" I ask Chris.

"It's just one of those things you don't do," he says. "It's all about creating the 'third place' experience. That's what Starbucks is all about. Creating the third place that's not home or work; it's the third place. Pushing [customers] to leave a tip might violate that experience."

If you ask me, some customers have gone beyond making Starbucks their "third place" and have turned it into their *only* place. Ever try finding a free seat at a Starbucks in Manhattan? Good luck. Hipsters with iPods snap up all the comfy chairs, and students and corporate types trying to look like they're doing something important with their laptops hold on to those tables for dear life.

"You'll get the folks who come in the store and camp out for hours and hours and hours," Chris says. "They'll bring in their entire office setup. You know, their printer, their laptop. If you have a registered Starbucks card you get free refills. Endless coffee." Those caffeinated campers Chris is talking about really annoy the shit out of me, and what I found fascinating is how Starbucks manages those "nonexistent" tip jars.

Let's say you give the cute barista who whips your foam a

crisp buck for her troubles. Does it go straight to her? No. All the tips at Starbucks are pooled, number-crunched, distributed by check every week or two, and then taxed. At the end of the workday, tips are placed in bags separate from the day's cash receipts and dumped into a drop safe. At the appointed time of the week, the money is counted, all the hours every employee worked are tabulated, and the tips are distributed according to how many hours each employee worked. So if a barista works 5 percent of the hours in a store, she'll get 5 percent of the tips. "It's pretty socialist," one barista told me.

"So, what happens if I give that cute barista a nice tip and she puts it in her pocket?" I ask Chris. "Is that a problem?"

"I believe Starbucks is very much like a team in everything they do," Chris says. "Everything they do is kind of for the team and the partners. They prohibit one person setting out and keeping everything they get. So if one person hands someone a five they're pretty much required to put it in the jar. It's looked down upon to keep it for yourself . . . There probably will be a corrective taken." What is this? Caffeinated communism? The "third place"? Collectivism? This is all starting to sound very Chairman Mao to me.

As mentioned, baristas' tips are taxed. "It's called allocated tips," Chris tells me. "The way Starbucks looks at it, they'll take an average for an area of what they believe the baristas get tipped. And they will add tax on that per hour to a barista. In our area it's right around fifty cents an hour they're paying taxes on. They're saying, 'You're going to make at least fifty cents an hour in tips, so we're going to tax you fifty cents an hour in tips.'"

When I asked what Starbucks baristas are paid, I learned that this can vary depending on what region of the country the store is in. Chris's store pays its baristas $7.25 an hour, while a Starbucks in Massachusetts might pay a new coffee slinger $8.25 an hour. If a barista in Chris's store worked forty hours a week, fifty-two weeks a year, that would come out, pretax, to

$15,080 a year. The same deal in Boston yields an annual salary of $17,160. So are tips important to Starbucks baristas? You bet your ass they are. As Chris says, "At the end of every week people go, 'Are the tips done yet? Are the tips done yet? Are they ready yet?' They're counting on it."

"Let's call it an average of fifty dollars a week in tips," says Zach, a barista in Boston. "I don't like to think high. Sometimes I'll get thirty to forty, but I'm more likely to get fifty or sixty." Zach works forty hours a week, so he pulls down $1,300 a month. If he gets $50 a week in tips, that's an extra $200 a month. He tells me he uses his tip money to pay for his cell phone and take his girlfriend out to dinner every once in a while.

"Nine times out of ten a customer's going to tip whatever we give back to them in change," Zach says. "Unless you get a regular, whatever you give them back in change is going to be it. If you don't get any change and it's a large order, you might see a dollar. That happens a lot, too."

"I usually tip fifty cents on a cup of coffee," I say.

"On a cup of coffee fifty cents is *amazing*," Zach says. "Fifty cents for two dollars is really generous." A small coffee is $1.73. If someone tips the $0.27 in change, "that's nice of them," Zach says. "I've had people come into the drive-thru wanting five frappuccinos and I have only two blenders. So I'll do five fraps, it's a sixteen-dollar order, these guys will hold up traffic, and we will still be nice, and then you get fifty cents and you're like, 'Thanks for tipping anyway.' No one ever says, 'I can't believe you only left fifty cents.' But then again, I'm also one of those people who think any tip is awesome."

The baristas I spoke to believe that customers who tip at Starbucks know they're going to do so before they walk in the door; their minds' are already made up. If you buy a $1.93 cup of coffee and tip only the $0.07 in change, either you don't care about tipping or you can live with feeling like a cheapskate. But some customers come prepared to tip. Whenever I buy a two-dollar cup of java, I stash a couple of quarters in my pocket.

Another reason why you have to be prepared to tip is because of how Starbucks operates: the only way you can leave a tip is in *cash*. If you sit in a Starbucks in any large city you'll see countless customers buying their caffeinated treats with a credit or Starbucks card. In Manhattan, a town where nobody seems to carry real money, this practice is endemic. But there's a big problem with credit and keychain cards at Starbucks. There's no space on the credit card slip to leave a gratuity.

"It kind of sucks," Zach tells me. "I've actually had people get annoyed with me over that. 'What? I can't leave you a tip?' And I'm like, 'No, they don't let us do it. Sorry.' They feel bad because they don't have any cash, and then they kind of direct that anger at us." So some people in our burgeoning cashless economy get pissed when there's not an opportunity to leave a tip with a credit card!

Zach also gives me the best answer I've heard yet regarding when and where tip jars are appropriate. He contends that because tipping's involved at Starbucks, a higher level of service is expected there. "If I fuck up your drink you can send it back," he says. Meanwhile tip jars at fast-food joints piss Zach off, because he says you'll never get the level of service at such places that he provides his customers. "I can't eat mayonnaise," he explains. "And if I get a number-four combo [at a Wendy's] and they put mayonnaise on it, I have to go back—and then *I'm* the jerk. I get treated like shit for that."

Many customers believe that the level of service at Starbucks doesn't merit a tip. Chris begs to differ. "I would ask [customers] if they tip at a bar? It's the same exact thing. We're doing shots of coffee versus shots of vodka."

Ah, bartenders! For many of us, they're the tipped workers we encounter most often in daily life. So, no tipping quest would be complete without delving into the world of the people who keep us inebriated. It's a tough job, but I figured I'd better get a good, close look into their world. And the best thing about this kind of research is I get to write off my dirty martinis as a business expense.

"What do you consider a good tip on a drink?" I ask Seamus, an older Irishman tending bar in Midtown Manhattan.

"Twenty percent," he says, shocking the shit out of me.

I've always thought that a dollar per drink was a good tip. I've given better tips since I've been in the service industry. Still, I've considered a buck the standard since I bought my first underage beer in 1986. Have I been wrong all these years? Seamus sets me straight.

"You go to a restaurant, right?" he says. "Let's say you order two ten-dollar martinis and eighty bucks of food, so your bill's a hundred. What are you going to do? Only tip on the food?" It's then that I realize I haven't heeded my own advice: as I stated earlier, at a restaurant you *always* tip on wine and booze.

"[It] drives me nuts," Seamus says. "People will tip twenty percent on a drink when they're eating dinner, but when they're sitting at my bar they'll only give me a buck. Why am I any different from a server? On a ten-buck drink I should get anywhere from a dollar-fifty to two dollars."

"Seamus," I say, sipping my dirty martini, "it looks like I might've been shortchanging bartenders for years."

"Don't worry, kid," he says. "Lots of people don't know how to tip."

Seamus's words sting. I'm on a journey to become a guru of tipping and I don't even know the right way to tip bartenders— one of the oldest tipped professions in the world. I should have known that fact already. So much for my knowing the meaning of *trinkgeld*.

"But how about when people are just getting a beer?" I say. "Isn't a dollar enough?"

"Most of the time a beer will cost about five bucks. So if you leave a dollar you're in the ballpark." Maybe Chris from

Starbucks's barista/bartender comparison was correct. If a soy-milk latte runs you five dollars, then a dollar tip is appropriate. But when you're paying for a mixed drink in a bar, good old George Washington just doesn't cut it.

"Listen," Seamus says, "if you pay me a dollar for a martini and then run off to chat up some chick, that's not the worst thing you could do. But what I hate is when some jerk warms my barstool for three hours, slurps five drinks worth sixty bucks, and then leaves me five dollars. That's insulting."

"You'd want him to leave you twelve," I say.

"Damn right," Seamus says. "Think about it. You're taking up real estate at the bar. I'm chatting you up, telling you stories, listening to you bitch about your wife or girlfriend or whatever. I'm your entertainer, confessor, and your temporary friend. Why shouldn't I get tipped for that?"

Seamus isn't far off the mark. In fact, he's dead-on. Waiters hate it when patrons "graze" at tables for hours and hours and then don't increase their gratuity to make up for the fact that they're denying the server the chance to turn the table and generate more income. A bar stool is just like a table in a restaurant. It's a place of business. And bartenders aren't there for their health.

"When I started out in this business," Seamus says, "I was working in this bar in Hell's Kitchen on Wednesday nights. Well, the place was dead on Wednesday nights, so I wasn't making any money. So I went to all the bars where waiters hang out and started chatting my place up. Before you knew it, Wednesday at my bar was where all the waiters came to drink after their shift."

"You established a stable of regulars. Smart move."

"Not only regulars," Seamus says, "but good-tipping regulars. Waiters are the best tippers in the world."

I peer into the remnants of my drink. Not all waiters are the best tippers in the world. I guess I'm going to have to face my own gratuity inadequacies as I journey to become the master of the tip. The truth hurts, but the lies will kill you—or get you bad service.

"So, what do you like better?" I say. "When a person pays you per drink or when they set up a tab?"

"I love running tabs," Seamus says. "That way I can keep track of who orders what. There's none of this 'How many drinks did I get?' shit at the end of the night. And when the bill's a nice large figure on a piece of paper, I stand a better chance of getting my twenty percent." Again, something I didn't know.

Seamus also tells me ways bartenders can coax a good tip out of a customer.

"You pay for your drink, see? And I have to break a twenty. Well, I'm going to put a five or a ten on top of the singles and hover over you when you're thinking about what to tip. That forces the guy into a situation where he has to decide if he's going to give me some singles from the bottom or the larger bill on top."

"So you're guilt-tripping him."

Seamus laughs. "Guilt is a bartender's best friend."

"But I've seen guys leave bartenders huge tips before," I say. "Usually because they're women."

"Yeah, yeah," Seamus says, shaking his head dismissively. "You get a girl with nice tits and suddenly she's raking in all the dough. But let me ask you something. What would you prefer, a bartender who gets your drink right or eye candy?"

I know there are smoking-hot bartenders out there who can mix a drink with the best of them. But when I was a waiter, I'd get my post-shift buzz on at the place with the hottest female drink slinger in town. Most of the guys at the bar were so mesmerized by her beauty that they overlooked the fact that this girl couldn't have made a Shirley Temple if her life depended on it. Even pulling a beer was a stretch for her. But what really drove me up the wall was how she expected men to tip her lavishly. If I gave her a twenty for a beer, she'd put it in the register and then take her sweet time bringing me my change. It was like she expected me to tip her sixteen bucks on a four-dollar beer. I don't care how good-looking a bartender is—unless she's my inamorata, a 400 percent tip is out of the question.

"I guess I'd like both," I say. "No offense."

Seamus chuckles. "Maybe I could stuff my shirt for ya."

"If you're a good tipper," I say after Seamus sets me up with another drink. "What does that get you?"

"I'll remember your name, what you like to drink, and maybe even give you one or two on the house."

Ah yes, the infamous buyback. "But if you give someone a free drink you want to be tipped on it."

"Of course," Seamus says. "But I'm also doing it because I probably like you."

"What if there's a long line at the bar?" I say. "Will you take care of a good tipper first?"

"No way," Seamus says. "The other people have been waiting, so I'm not going to jump over them. You want to impress your bartender? Wait patiently for your drink and then tip me heavily. Brother, I'll always remember you." So, paying extra might bump you to the head of the line at Disneyland or the car valet—but not at a bar. I guess there's only so much that money can buy.

"And here's another thing," Seamus says. "When you go to a wedding and there's an open bar? Tip, for Christ's sake! The booze is free, ain't it?"

A few months after my encounter with Seamus, I met a man who showed me what being a bartender is all about: Manny Aguirre, the barman at the legendary Musso and Frank Grill in L.A. When I walked into the place on that rainy Southern California day the last thing on my mind was tipping. For the first time in my travels, I had taken a break from my tipping quest and decided to be a tourist for a while. After visiting Grauman's Chinese Theatre, standing in Bogie's footprints, and visiting Raymond Chandler Square on the corner of Hollywood and Cahuenga boulevards—the site of the legendary detective Philip Marlowe's office—I sauntered into Musso for a late lunch.

After eating my filet mignon and being regaled by my waiter, Panama, with stories of the film legends who had eaten there, I walked into the barroom to have an after-lunch drink. The bar was empty and a little old man was standing behind the counter polishing glasses.

"How can I help you, sir?" he asked.

Raymond Chandler is my favorite author and he ate at Musso long ago. So, since I was in a 1940s kind of mood, I asked, "Do you know how to make a sidecar?"

The bartender beamed. "Not too many people ask for those."

"Not many people know how to make them."

The bartender smiled. "Don't worry. I've been doing this since before you were born."

I watched in awe as he performed his alchemy with cognac, Cointreau, and lemon juice and then poured the result into a chilled sugar-rimmed glass. And when I took a sip I realized I was drinking one of the best cocktails I'd ever had in my life.

"This is amazing," I said. "And you didn't use a drink measure or anything."

"It's all in my head," the bartender said, tapping his skull.

"My name's Steve," I said, extending my hand. "What's yours?"

"Manny."

Since I was the only customer in the bar, Manny and I got to talking. It turned out he'd worked at Musso and Frank since 1989, and had been the head bartender at some of L.A.'s finest eateries.

As he made me another sidecar, he told me stories about all the famous people he'd waited on: Keith Richards, Harrison Ford, Francis Ford Coppola, and Nicolas Cage, to name a few. And as I sipped my drink I realized something: while Manny was talking to me, I was the only person in his *universe*. Even though I was fresh off the street, he was lavishing as much attention on me as he would have on any movie star. He had a great gift: the gift of being *present*. And this is an ability not too many people have. We've all talked to people who pretend to listen to us only so they could think of what they're going to say next. They might be right in front of us, but mentally they've checked out. Not Manny. He was all there.

Two men walked into the bar, and Manny went to take care of them. For a moment I was jealous that he was being taken away from me. But after he set them up with their drinks, he came back to me, fully present again. In the center of his world, I felt surrounded by a warm sense of well-being—and that wasn't the booze talking.

There's an amazing scene in *The Empire Strikes Back*. Luke Skywalker crash-lands on a jungle planet while searching for Yoda, the legendary Master of the Force, whom he needs to find to become a Jedi Knight. As he's trying to extricate his spacecraft from a lake, he runs into a wizened old green gnome. At first Luke thinks he's just a crazy codger alien—small, weak, and unable to teach him anything. But when the old gnome levitates Luke's ship out of the lake and sets it safely on the ground, Luke realizes that this small little creature is Yoda, the Jedi Master he's been seeking. As I sat at Musso and Frank's bar, I realized this old man was the master *I'd* been seeking. Manny had seen the rich and famous rise to the top and fall to the bottom. He'd seen the unknown kid from Kansas rise from obscurity into stardom. His head was full of wisdom, humor, and every drink recipe ever conceived by the mind of man. He was the Yoda of Hollywood Boulevard.

Three sidecars later, and I was in the bag. After Manny rang up my bill, I tipped him fifty bucks. Of course I overtipped him, but he had taught me that even a bartender on a rainy L.A. afternoon could become a friend for life. That's because friendship is all about being present. Manny's gift of presence meant he could form a bond with almost any person he met. Seamus may have said that a bartender is your temporary friend, but when I return to L.A., I know I'll journey to Musso and Frank just to see Manny. And I will remember him for as long as I live. Because of that, he deserved a great tip. Not because I felt bad for him, nor because I wanted to impress him, but because it was the right thing to do. And that's part of what tipping is all about. That's what the Yoda of L.A. taught me.

Drunk and content, I walked back to Raymond Chandler Square and looked up at the building where Philip Marlowe's office never really existed. And as the cars hissed along the rain-swept boulevard, I swore I could see Marlowe looking out his window and smoking a cigarette while watching the gray twilight play on the Hollywood sign in the distance. Popping open an umbrella, I lit up a cigar and smiled to myself. While taking a break from my quest, my quest had come and found me.

That was a very good day.

Sitting in my local Starbucks one day, I thought about those customers who loathe the tip jars and think the service that baristas provide doesn't warrant a tip. My kneejerk reaction was to dismiss them as cheap bastards. But then I thought to myself, "What the hell do I know?" I've whipped up a few cappuccinos in my time, but I have no clue what it's like to work in a fast-paced java joint, much less if baristas really deserve tips. So I decided that I had to take the plunge and sling coffee for a few days. And I had to travel almost three thousand miles to do it.

I decided to look for an independent coffee shop that would let me try my hand at the coffee arts. After getting a tip about an excellent coffeehouse called Ristretto Roasters in Portland, Oregon, I emailed the owner, Nancy Rommelmann. Without reservation, she and her husband, Din, enthusiastically agreed to let me spend a few days working in their store.

In Portland, coffee is practically a religion. Even the *bad* coffee there is good. And with well over three hundred coffee shops to choose from, Starbucks are as outnumbered there as Custer was at Little Big Horn. After I check into the Ace Hotel in the Pearl District, I wander over to Barista, an über-coffee shop on Northwest Thirteenth Avenue. I'd heard that the store's owner was a hotshot who had won the World Series of Baristas or something. If you go to their website, it reads, "Preparing coffee is not just something that we do in between gigs or something to get us through college. Instead, we take pride in the craft of being *BARISTA*." And man, don't try phoning the store. "Please DON'T call us," the website also reads, ". . . as it will just ring and ring, and you'll be frustrated." I guess they're just too busy being *BARISTA*.

When I walk into the shop I'm immediately struck by the monastic look of the décor and of the workers themselves: a skinny man and woman both dressed in black and looking very, very serious. I have to tamp down the urge to shout, "Now's the time on *Sprockets* ven vee dance! Would you like to touch my monkey?" But that'd probably get me tossed out on my ass, so I decide to order a nine-dollar cup of coffee instead.

No, that's not a misprint. The coffee really costs nine bucks. The coffee I ordered is called Ethiopian Beloya. "It has almost a tealike consistency, with flavors of sugarcane and dark berry," the female barista, a very pretty but severe brunette, tells me. "And it'll take about ten minutes to make." Now, I'm from Jersey, so I'm used to getting my "regular with two sugars" in less than thirty seconds. The reason the java takes so long here is because the barista is using a vacuum coffee brewer. Part Japanese tea ceremony and part freebasing ritual, the coffee preparation involves a device comprised of two glass globes. Coffee goes into the globe on top, water goes into the globe on the bottom, and then heat is applied. As the water gets hot, it goes into the upper globe and brews the coffee. Then, when the heat is removed, the vapor in the lower globe cools and contracts, forming a vacuum that sucks the coffee though a filter and back into the lower chamber, and *voilà*: a nine-dollar cup of coffee. After I thank the barista for patiently explaining the process, I take my oversize cup of coffee and toy with the idea of adding milk and sugar, but something tells me the brunette would decapitate me with a samurai sword if she saw me doing so. Then I discover there's no need. When I put the cup to my lips and take a sip, I realize I'm drinking one of the best cups of coffee I've ever had. Say what you will about their being all *BARISTA*, the people at Barista make a damn good cup of coffee. If you're ever in Portland and have nine bucks to burn, give them a try.

When I get over to Ristretto on North Williams Avenue the next day I'm instantly impressed with how beautiful the store is. Painted in soft whites, the space features exposed rafters holding up a high ceiling. Sunlight streams through the windows, washing the black walnut counters and tables in a soft, inviting glow. With the skylights in the center of the roof casting altars of square light onto the concrete floor, the entire space feels like an airy, welcoming cathedral. Like I said, coffee's a religion in Portland.

When Nancy throws me behind the counter just before the morning rush hits, I learn that I don't know a damn thing about making coffee. At Starbucks everything is automated, but at Ristretto, the baristas do things the old-fashioned way, and the first skill I have to learn is to "pull a shot." If you don't know how to brew a perfect cup of espresso, you might as well hang up your barista apron and go home.

The two baristas working the counter today are Rachel, a slender blonde who's also an artist, and Ryan, a thin, fashionably dressed fellow wearing a porkpie hat and a slightly bemused expression on his face. Lucky Ryan gets tasked with teaching me how to work the espresso machine. Despite his kind and patient instruction, within ten minutes my head is swimming. Since this pulling espresso thing's kind of complicated, let me boil it down for you. Before pulling a shot, the first thing you do is put an espresso cup under the spigot and preheat it by filling it a third of the way with hot water. Then you pick up a "portafilter," a metal basket with a handle, and knock out the compressed puck of old coffee left over from the previous brewing. Then you have to ensure that the portafilter is clean and dry, because when coffee is ground it releases lots of oil, and oil and water just don't mix. So you run the portafilter under hot water and dry it thoroughly. After that's done, you place the portafilter under the grinder's funnel and flick the lever two or three times to drop a "dose" of loosely ground coffee into the basket. The next stage in the process is to compact the coffee—but if you do it at this point you'll just screw everything up. That's because if the coffee bed isn't nice and even in the portafilter, compacting it will create uneven densities in the grind. That's a problem, because when the hot water flows through the coffee at high pressure, it will "under-extract" the less dense coffee and "over-extract" the denser coffee, resulting in a crappy espresso. To avoid this problem, gently sweep your index finger across the basket to distribute the coffee evenly and wipe away any excess. Now you're ready for the compacting part. Of course this isn't a simple process either.

First you give the coffee a *gentle* press with a metal hand tamper, and then give the portafilter a gentle tap so any coffee sticking to the basket's side walls slides off. Then you press down on the tamper with roughly thirty pounds of force to achieve a level and firm compaction. If you screw up the tamp, you're back to the whole density problem again—and will yield weak, flavorless espresso or bitter, black sludge. Either way you'll have a pissed-off customer. After the coffee has been properly tamped down, you twist the portafilter into the machine, press the button, and blast hot water through the grinds at 135 pounds of pressure.

Are we done yet? You wish.

A barista has to watch the espresso stream closely, because as it flows it should have the consistency of maple syrup. If it doesn't, you've screwed something up. The time it takes to extract the coffee is vital as well. A one-ounce shot of espresso should take twenty-two seconds to extract. If it takes nineteen seconds, you've screwed something up. If it takes twenty-five seconds, you've screwed something up. And as Ryan watches me trying to master this most basic of barista skills, I just keep *screwing things up*.

"Don't worry," he says, "you'll get it eventually."

I've made about twenty espressos and have messed up every one. My extraction times are either too fast or too slow, resulting in weak coffee or viscous goo. And not a single shot I've pulled has had the fine brown foam of oil that contains the tastes and aromatic properties that are the hallmark of a good espresso: the *crema*.

"I have no idea what I'm doing wrong," I say, wanting to take a baseball bat to the espresso machine.

"Try it again," Ryan says. But the result is the same: crap.

"Maybe it's not what you're doing," Ryan says. "Maybe it's the grind."

He explains to me that pulling a shot is more of an art than a science, and every barista does things a little differently from every other. Even if the coffee they're using is ground in exactly the same manner, one barista might tamp the coffee with a little more pressure than another, producing different flow times and results. At Ristretto, there are two coffee grinders behind the counter, one for each of the two baristas working a shift. Both are set to grind coffee almost the same way, but not quite. Because their barista styles are unique, Rachel's machine grinds a little bit finer, while Ryan's grinds just a smidgen coarser. And they'll use coffee only from the grinders they've tweaked to suit their own personal style.

As Ryan explains this to me I'm reminded of something I read a long time ago. Back when people used to communicate over telegraph wires, each telegraph operator had his own unique style and pattern when transmitting a message. Among telegraphists, this unique style was known as a "fist," and it could be used to identify which operator was sending a message. In wartime, analysts examining signals traffic could cull valuable intelligence by identifying individual enemy telegraph operators by their "fists." So, when it comes to making coffee, you could say that every barista has his or her own "fist." It's a fingerprint as unique as that of those old-time telegraphists.

Ryan thinks my coffee is being ground too fine for my "fist," and he makes a minor adjustment to the grinder. I measure out a dose, twist the portafilter into the machine, and hit the button. Twenty-two seconds later a beautiful espresso with a luscious *crema* forms in the demitasse cup.

"You got it," Ryan says. "That's perfect."

I pick up the espresso cup and take a sip. It's delicious. It only took me an hour and three pounds of Ristretto's coffee beans, but I did it. Still, Ryan and Rachel aren't crazy enough to let me brew espresso for their customers. "Keep practicing," Ryan says.

The morning rush hits, and soon Rachel and Ryan are whirling like caffeinated dervishes behind the counter. Knowing that I'll only get in their way, I pull back and watch in awe as they work with astonishing speed and accuracy. Without missing a beat, they give me a play-by-play of the action.

"This person wants two cappuccinos," Rachel says, prepping a double-spouted portafilter to pull two shots. "A perfect cappuccino's made of one third foam, one third milk, and one third espresso." She grabs a chilled metal pitcher, adds cold milk, brews the coffee, and starts frothing the milk with the espresso machine's steaming rod. As the wand hisses, the swirling milk magically transforms itself into a silken dairy mousse, and, since she's timed it perfectly, it's ready the moment the espresso stops brewing. Putting the coffee cups on the counter, she slowly streams the foamy milk into the espresso with a slight waving motion, creating a beautiful pattern in the *crema*. Then she takes a plastic stirrer and pulls some of the *crema* into the shape of a flower.

"Wow," I say. "How'd you do that?"

"Practice," she replies.

I later learn that cappuccino or latte art is a big deal in Portland. Baristas have been known to fashion images of hearts, dogs, cats, smiling devils, bunny rabbits, starbursts, teddy bears, flowers, and haunting abstract shapes atop their floating canvasses of coffee and foam.

As Ryan and Rachel perform their well-practiced ballet, I try absorbing all the information and tasks they're throwing at me. Soy lattes are harder to make than regular lattes, because soymilk's fat content is so low. And rice lattes? That's like trying to whip an underfed supermodel into Santa Claus. Prep the espresso cups on top of the machine so they're warm. Clean out the grinders so no one gets stale coffee. If a customer wants you to grind coffee for them to take home, you have to know what kind of coffee maker they use. It's the coarse setting for press pots, medium for drip, and fine for espresso. And if they want Turkish coffee, grind it into particles of quantum dust! Put the dishes in the dishwasher! Here's how the credit card machine works . . . and on and on and on.

When there's a lull in the action, I glance at the tip jar filled with money and finally get around to the reason I've traveled three thousand miles to be here. "So, what's the deal here with tips?"

Ryan and Rachel explain that in addition to the wages Nancy and Din pay them, they take home all their tips at the end of every shift. "How do you keep track of who gets what tips?"

"It's simple," Rachel says. "When Pamela comes in to work the swing shift at twelve thirty, Ryan and I will empty the tip jar and divvy up the tips between us. Then I'll go home and Ryan and Pamela will keep all the tips they make while working together. And when the next barista comes in, they'll empty the tip jar again and divide it between themselves. Then the process repeats itself." I like how Ristretto does things. Unlike the "socialist" tip system at Starbucks, the baristas here get instant monetary gratification for their hard work.

"What percentage of your income is tips?"

"About forty percent," Ryan says, a much higher percentage than at Starbucks.

"And what do you guys do with your tips?" I ask. "What do they pay for?"

Rachel tells me working at Ristretto gives her a flexible schedule to attend to her artistic pursuits and that gratuities pay for all the little extras in her life: clothes, jewelry, beer, and going out to eat. Her paycheck goes to her landlord.

"Tips pay for my food, transportation, and cell," Ryan says. "And my paycheck goes to pay the mortgage on the house I share with my lady friend." The fact that Ryan can afford to buy a house while working as a barista astounds me. And in his spare time he's a musician to boot.

When the morning rush fades into a murmuring echo, I'm exhausted and my brain hurts. I had no idea how hard a barista in a shop like Ristretto worked. Now I know. Since I need to reboot my crashed neural net, I decide to make myself a latte. But when I try doing some latte art, my doodles look like the finger paintings of a deranged psychiatric patient.

At 12:30, Pamela, the swing barista, arrives, and Ryan and Rachel divide up their tips. In four and a half hours they've made thirty-two dollars in tips apiece. Compare that to the fifty or sixty bucks in gratuities Zach gets by check—a week. I'll bet Zach would love to work *here*.

I introduce myself to Pamela, a pretty young woman with a tattoo on her arm, a nose ring, and a wicked folding knife clipped to her right hip pocket. Pursuing an engineering degree, she often does differential equations when things are slow at Ristretto. Differential equations? I can barely balance my checkbook. "Pamela's the mouthy one," Nancy tells me. "She's opinionated and sassy and doesn't have much tolerance for fools. She tells it like it is." When I talk to Pamela about tipping, I discover Nancy's assessment is spot on.

"The tips at this location are very good," Pamela says. "But they kind of suck at our other store on Forty-second Avenue."

When I ask why, she says, "Because the rich people live over there and they have no idea how to tip. We get a younger, creative crowd here, and they're much better tippers." That's probably due to the fact that most "creative types" have worked as waiters at some point in their lives. Nancy later tells me that tips are lower at the other store because most of the customers there are just running in to get freshly ground coffee to take home. They don't have time to form relationships with the baristas. "But at our second location it's like a nonalcoholic daytime bar," she tells me. "People form bonds with the baristas. It's kind of like the bar in *Cheers*."

A fussy-looking woman squawking on a cell phone comes in, orders a rice milk latte to go, and acts as if Pamela doesn't exist. Because I'm attuned to servers' emotional states, I pick up on Pamela's annoyed vibe, but she keeps her game face on. "One rice latte coming right up," she says, smiling sweetly.

"How do you handle people like that?" I whisper to Ryan.

"I just get into a mental safety zone and treat all the customers the same," he says. "You can't take things personally, because that'll just slow you down, and speed is the name of the game. And if you're too busy getting angry at the customers it'll screw up your mojo and you'll make a bad product." As I watch rice latte lady leave, I notice she doesn't leave a tip. I shake my head.

"What do you think is a good tip for the service you provide?" I ask Ryan. "What would you like to get?"

"A dollar a drink," he says instantly. "Just like a bartender." After watching Rachel and Ryan professionally turn out drink after drink all morning, I'd say they deserve it.

When I leave Ristretto, I'm exhausted. I crash into my hotel bed covered in coffee grinds. (I had better remember to tip my maid extra.) After a long nap, I take an evening walk through the city and find myself inside a Portland institution: Voodoo Doughnuts. Despite the fact that some of their doughnuts have perverted names like The Dirty Snowball and Cock and Balls, the place is jammed. After waiting in line for twenty minutes, I get a Voodoo Dozen and head back to the Ace Hotel. Don't worry. All those doughnuts aren't for me. I'm trying out a new way to tip hotel staff.

"These are for you guys," I say, handing the box of goodies to the friendly redhead manning the Ace's front desk.

"Voodoo Doughnuts!" she says, a smile lighting up her face. "Thank you!" Tipping people in glucose and empty fats will work for you every time.

The next morning I'm back behind Ristretto's counter trying to perfect my "shot-pulling technique" when Nancy suggests we play hooky and go for a walk. Honestly? I think she's trying to keep me from wasting her coffee beans.

I really like Nancy. In addition to being a lovely woman she's also a journalist and a *New York Times* bestselling author to boot. I've read some of her stuff, and she's a fantastic writer. As we walk in and out of the quaint stores near the coffee shop, I ask her about Ristretto's pay policies.

When she tells me how much she and her husband pay their employees, I'm amazed by the disparity between Ristretto and Starbucks. The minimum wage in Oregon is $8.40 an hour. Ristretto, however, starts its workers at $10.50 an hour, and some of their baristas make up to $16.00 an hour. "We're pretty liberal with pay raises," she tells me. "Because we believe you have to pay people for a job well done." And in addition to the above-average wages they pay, they also provide baristas who work more than thirty hours a week with health insurance. "It's a great plan from Kaiser Permanente," Nancy says. "We take a hundred dollars a month out of each of [the participating] baristas' paychecks, and Din and I cover the rest ourselves."

"That's got to be tough when you're a small-business owner," I say.

"It is," Nancy says. "And we could put that fifteen thousand a year we shell out into our pockets, but we won't. My father always said you do the right thing because it's *the right thing*. And taking care of our people is the right thing. And nobody ever did it for Din and me."

When I tell Nancy how some people think that people who work for tips are "shiftless losers" or "parasites" living off the largesse of other people, her eyes light up.

"There are a lot of slackers in Portland," she says. "But none of them work for me. I mean, look at the people who work for us. Ryan's a real, live rock star! Rachel's an artist, and Pamela's an engineering student. We've even got a barista who's working her way through nursing school. All my baristas are smart and interesting people." That's a far cry from the characterization some people have of tipped workers being lazy bums living off the tipping dole. When I ask Nancy about the importance of tips to her employees she says, "I've got a manager whom I pay twenty-eight thousand dollars a year. But because tips make forty percent of our baristas' incomes, she's making an additional eleven thousand dollars on top of her salary before taxes—almost thirty-nine thousand a year. That's not too bad for a twenty-three-year-old." Nobody paid me that well when I was twenty-three.

"And I welcome my staff's ideas," she adds. "I *want* them. Din and I want our people to grow with the company and pursue their own dreams. We have no interest in being dictators."

After our little walk, Nancy and I head over to a microbrewery to meet Rachel and Ryan for burgers and freshly made India Pale Ale. The crowd sitting on the picnic benches outside is an interesting mix of people. There are tattooed biker dudes, pretty women in long flowing skirts, a smattering of professional types, and skinny guys wearing the Portland uniform of lumberjack shirts who probably don't know the first thing about wielding an ax. As I enjoy the warm sunshine and beer, I think about how whenever I've traveled to a strange city, I've felt just like that, strange—a foreigner in a foreign land. But the moment I arrived at Portland I felt right at home. I don't know if it's Nancy, the gang at Ristretto, the friendly staff at the Ace Hotel, Voodoo Doughnuts, or the city's vibe, but for the first time in my life I realize I don't always have to live in New Jersey. But if I'm going to go native I'd better learn to pull the perfect shot in case I have to hit Nancy up for a job.

After I say my good-byes to Nancy and Ristretto's staff, I realize I have one more stop to make. A few months earlier, my agent sent me a galley copy from a publisher looking for a blurb. It was for a book titled *Tattoo Machine*, by a guy named Jeff Johnson. I'm not a big fan of tattoos, but I enjoyed his book so much I was happy to write my very first blurb for another author's book. *A wry, tender story about the tribulations of flesh and ink*, I wrote. *And funny as hell. I've never understood why people get tattoos, but after reading Jeff's excellent book I may just get one myself.* I call Jeff up and we agree to meet at the Sea Tramp Tattoo parlor and go out for a drink. When I arrive at the shop Jeff gives me a quick tour of the facility. Of course the conversation soon turns to tipping. I have it on the brain.

"You have to understand that tattoo artists never used to get tipped," Jeff tells me. "Let's face it, the only people who used to get tattoos were bikers, sailors, ex-cons, and skinheads. But as tattoos became more mainstream, and middle-class kids started getting them, they brought their sensibilities into the business. Now we get tipped."

When a profession starts out not being tipped it's unusual for gratuities to make inroads into that profession. (A perfect example of this is flight attendants. Since the early days of flight, these airborne workers have never accepted tips, and still don't to this day.) But like the relentless spread of tip jars, the appearance of gratuities in tattoo parlors is another example of how tip creep is playing out in America. After looking at the excellent work Jeff does, I can fully appreciate why a tattoo artist deserves to be tipped. Dude, when a guy is inking something permanent into your skin, that's not the time to get cheap! "And remember," Jeff says, "the true meaning of the [Latin root of the] word *gratuity* is 'thank you.'"

I'd like to be able to say that Jeff and I spent the rest of our time together waxing philosophical about tipping. We didn't. We just prowled around Portland's bars and got hammered.

"You know," Jeff says, nursing a Jameson, neat, "I drew up a tattoo just for you. But the moment I saw you I knew you'd never get one."

"Was it my Young Republican haircut?"

"Basically."

Twelve hours later I'm on a plane flying above the Cascade Mountains heading for home. As I drink bad airline coffee and munch my prefab breakfast, I think how it's a good thing that flight attendants don't get tips. With food like this, they'd never be able to pay their bills. And as I look at the rugged scenery flowing beneath me, I also think about what tip jars are and what they are not.

Tip jars can be annoying, especially in places where your tip is nothing more than dropping a coin into a collection box. I know, service has little or nothing to do with how much people tip, but we've got to draw the line on tip jars somewhere. So here is my guru proclamation on the subject. If an establishment with a tip jar provides you with care and attention, then you should tip. But if they don't and their tip jar seems like a glorified beggar's cup, then you're off the hook. Having said that, tipping is also a form of giving alms—*baksheesh*. And the reason you find tip jars in so many inappropriate places is because the workers there aren't making enough money. So if you find it in your heart to spare them some change, your reward in heaven will be great.

After talking to the baristas at Starbucks and Ristretto, I

discover that while we are indeed subsidizing their wages to a degree, that's not the whole story. The gratuities baristas make, large or small, help subsidize their hopes and dreams—whether it's playing in a band, becoming an artist, getting a college degree, or just taking a girl on a date. Everybody needs a little help now and then, and when you drop a few coins into that tip jar, even that nonexistent one at Starbucks, you're helping someone get a leg up in life. Nancy and Din somehow found the grit to create a wonderful company that doesn't press people into molds and that allows them to realize their potential. Why should we get all cheap and be any different? Oh, sure, there are some slackers, but then again, look how the SEC let Bernie Madoff scam people for years. Slackers are everywhere. But don't let that stop you from putting your change or a nice crisp dollar into that jar. Whether you're benefiting from the automated machinations of a well-oiled coffee juggernaut or the subtle latte artistry of baristas working at places like Ristretto, these people are working hard to keep you caffeinated. And they deserve that thank-you Jeff was talking about.

Oh, and one more thing. At Ristretto you can leave a tip when paying with a credit card. Now, if only Starbucks would get with the program. It's not about creating the "third place," guys. It's about creating the "right place."

What Price Beauty?
Massage Therapists, Barbers, Hairstylists, Beauticians, and Pet Groomers

I'm lying naked on a table as a guy is pressing his thumb deep into my inner thigh just below my scrotum. And, man, *it feels good*.

"Does that hurt?" Dave, the massage therapist, asks.

"No," I say. "It burns, but it's a good kind of burn."

"You store a lot of tension in your inner thighs," Dave says, sending another wave of rippling heat through my abductor muscle.

"Probably from sitting down all the time."

"Well, you're handling a lot more pressure than I thought you could," Dave says over the soft music playing in his studio. "You're not pushing back too much."

"You can go full force if you want."

"No," Dave says, "this is as hard as I'm going to go."

"Okay," I murmur, feeling kind of sleepy.

Dave's talented hands move upward and start massaging the steel hawsers that my neck muscles have become. "When you write you have your computer on your lap," he says matter-of-factly.

"How can you tell?"

"Because your neck muscles are very stiff. It comes from looking down all the time. When you write, the screen should be level with your eyes."

I can feel the tension flowing out of my head.

I'm forty-one years old and I've never had a massage. Not a professional one, anyway. And for the record, I'm not completely naked. According to New York State law, when receiving a professional massage, your entire body, except for the part the masseuse is working on, must be draped with a cloth. If you're expecting to get a massage totally nude, you're looking for another kind of rubdown.

Why am I here? To discover how to tip on beauty.

Every year millions of Americans plunk down billions of dollars to look and feel good. And whether you're spending your hard-earned nickel at a barbershop, a hair salon, a day spa, or a massage therapist's office, guess what? Tipping is a big deal for the people who make you look gorgeous.

To get the scoop on beauty and gratuities I've decided to get all metrosexual. Like most men, my only concession to grooming is usually to get a haircut. Once a month I drive over to the Acropolis, a men's hair salon in Clifton, New Jersey, to get a trim and my nose hairs shorn. Except for a short time after college, I've been getting my hair cut at the Acropolis for almost thirty-five years. The owner, Gerome, started cutting my dad's hair in 1972, and even though Pop's retired to Pennsylvania, he still drives up just to see Gerome and his partner, Spiro. Talk about loyalty. In fact, Gerome gave my younger brother his first haircut and then gave my nephew *his* first haircut. Going to the Acropolis is a family tradition.

When I graduated from college I was so broke that I stopped going to the Acropolis and subsisted on seven-dollar haircuts that made me look like a hedgehog. But when I was twenty-six and trying to woo a girl, I decided my image needed a make-over. So I walked into a random shop in my hometown and met an excellent barber named Tony.

"Why's your hair so dry, kid?" he asked after assessing my follicular damage. I explained that I had had horrible acne as a teenager and now thought that using a shampoo for oily hair would keep the zits away.

"No, kid," he said, without judgment. "You have dry hair. You need to use something with a moisturizer."

After Tony gave me a new hairstyle, I left his chair feeling reborn. When he sold his shop soon afterward, he got a part-time gig working alongside Spiro and Gerome, and I was back at the Acropolis again. And when Tony hung up his shears for good, Spiro became my barber.

Back when I first sat in Tony's chair all those years ago, he gave me another piece of invaluable advice: "You give a barber fifteen to twenty percent, kid," he said. "And at Christmas you give him the price of the haircut." So now, when Spiro cuts my hair, I give him a five-dollar tip, and I give him twenty-five bucks at Christmas.

In fact, the 15–20 percent rule is pretty standard in the industry. But as women know all too well, tipping for beauty services can be a sticky wicket. Sure, you can tip 20 percent on a $50 cut, but does the same rule apply for a $400 cut, color, and highlight job in a fancy New York salon? And what do you tip the shampoo girl? The lady who waxes your bikini line? What do you tip for a massage or a mani-pedi? A facial? With more and more men getting in touch with their feminine side, they're encountering the same kind of confusion as women.

Still, I don't want to risk overgeneralization. Women's haircuts are a different animal from men's. I once had a girlfriend who wanted me to give her a "new hairstyle" for her birthday. So I handed her my credit card and told her to get done whatever she wanted. "How bad could it be?" I thought. When she got back from the salon she looked great, but when I got my credit card statement, I got the shock of my life. My girlfriend's new do had set me back $300.

"That's nothing," Claire, a hairstylist in Chicago told me when I recounted that story. "Women can spend five hundred bucks, easy, in our salon. And New York prices are even crazier."

"So, what's the deal with tipping in a high-priced place like yours?"

"I think most women get confused by all the people you have to tip in a salon," she says. "There are just so many people involved in the process: colorists, cutters, shampoo girls, assistants, the person who blow-dries your hair. It's hard to keep track of who gets what."

Claire tells me that everyone at a salon should get tipped 15–20 percent for the service they provide. Now, these salon prices are sort of urbancentric, and costs vary across the country, but here's a tip breakdown.

COLORIST: The person who touches up your roots, colors your hair, and does those fancy highlights with the tin foil wraps that keep the aliens from controlling your mind. "It's important they don't give you an all-over color," Claire explains, "but something with more dimension." This process can take up to two hours, and at Claire's salon it costs $200. The tip for this service should be between $30 and $40.

AESTHETICIAN: The person who waxes and tweezes your eyebrows and gives you a facial. Skin treatments can start at sixty dollars, and the tip should be between twelve and sixteen dollars.

BIKINI WAXER: "Well," a spa worker told me delicately, "how long the process takes depends on how much we have to do.

Sometimes it takes ten minutes. Sometimes it takes, uh, half an hour." (Ouch.) The price at many spas starts at thirty-five dollars, so the tip's between five and seven dollars. "But some places charge as high as seventy or a hundred dollars," the spa worker told me. And Brazilian waxes? They cost quite a bit more. Labor costs, you know.

LEG WAXER: Usually the bikini waxer. At a high-end salon this process can cost upward of thirty dollars for half a leg and fifty dollars for the whole thing. So, you're going to be tipping out anywhere from five to ten bucks.

HAIRDRESSER: Forty-five minutes of snipping and shaping costs sixty dollars. The tip should be between nine and twelve bucks.

SHAMPOO GIRL/ASSISTANT: The worker who washes your hair and/or rinses your color. The tip is between three and five dollars.

BLOW DRYER: If the person who blow-dries your hair is a person other than the hairdresser, the appropriate tip is between three and five dollars.

RECEPTIONIST: If the receptionist checks your coat for you, a one- to two-dollar tip is appropriate. "But that doesn't happen very often," Claire tells me.

MANICURIST: A straight manicure at a spa can be as high as twenty dollars. The tip's between three and five. Of course at those nail salons that pop up like weeds, the prices are usually lower—maybe fifteen dollars. Three dollars is an appropriate tip.

PEDICURIST: This can cost seventy dollars at an über-salon, so the tip's between eleven and fourteen. Cheaper places may run you thirty bucks or less, so tip between five and six dollars.

Of course not every woman goes to a high-end salon to beautify herself. For many, going to a spa is a rare treat. But whether you go to a day spa or get your hair cut in some lady's house, the 15–20 percent rule still applies. The trick is to know the prices of every service you receive so you can tip accordingly.

How haircutters get paid varies from place to place. Some shops pay their workers an hourly rate. Other shops let workers make a commission on the cut and pay them a salary. At still other shops there's a percentage split, sixty/forty or some similar formulation. In all these cases the hairstylists keep their tips. And then there's booth rentals—that's when a stylist "rents" space in a salon, keeps all the money she makes, but has to provide all her own products and equipment. And that stuff isn't cheap. Most salons want their renters to use quality hair care products or buy the same stuff the salon uses. Some of those shampoos and conditioners can go for fifty bucks or more a bottle. And scissors? Good ones start at $150 and can go as high as $400. "And if I have to sharpen them that costs me twenty-five dollars apiece," one hair stylist lamented. With booth rentals running from $200 a week and up, these operators are basically independent contractors.

"How much of your income is derived from tips?" I ask Claire.

"A haircut at my place costs sixty bucks," she says. "The salon takes sixty percent, so I keep twenty-four dollars. If a customer tips fifteen to twenty percent on top of that, I'll make between thirty-three and thirty-six dollars a cut." Tips account for one third of what Claire makes. Other hairdressers told me tips account for 25 to 33 percent of their compensation. So tips are very, very important.

"Tips tell me the customer appreciates what I do," Kelly,

a beautician from New Jersey says. "They tell me I'm doing a good job and they recognize the dedication I put into my job. I fly out to L.A. for hair conventions with my own money to learn about the newest trends and technology. I take my work seriously. I'm a professional. But tips also help pay my bills."

Beauty workers remember who tips and who doesn't. If you're a good tipper, hairstylists will see you at the last minute, cram you into their schedules, take extra care of your hair, and even do your hair after regular business hours. "But if you come in when the salon's closed, you should tip a little extra," Claire says. Bad tippers, however, can find themselves blackballed or unable to secure last-minute appointments. "That all depends if the receptionist and the owner are on your side," Kelly says. "If a bad tipper is friends with the owner or something, you're stuck."

"How do you handle that?"

"Roll your eyes, deal with the client, and move on."

What every hairstylist hates are customers who are late for their appointments. "I'd rather you not show up than come late. If you cancel, I can take a break or do a walk-in," Kelly says. "But if you're late, then I have to spend the rest of the day playing catch-up." Many of us have been late for a haircut. It happens. But if a customer is habitually late that means they're inconsiderate and they run the risk of being told never to come back. "No-shows" hurt both the stylist's and salon owner's bottom lines. Don't be that guy. (Or lady.)

"But what really drives me nuts," Claire says, "is the lack of communication. Some women come in and go, 'I don't know what I want.' If I ask if you want your hair set to your chin, don't tell me you don't know. You've got to give me something to work with."

"What if a woman comes in with a magazine and says, 'I want this'?"

"That's actually very helpful," Claire says. "It helps me

know what you want. But don't expect to end up looking like the model."

"So if a woman shows you a picture of Charlize Theron's hair, it doesn't mean she's going to end up looking like her."

"Some people come to us as though they want us to change who they are, and a haircut's not going to do that," Claire says. "And when it doesn't do that and you're finished with your service and the client's disappointed, it's a very difficult thing to have to deal with, because you cannot tell your client, 'I can't change who you are on the inside.' You're coming in for a haircut. I don't do plastic surgery."

Let's face it: women have historically been more concerned with their looks than men. The media constantly bombard women with images of supermodels with kick-ass bodies, flowing tresses, perfect skin, and gleaming white smiles. And despite the fact that many of the women you see in the pages of *Vogue*, *Glamour*, or *Cosmo* have been PhotoShopped into supernatural unreality, many women buy into the fiction that they have to look *perfect*. I once worked in a psychiatric hospital and saw women struggling with bulimia and anorexia. Once you've seen a young woman who looks like a concentration camp survivor you realize the terrible price some women pay to chase an impossible dream. Beauty is nice; let's not kid ourselves. But who among us doesn't have a little jiggle in their wiggle? A pimple on our ass or hair where it just shouldn't be? But it's the flaws that make us endearing.

When women visit a salon or hairdresser it can be a very personal thing. They're entrusting their looks to another person and have come face-to-face with the reality of their physical self in the glaring lights of the makeup mirror. It's a vulnerable space, like when you reveal your nakedness to another person. And let's face it, it doesn't get more up close and personal than when a spa worker's ripping out your pubic hair. Is it any wonder so many women see the same stylist, colorist, and waxer over and over again? "Eighty to ninety percent of my business is regulars," Kelly told me. That's because women can form intense personal bonds with beauty workers and will follow hairstylists from salon to salon. And whenever a salon puts out a "Help Wanted" sign it usually includes the phrase "Following preferred."

"So do hairstylists take revenge on obnoxious customers?" I ask Claire. "I mean a hairdo is a walking billboard."

"That's true," Claire says. "But if the client's a real asshole, you never want to see them again, so you can totally fuck up their hair." She then tells me about a woman who always castigated her whenever she blow-dried her hair. "She'd explain to me how she wanted it, and I'd do it," she says. "And at the end she'd always complain over this one piece on the top of her head that she didn't like. But once the hair is dry, I can't go back and blow it again." Eventually Claire had enough of this woman's insanity and screwed up her hairdo. "I just burned her hair," Claire admits. "She didn't notice it necessarily. Probably until the next day or whenever she washed it again. *But I watched her ends burn as I wrapped it around the brush . . .* I never saw her again."

Male hairstylists aren't above a little vengeance either. "I won't mess a guy's hair," Spiro tells me. "But I'll rush through the job. I won't give them the attention I give you."

Now, interviewing salon workers is nice and all, but when you come down to it, talk is cheap. I knew I had to experience what women go through, so I booked a "Day of Beauty" for myself at a day spa where my friend Sasha works.

When I pull into the spa's parking lot I'm a tad nervous. Despite the fact that many men are availing themselves of spa treatments nowadays, I can almost hear my poker buddies laughing their asses off. And many women would be laughing along with them. When I was at the mall a few months ago I stopped in front of a store called The Art of Shaving. They sell all sorts of expensive beard-removal accoutrements and they even shave customers right in the shop. As I was admiring the boar bristle brushes, a girl and her boyfriend stopped in front of the store window. "Look at that faggot," the girl said, pointing to a man getting a shave in the chair. "If you ever do that I'll break up with you."

My first thought was, "What the hell? Men shave themselves every day. When did that become a 'faggy' thing?" And there's nothing like a barbershop shave. It's a luxury even the manliest man would enjoy. Heck, John Wayne got them.

"Yeah, babe," the girl's boyfriend said with a smirk. "I'd never do something as gay as that." As I watched them walk away I felt sorry for the boyfriend. What he should have said was, "Honey, you don't know a goddamn thing." But he was young and probably still figuring out what it means to be a man.

When I walk into the day spa, the receptionist's eyes spark with surprise. "We don't get too many men in here," she says sweetly. Just great.

"Would you like some herbal tea?" she asks, taking my coat. "Sparkling water?" I feel like asking her for straight bourbon in a dirty glass, but I go with the water instead.

"So you're here for a facial, manicure, pedicure, and a cut?" she asks, looking at my appointment card. I say I am.

"Just wait here," the receptionist says, pointing toward a comfy chair. "Sasha will be with you in a few minutes." As I sip my Perrier, I look at the magazine choices: *Elle, Vogue, Modern Bride*, and *Us*. What I wouldn't give for a copy of *Guns & Ammo* right now.

After several minutes Sasha emerges from the back of the woman cave. "Hey, Steve," she says. "Come on in. We'll do your facial first."

As I walk into the heart of the spa, a young woman drying her fingernails under a blower casts me a curious look. Even though Sasha's spa does offer men's services, it's rare that a male of the species makes it inside. I'm invading her space.

"Man on the floor," I say, trying to break the tension. The young woman quickly averts her eyes.

"Sit here a moment," Sasha says. "I have to get the room ready for you."

As I watch the woman drying her nails, my anxiety level ramps up. To paraphrase Raymond Chandler, I belong in this place like a pearl onion on a banana split. Finally, Sasha waltzes back into the room. "Okay, all ready," she says gaily.

Once I'm in the skin treatment room, Sasha tells me that I have to take off my shirt and get under the heated blanket on the table. "I'll wait outside until you're done." So I strip off my shirt and hop under the covers. When I'm comfortably situated, Sasha walks back into the room.

"The first thing I'm going to do," she says, smearing some goop on my face, "is to cleanse your skin."

"What are you using?"

"Oh, just some oils and cleansers," she says. I'm afraid to know what's in them. With my luck it's some exotic reduction of lizard piss.

After the cleansing, Sasha applies a gravelly mixture to my epidermis. "This is to exfoliate your skin," she says.

"OWW, OWW, OWW!"

"What's the matter?"

"That stuff got into my eye!"

"I'm sorry!"

"It's rubbing up against my contact lens!" It feels like broken glass.

After the intruder is washed away, Sasha takes a sinister metal tool and holds it near my face.

"What's that for?"

"I'm just going to dig out a few blackheads," she says soothingly.

While she digs away, my mind flashes back almost twenty-nine years. When I hit puberty I developed a terrible case of acne. How bad? Think of the most zit-pocked kid you knew in high school and square it. One time I had a pimple on my nose that was so bad it made me look like Rudolph the Red-Nosed Reindeer. I begged my parents to let me stay home from school that day, but they made me go anyway. Of course my eighth-grade classmates, who were blemish-free, mocked me mercilessly. When you're a gawky teenager with a head too big for your body, things are tough enough. But being called Pizza Face and Zit Boy will do wonders for your self-esteem.

To combat my affliction I had to go to a dermatologist once a week for several years. During every visit, the doctor would dig out the legions of blackheads, inject stuff into my face, and then bake me with a UV lamp. It was pure torture. And by the time my acne cleared up at age twenty-one the psychological damage had been done. Even though some girls actually thought I was cute and asked me to take them to high school dances, I could never shake the feeling that I was *ugly*. So as Sasha digs a big one out of my nose all those terrible feelings start stirring again. And it's then that I realize how vulnerable women are in those moments, when their flaws are being examined, yanked out, and smoothed over.

When Sasha is done excavating, she smears a thick cream on my face. "This is a moisturizer," she says. "I'm going to let it soak into your face for fifteen minutes."

"It kind of burns."

"I'm not surprised," she says. "Your skin's very dehydrated."

Sasha leaves to let me stew. And as I listen to the New Age music being piped into the room, my old adolescent emotions fade away. Even though having acne was quite the whack to my self-image, I got over it. By the time I was thirty my feelings of ugliness were replaced by confidence, and now, at forty-one, I know I'm scrum-deli-icious. I don't think I'm Adonis or anything, please. I could lose some weight, add muscle tone, eat better, stop smoking cigars, and improve my wardrobe. But as I've gotten older I've become a lot more accepting of who I am and what I look like. Besides, what can I do? This is the only body I have.

"So why do you like doing this kind of work?" I ask Sasha when she returns.

"Oh, I get to be all girly-girl and make people pretty," she says.

"What do you do when your clients are, well, ugly?"

"I make them prettier," Sasha replies without skipping a beat.

But money is also why Sasha likes her work. In addition to her base salary and tips, she makes a commission on every bottle of expensive lotion and cream she sells. "I move a lot of product," she tells me when I ask about her compensation. "So when you add it all up I make two thousand dollars a week." Yet again, I'm in the wrong business.

"But don't worry," Sasha says, "I won't try and sell you any stuff. Besides, I don't think we have anything for men."

After an hour and a half of her attentions, she whisks me in to see Marisol, the manicurist. When I look at myself in the mirror I heave a sigh of relief. I don't look like a character from *Star Trek*.

As Marisol gently puts my feet into a swirling warm bath I look around and say hello to the female customers in the room. The youngest of them, a girl around twenty-five, doesn't say a word. But the older women are polite and wisecrack about how nice it would be if their husbands followed my example and got a pedicure. "He's always stabbing me with his toenails," one woman with a Brooklyn accent says.

"Takes a tough man to get a pedicure," I reply.

After Marisol clips my nails, trims their cuticles, and buffs them to a high gloss, she rubs the calluses off the soles of my feet and then starts a hot stone massage. I could get used to this.

"You have very nice feet," Marisol says. "Most men have nicer feet than women."

"Really?"

"Sure. You guys wear sensible shoes that cover your feet and protect them from the elements. We're cramming ours into high heels, sandals, open toed-shoes, and they're *always* getting dirty." Marisol has just confirmed my suspicion that guys who wear Birkenstocks are girlie-hippie dweebs and they'll end up with the feet to prove it. Once my feet are done, Marisol takes me over to the manicure table and starts on my fingernails. They need work.

Manicures have an interesting history. The practice has been around since Indian women tricked out their nails five thousand years ago, and ancient Chinese empresses were known for their intimidating set of claws. Of course, the practice has been in the United States for years, but it was once something you could get done only in an expensive salon. Back in the 1970s a salon manicure could cost $60. If you adjusted for the cost of inflation, $60 in 1970 would be $337 today. So why are there low-cost manicure parlors run by Asian women all over the United States where they charge $13 instead of $1,000? Thank Tippi Hedren. You remember her; she was the chick in the phone booth getting attacked by a legion of demonic poultry in Alfred Hitchcock's thriller *The Birds*.

According to an article in the *Los Angeles Times*, Hedren became involved with the plight of Vietnamese refugees flocking to California after the fall of Saigon in 1975. And as she worked with some of the women, she noticed that they had beautifully sculpted nails, "long, oval and the color of coral." So Hedren flew in her personal manicurist to teach a group of twenty women the trade and used her fame to get beauty schools to find them jobs. Because of their limited English skills, these women couldn't compete with the higher-end salons, so they did what any driven businessperson would do—drastically undercut the competition. Within a few years Vietnamese women had a lock on the nail business in California. And that process repeated itself with other immigrant groups, especially Koreans. In my town alone there are ten nail salons, all run by Korean women.

And with so much competition, they're always engaged in one kind of price war or another, so their prices remain low. So this influx of Asian nail technicians took what was "an indulgence for the pampered and wealthy," according to the *Los Angeles Times*, and made it into "an affordable American routine." While these nail workers face resentment from their pricier comrades, and sometimes suffer from poor working conditions, American women can now get their mani-pedis on the cheap, thanks to Tippi Hedren.

After Marisol makes my hands and feet pretty, it's time to do my hair. A shy-looking Latina shampoos my hair, and when she's done I hand her five dollars.

"Thank you, sir," she says, looking absolutely shocked. Maybe the lunching ladies who go to this spa don't know they have to tip her.

Soon I'm in the chair, where a thin, taciturn stylist named Sebastian asks me, "So, what are you looking for?"

"Something different," I say. "Something that's new but doesn't make me look like a forty-year-old trying to be twenty."

"Gotcha."

After Sebastian gives me a new do, my little day of beauty is finished and I go to the receptionist to pay up. Because Sasha's a friend of mine I get a bit of a discount, but the bill's still almost $200. If I were a woman getting a coloring and a massage the bill would be stratospheric. Thank God I'm writing this off as a business expense.

Now it's time to give everyone a tip. When I called the spa earlier to do some reconnaissance, they said they prefer all tips to be in cash. In fact it's impossible to leave a tip here any other way. Just like at Starbucks, there's no line on the credit card slip to leave a gratuity. I have to put everyone's tip in an envelope, write down my name and whom the tip is for, and drop it into a locked box. For beauty workers this is the stage in the process where things get hairy.

Some salons do indeed accept credit card gratuities. But then you have to tell the receptionist who gets what, and as some stylists told me, there are often lapses in communication. If you can leave gratuities only in cash, and the salon doesn't have a tip box and envelopes, you have to give the receptionist your money and tell her how to distribute it. Again this leads to communication errors and occasional pilferage. Now, the vast majority of salon receptionists are honest, but as Kelly tells me, there are some occasional bad apples. "We had a receptionist who thought when someone handed her a twenty-dollar bill and said, 'Can you split this up between the cutter, stylist, the colorist, and the assistant' that she was included. She was a psycho junkie with a lot of issues. I got her fired in the end, because we finally woke up and realized what she was doing."

I'd like to say you could cut down on these shenanigans by going into the salon with cash ready to press into everyone's palm. But as one worker told me, "It's a salon. Not a strip club. You don't go in there with a wad of singles." Also, you may not know what everyone deserves to be tipped until you get an itemized bill. But there's a problem with the tip envelopes, too: they create distance between the customer and the beauty workers. Instead of looking them in the eye, saying thank you, and handing them a tip, you're one stage removed from the process. And this lack of human interaction at tip time has a funny way of making people suddenly cheap. "Sometimes I'll open an envelope expecting a fifteen- or twenty-dollar tip and they've left me five dollars," one haircutter told me. "Sometimes I want to mail that envelope back to them and say, 'Hey, you must need this more than I do.'" Occasionally a customer will write the worker's name on the envelope but not their own—undertipping them in quiet anonymity. But don't worry, the workers eventually catch on.

I examine my bill and, since I'm getting a discount, tip

heavier, stuff the money into the little envelopes, and leave. I think they will all be very happy with what I've left them. Just like when I walked out of Tony's shop years ago, I feel like a new man. I've also come to a conclusion: if you can't afford to tip the workers at a salon or day spa, then you can't afford to go there. When I get home I pick up some of the moisturizer Sasha recommended. Maybe there *is* something to all this metrosexual stuff. Just don't tell my friends I said that—ever.

Of course beauty is not limited to human beings. Many people like their pets looking gorgeous as well. Americans spend $45 billion a year on their pets. That's more than the GNP of all but sixty-four of the world's nation states. Long gone are the days when Fido slept outside and waited at the table for scraps. Lavishing attention on their surrogate children, American "pet parents" now feed their pooches locally sourced food, treat them to "spa days," replace neutered testicles with prosthetic ones so poor Spot doesn't feel "emasculated," dress their dogs up in fancy clothes, buy them jewelry, and even drop hundreds of dollars on bottles of canine perfume. Egged on by that televised marketing machine called *Animal Planet*, Americans have begun projecting their narcissistic impulses onto their dogs in much the same way hypercompetitive parents micromanage their overscheduled kidbots' lives, even arranging doggy play dates and "stimulating" enrichment programs. No wonder vets are prescribing animals Prozac and pet psychiatrists are springing up all over the place. What's next? Doggy rehab?

Because we're talking about such serious amounts of cash, it should come as no surprise that pet care has become a *huge* service industry in this country, with pet grooming, day care, and boarding accounting for a $3.5 billion slice of the critter-care pie. With that kind of money floating around, significant amounts of tip cash must be involved. If everyone tipped groomers and dog hostelry workers 15 percent, we're looking at over $500 million in gratuities changing hands. With this in mind, I decided to ask the ladies at Pampered Pooch, the people who groom my dog, Buster, if I could spend the day working with them.

"Sure," Alicia, the owner, says. "Why don't you come the day before Super Bowl Sunday. People have lots of parties and they want their dogs looking nice. We'll be packed." True to her word, when I arrive at Pampered Pooch on the appointed day the lobby is crammed with dog owners.

"Can you get Princess done in an hour?" an anxious-looking woman says, holding a cocker spaniel.

"No, ma'am," Alicia says. "It'll be three hours before we're done with her."

"Can I stay while you groom her?"

"You can," Alicia says. "But we prefer that you don't. When owners hang around it just makes the dogs nervous."

"But you can have her ready in an hour, right?" Doggy Mama says.

"We'll call you when she's done."

After the woman reluctantly leaves, Alicia says to me, "Some dog owners are complete neurotics. And a cocker spaniel is one of the toughest dogs to groom."

"Why's that?"

"Because their hair is so thick. Lots of groomers try cutting corners and just stick them in a cage dryer to save time. But we don't do that. If you don't manually brush the dog's hair as it's drying it'll come out terrible."

"So some dogs take longer than others?"

"Oh, yeah," Alicia says. "And we like to do things right here. But you see Daisy, the Rottweiler over there? She's what we call a 'trophy dog.' We just have to soap her up, clip her nails, and she's done."

"I'll bet you love those."

"You bet," Rachel says. "In fact, I'm gonna knock Daisy off first. Could you go get her?"

"Sure."

I approach the cage with some trepidation. Daisy, a big, powerful dog, is pacing nervously in her pen; it's obvious all the other dogs barking have made her nervous. Remembering that dogs smell fear, I talk to Daisy in an even, firm voice.

"Good dog, Daisy. Don't kill me."

Daisy's ears prick up at the sound of my voice. I offer my closed fist and let her snort it. Suddenly her stubby tail starts wagging. I smile. Most dogs like me.

As I help the girls by cleaning up a mountain of dog shit (ah, the glamorous life of a writer!), I find out that grooming dogs is a hell of a lot harder than grooming human beings. First off, dog hair gets up your nose, saturates your clothes, and induces a constant, maddening itch. There's also a lot of heavy lifting, wrestling with big dogs, and the occasional bite. "When I get out of here," Bernice, the assistant groomer, says, "all I want to do is drink a glass of wine and go to sleep." Both she and Alicia tell me they've suffered from aching feet, bad backs, and even one torn rotator cuff.

For eight hours I help the groomers greet customers, wash dogs, sweep up hair and unclog tub drains filled with wet masses of the stuff, and clean up more canine shit, all the while getting doggie nail clippings down my shirt. ("They're in my bra when I get home," Alicia tells me.) And I learn which dogs are easy and which are tough to groom. "Trophy dogs" include boxers, bull-dogs, pit bulls, beagles, and Chihuahuas. The toughest dogs are cockers, Wheaton terriers, standard poodles, sheepdogs, and, with apologies to President Obama, Portuguese waterdogs. By five o'clock the shop's almost empty, and I'm a sodden, urine-scented, dog-hair-covered mess. But we're not done. There's one appointment left.

"Here," a fat man with a Russian accent says imperiously, handing Bernice a shaggy-looking Maltese puppy. "Clean up my dog. And don't take off all his hair."

"Certainly, sir."

After she examines the puppy she waves me over. "Feel this," she says, placing my hand on the quivering pup's fur. "See how the coat's smooth on top but matted underneath? That's a sign the owner's not taking care of the dog."

Upon further inspection she discovers that the Maltese's condition is more serious than she initially thought. The dog's hair is so matted that it's at risk of developing dermatological problems and infection. "A dog's hair has to breathe," she explains. In a case this severe the proper thing would be for the owner to take this dog to a vet, have it anesthetized, and then remove the hair with surgical shears. But Bernice knows this owner will never plunk down the $200 this procedure costs, so she decides to shave down the dog herself. It won't be fun for the dog, and it won't please the owner, but in the end it'll be the best thing for the animal.

Because the dog's frightened, and shaving him is painful, it takes over an hour to get the job done. After holding a whimpering, scared dog while Bernice gently works her clippers, I have tears in my eyes. I'm also very, very angry. I'm not alone.

"You took off all his hair!" Fat Russian shouts when he comes to collect his dog.

Bernice quietly tries explaining to the man that it was for the dog's own good, but the man will hear none of it. "You're lazy," he says. "You took easy way out."

As Bernice prepares the man's bill he takes turns verbally castigating her and talking in rapid-fire Russian into his cell phone. As I pet his dog soothingly I can feel my anger reaching its breaking point.

"I never come here again," the man spits out. "You're no good."

I move into the man's cone of vision. Our eyes lock and I give him my "I'm gonna take a tire iron to your kneecaps" stare. That shuts him up. After I hand him his dog, he throws a fifty on the counter and leaves. There's no tip, obviously.

"What an asshole," I say, feeling very sorry for the dog.

"We get people like that all the time," Bernice says.

After I say my farewells and get home, I pick up my dog Buster and give him a kiss. "You don't know how lucky you have it," I say. Grooming a dog is much harder than grooming a human.

While I enjoyed being around animals all day, I realized that the human component was the toughest thing Alicia and Bernice had to deal with. Most of the dog owners were nice, decent people who took care of their animals. But some of them were insane.

So, what to tip a dog groomer? After seeing how hard these ladies work: 20 percent—always. Sure, dog grooming is expensive, but if you can't afford to tip these workers, you can't afford to take your pooch to the groomer. And if you can't afford to go to the groomer, you can't afford to own a dog.

Back in Dave's massage studio I'm completely blissed out. After an hour being underneath his strong hands, I feel loose, relaxed, and that annoying twinge in my shoulder is gone.

"So tips are important to you," I venture.

"Very important," Dave says, stating that gratuities account for a third of his income. While the vast majority of his clients tip, there are some cheapskates out there.

"It's the people who don't get massages very often or got a gift certificate from their boss or something," he says. "Out-of-towners or inexperienced people who don't give a shit . . . and if someone else is paying for the massage, they're going to hand over their gift certificate and run out the door."

"How does it feel not to get tipped?"

"It *pisses* me off," he says. "Tipping is part of the beauty culture. It's part of the deal. If you can be part of it, if you can afford a massage, you can afford a tip. I think it's categorically rude for you to buck the system and say, 'I'm not going to tip.' It's like that scene at the beginning of *Reservoir Dogs* where

Steve Buscemi is railing against tipping. That's the kind of attitude that pisses me off."

He explains to me that he wants a 15 to 20 percent tip when he works at the spa. And if he senses a customer is ignorant about tipping on a massage, he'll work it into the conversation.

"I can ask leading questions with the best of them," he says. "A big thing that's come up lately this year is 'Oh, how are you guys doing in the recession?' And that enables me to say. 'Just like everyone else, we're slow, too, yada yada yada, and I work for a pretty good company and the fact that we make gratuities helps a lot, too.' I can say things like that without being a schmuck about it, without being obvious." He tells me that having the receptionist on your side when it's time to pay the bill helps out a lot. If she says, "Would you like to add on a gratuity for the masseuse?" that means she's worried you might be a cheapskate.

"What do you do when your clients are unappealing physically," I ask Dave. "What do you do if they're ugly?"

Dave tells me that being a massage therapist means you won't be able to work with pretty people all day. You have to be able to deal with humans of every stripe—gay, straight, black, white, well-toned and attractive, flabby, healthy, or sick. It's a job, and you have to leave your squeamishness at the door. Dave learned this lesson when he was just starting out and volunteered his time at a wellness center for people with HIV. One day an almost skeletal man covered all over with Kaposi's sarcoma lesions came in for a massage.

"I've known lots of people who have HIV," Dave says. "But I've never known anyone who's had full-blown AIDS. So for the first and only time in my entire career in massage therapy I put on rubber gloves. To protect me and to protect him."

At first the man whined and complained. "He had a bad attitude at the very beginning," Dave says. "And I just said to myself, 'This guy needs me . . . he needs my energy. He needs me to be there and be present.' So, what happened in the next hour was I just connected with this guy and gave him the same kind of treatment I'd give anybody else . . . And by the end, his attitude was so different. He was like a completely different person. He was like, 'That was so wonderful. Thank you so much.' He hadn't been touched like that in a long, long time."

I get dressed, pay my bill, and tip him 20 percent.

As I walk along around Union Square, I light a cigar and enjoy the young girls walking by in their chic clothes. Feeling loose and relaxed, I puff on my cigar and think about beauty.

Beauty workers can't fix who you are as a person. They can only burnish what physical attributes you have, not transform you into a supermodel or turn back the clock. Like Sasha and Dave, they can work to make you feel "pretty," and they deserve tips for their hard work. But beauty comes only when you accept who you are. When you accept the truth of yourself. It's a journey we all have to make. I'm still working on it.

As I puff on my stogie a woman in her seventies walks past and winks at me. I wink back. I can tell that she was once a beautiful woman, and her eyes still hold the joyous luminosity of her youth. This woman, I suspect, gets what beauty is all about. I hope I'm like her when I'm old and gray.

"Beauty is truth, truth beauty," I murmur to myself as I watch the beautiful people stroll around Union Square. "That is all ye know on earth, and all ye need to know."

CHAPTER 7

Abode of Riches
Deliverymen and Movers

It's Saturday morning and I'm sitting in a furniture delivery truck that's idling in front of a monolithic apartment complex in Dumont, New Jersey. Things are not going well.

"Lady, I just deliver the furniture," the driver, a compact man with thinning hair named Liam, says into his cell phone. "If you want to dispute the delivery fee, you'll have to call the store."

I shift uneasily in my seat. It's our first delivery of the day and we're already falling behind schedule. And because I'm riding shotgun as an observer, Liam's two sons have been forced to sit wedged between several pieces of furniture on the cold van floor.

"You guys okay?" I whisper, feeling guilty.

"We're okay, sir," says Patrick, a strapping twenty-year-old college quarterback. I don't know what bugs me more, that I feel guilty or that Patrick calls me "sir." Have I gotten to the age where college kids think I'm an old coot? Then again, I'm not much younger than Patrick's father.

"Ma'am," Liam says, sounding exasperated, "there's a thirty-dollar delivery charge. They told you that when you bought the piece."

I strain my ears to hear what the woman on the other end of the line is saying. I can't make out the words, but from the rapid and pressured noises emanating from the earpiece, she sounds like a manic-depressive on crack.

"Listen, this is my time, too," Liam says firmly. "I have other deliveries to make. I'll wait here for ten minutes while you call the store and sort this out." High-pitched, angry sounds warble out of the cell phone.

"Well, if I have to come back here again you'll get charged another delivery fee," Liam says, looking at me wanly. "Then you'll be out sixty bucks." The woman's screeching reply would've given the Harpies of ancient Greece a run for their money.

Liam winces, listens for a few moments, and then hangs up.

"I knew this lady was going to be a problem," he says. "There'll be no tip from her."

Liam and his two sons work for a store in North Jersey that specializes in reupholstering antique furniture and crafting custom pieces. I bought a sleigh bed from them a few months back and Liam delivered it. While his crew was setting up my bed, we got to talking, and after Liam cleared it with his boss, I got the green light to ride along with him on a delivery day. The only caveat was that I had to provide the store with a letter releasing them from any liability if I got my brain depanned from a falling credenza.

"Why is this lady being so difficult?" I ask.

"The owner of our store usually waives the delivery fee," Liam explains. "He tells customers, 'Just be sure to tip my guys.' But if he thinks the customer's gonna stiff us, he slaps on a delivery charge. He thinks this lady's cheap."

"The delivery price sounds very reasonable," I say. "When I got a couch delivered last year I was charged a hundred bucks to get it in the door."

"Where'd you get it from?" Liam asks. I tell him I bought my couch from a nationally recognized chain.

"You're lucky that's all they charged you," Liam says. "One

of the biggest scams going is delivery charges for furniture. Have you ever wondered why some stores can move a bedroom set for six hundred bucks?"

"Why?"

"Because they don't pay a dime to deliver it. They farm it out to some no-name guy with a truck and three Mexicans. That way the store doesn't have any payroll, insurance, or liability costs associated with shipping.

"And here's the kicker," Liam says. "You buy that bedroom set and they tell you the delivery fee is ninety bucks. But that ninety only covers delivery to your door. If you want them to bring it into the house, they'll stick it to you for another ninety. If you don't pay it they'll just leave it on the sidewalk. So, what you gonna do? Now your six-hundred-dollar bargain's costing you eight hundred."

"That sounds like extortion."

"There are plenty of 'man with vans' out there," Liam says. "They don't care about your furniture or the store. They just want the money."

"So why isn't there full disclosure about the delivery fee at the store?"

"Because furniture salesmen rank just below used-car salesmen on the food chain," Liam says. "They're bottom feeders who will say anything to make a sale."

The furniture store calls Liam and tells him they'll work something out with Ms. Manic-Depressive and to proceed with the rest of his deliveries. "We'll make her our last stop of the day," Liam tells me.

"So where are we off to now?"

"Da Bronx."

"Lovely."

Quickly discovering that we both aspired to be Catholic priests at some point in our lives—I for a New Jersey diocese and he with the Franciscans—Liam and I hit it off right away.

"After I punched out one of the friars, I began to think that that life wasn't for me," Liam says. I never laid a beating on one of my professors, but Lord knows I wanted to.

Liam came to New York City with two friends to start a new life when he was nineteen. "When we got off the plane we were three illegals with a hundred and twenty bucks between us. That's the exuberance of youth: thinking you can get by on that amount of money. We were so broke we couldn't even stay at the YMCA for nineteen dollars a day. So we ended up living in a flophouse, next to an old hooker and a heroin addict. It was grand until our money ran out. Luckily, the Irish immigrant community in New York is very tight. People would put us up in their basement, an extra bed, on the floor—wherever there was room. I moved nineteen times in three months. It was fantastic. But now that I'm older I'd never want my sons to go through that."

Liam's one of those Irish charmer types, complete with a lilting Galway accent. Throughout his life he's worked as a moving man, waiter, and bartender, sold caskets, toiled in publishing, and dealt in real estate. He's made money, lost money, married, had five children, gotten honest, become a citizen, and he now runs an import/export company. He's a good man, but a hustler through and through. A born salesman, given half the chance he'd sell me the coat I was already wearing. He works for the furniture store on the only day they make deliveries, Saturday.

"I've got five children," Liam says, "so the extra money's good. Besides, what would I do sitting around home all day? Get fat?"

Liam and his sons get a hundred bucks apiece for a Saturday's worth of work. If the delivery schedule is light, they'll work in the shop. "But sometimes we'll spend more than twelve hours on the road," Liam says. "Start at ten a.m. and finish up around midnight."

"So tips are a big part of this job."

"It's the only part," Liam says. "Furniture delivery guys are lucky if they get seventy to eighty dollars a day. So, yeah, tips are very important."

Liam's first job when he got off the boat at nineteen was working for a moving company in Manhattan. When I was the same age I ran a little business specializing in doing odd jobs for a Catholic university and shuttling priests' belongings from rectory to rectory. Trust me, priests move a lot.

"I once won a bid to empty out the old ROTC building on campus," I tell Liam. "Over the years they had remodeled the space so many times that an old-fashioned Coke machine had gotten sealed up inside the attic. Since there was no way to get it down the stairs we popped out the windows and threw it into a Dumpster three stories below."

"Holy shit!" Liam exclaims.

"The *BANG* it made," I say, smiling at the memory. "It made everyone on campus jump. The president of the university even called to complain. If I tried pulling that shit today, the SWAT team would be called in to take us out."

But my moving stories pale next to Liam's tales of starting out as a poor immigrant trying to survive in the Big Apple. His first moving jobs were studies in malfeasance and greed.

"In New York City," he says, "movers get a lot of business doing evictions. If someone can't pay rent, the sheriff seizes the property and movers are called in to haul the tenant's possessions out and put them in storage. And if the tenant isn't able to pay back the landlord, he'll sell the belongings to recoup his losses. Ugh, it was a disgusting business. Sometimes we'd walk into apartments with twelve people sleeping on the floor and all we'd take out was piles of trash. Just awful."

As Liam explains how evictions work, it becomes apparent that, at least in his day, the process was riddled with corruption. "The guys doing eviction moves were poor like myself, so they'd 'augment' their income by taking anything of value from the apartments. We'd lift televisions, stereos—stuff like that. But it was the sheriffs who were the real scumbags. Since they sealed off the property, they got first look at what was inside and had first dibs on what was valuable. If they took the cream of the crop, we really couldn't take anything or we'd get in trouble. You couldn't be too greedy or people would notice. But we'd be dropping off televisions and electronics at the sheriff's office all the time. They didn't say anything. We didn't say anything. It was a corrupt little arrangement."

"So if you're being evicted you're looking at having stuff stolen."

"Basically," Liam says. "But there was this one time we were doing an eviction move. I was the 'ganger'; that's the guy driving the truck. I liked being a ganger because it meant I was the supervisor and didn't have to do any heavy lifting. Well, this one time we're working an eviction over in Stuyvesant Town. I'm by the truck having a smoke when one of the guys comes down and says, 'Liam, you've got to come upstairs. There's something you should see.' So I go up to the eleventh floor and there on the bookshelf is a picture of me. Turns out I knew the woman being evicted. She was a customer from the bar I used to work at on the side. She had fallen on hard financial times. Very sad."

"So, what did you do?"

"I made sure every last bit of her stuff was carefully taken out," Liam says. "I made sure no one, not even the sheriff, took a single thing from her. Then we locked it up in storage and I made sure I was the only one with a key. So when this poor woman managed to pay off her landlord, she got all her stuff back undamaged. Not a thing missing."

"I can't even imagine what it'd be like to evict a friend of mine."

"She looked me up and thanked me," Liam says. "She was convinced she was going to get ripped off. But she was grateful I took care of her."

As our truck slides across the George Washington Bridge, I look at the Manhattan skyline and wonder how many people are being evicted from their apartments today. Liam's story of organized thievery happened over twenty years ago, but there's a small, cynical part of me that knows human nature never changes. The same shit is probably happening as we speak.

"So, what do you think is an appropriate tip for moving men? The guys who move you from house to house?"

"Tips are feast or famine sometimes," Liam says. "I'd work jobs on Park or Fifth Avenue and get tipped three hundred to five hundred dollars. But sometimes I'd get nothing. Sometimes even rich people could be lousy tippers. Old money, new money—it made no difference. You just never knew what you were going to get."

He explains that moving men expect to be tipped. "The going tip rate today is fifty dollars a man for a full-day job. If it's a half-day job, like four hours, tipping twenty-five per man is good. Some jobs, however, take twelve to fourteen hours. On a job like that, a good tipper will give eighty to a hundred per man. But some people don't have lots of money, and the move's expensive enough as it is."

"What about furniture delivery guys," I ask. "What are they normally paid?"

"Our store is good to us," he says. "But other places? They pay their guys like seventy to eighty dollars a day. If they're working a twelve-hour day, that comes out to what, five and change an hour?"

"So sometimes these guys can make below minimum."

"And these 'man with a van' types have to pay for their own gas. And if they get into an accident, the liability's on them. Not the company."

He goes on to explain that big retailers like Best Buy and Sears abandoned using the "man with a van" concept long ago. "They'd get so many complaints from customers about damaged goods," he said, "that they realized it was cheaper in the

long run just to have their own people. But smaller outfits, especially discount stores, use independent contractors to lower
their costs. And what they charge can be completely arbitrary.
After a delivery they'll call their boss, who will ask, 'Whadidya
have to do extra?' If he learns his guys had to go up two flights
of stairs instead of one, he might charge you more." The lesson
here? When you buy furniture, make sure to get the delivery
price in black and white.

If there's one common thread I've found talking to delivery
people of all stripes it's that companies save money by making
contractors use their own cars and fuel to deliver *the company's*
goods and services. And nowhere is this dynamic more endemic
than among food delivery workers.

When it comes to getting food delivered, we've all experienced this kind of dilemma: It's a cold, rainy, windswept Saturday night, your fridge is bare, and you don't want to eat out.
So you call your favorite pizza, sushi, Chinese, or hippie vegan
soy burger place for takeout. When you hear the doorbell ring
your stomach starts rumbling, and it's not because you're hungry. What to tip the delivery boy? Most people have no clue
what the appropriate gratuity is. Since I've never worked as a
delivery boy, I knew that talking to pizza and Chinese food
runners would have to be part of my guru quest. And I found
that if you understand a few facts about the deliveryman's
plight, you'll find it in your hearts to open your wallet a little
wider.

"We have a dollar-fifty delivery charge for every pizza we
deliver," Sandy, a pizza delivery girl near Buffalo told me. "The
customers think we get to keep that money, but we don't. It goes
straight to the shop."

Pizza accounts for 25 percent of cheese consumption in the
United States. When cheese and flour prices went through the
roof in 2008, Sandy told me, her shop's owner had to "increase

prices without increasing prices," so he added the delivery fee as a sort of surcharge. This is a common occurrence in the restaurant industry. But now pizzeria owners are enjoying lower overhead. Cheese went from a May 2008 price of $2.28 a pound to $1.00 a pound in September 2009. But guess what? Many chains retained their delivery fees and surcharges. The delivery people, however, see none of that. In fact, their wages have stagnated.

"I get paid $7.15 an hour when I'm in the shop," Missy, a fifty-year-old deliverywoman for a Papa John's Pizza in Virginia, told me. "But I only get paid four dollars an hour when I'm on the road. So you better believe management makes sure we're out doing deliveries so they don't have to pay us a full wage."

"So the expectation is that you'll make it up in tips, right?"

"That's a laugh," Missy said. "Last night I made five dollars in tips."

"That's awful!"

"And we have to pay our own insurance," Missy said. "If I get into an accident, it's my insurance that goes up, not the company's." So when you factor in gas, wear and tear, insurance, and depreciation, delivery drivers are getting hosed. Just like those furniture delivery companies that use a "man with a van," many takeout places are using outside drivers to help bolster their bottom line. Yet another example of how businesses exploit tipped workers.

"I also deliver for a Chinese restaurant," Missy said. "But you know what they do there? If we get busy, the owner will make deliveries. But he'll only go to the houses where he knows they're good tippers."

Delivery drivers are exploited because what they actually make often falls below the legally mandated minimum wage. Sandy in Buffalo gets paid $7.15 an hour for working a five-hour shift. But if her tips are bad, and since car costs eat up a significant percentage of her earnings, she'll end up making less than the $7.15 an hour. In Kansas City, delivery drivers filed a class-action suit against Papa John's, alleging that paying them a small flat fee per delivery, irrespective of the mileage incurred, resulted in their earning less than minimum wage. If that's true it's a clear violation of federal law.

It could be worse. In January 2009, Saigon Grill in New York City was forced to pay a $4.6 million judgment for violating state and federal labor laws. The company's three locations were pulling down $2 million a month but paying their workers only $1.60 an hour. In addition, they forced their employees, mostly poor immigrants, to work eighty-hour weeks and levied fines on them for calling in sick. And if a worker was robbed and his deliveries stolen—not an uncommon occurrence—he was forced to pay for the cost of the lost food. As a result of this judgment, some noodle places in the city started paying their workers more and reducing their hours. But many restaurants are still pulling this scam today.

"I need to get out of this business," Missy told me. "Papa John's makes me buy this stupid uniform shirt jacket for seventeen bucks when it probably only cost them five. I could get something cute for seventeen dollars." I feel Missy's pain. When I waited tables at a restaurant in the Jersey 'burbs, Sammy, our shifty, sex-crazed manager, made us shell out eleven bucks for aprons that had probably cost the restaurant three. We were all sure Sammy was pocketing the difference. Of course the aprons were white, and if we got spaghetti sauce on them during the shift we had to buy new ones or go home. After being victimized by this shakedown several times, I eventually learned always to keep a backup apron in my car.

Missy's son, Adam, is also a pizza delivery driver for Papa John's. "You know what a good tip for a delivery driver is?" he told me. "Fifteen to twenty percent of the bill or the cost of a gallon of gas—whatever's higher."

"So if you deliver twenty-five bucks' worth of food to my house, a four- or five-dollar tip should about cover it," I said.

"That helps pay for my gas and puts a little extra in my pocket," Adam replied. That same mathematical formula applies to the urban delivery boy who pedals a bicycle to bring you your Pad Thai or burrito. These guys may not have cars, but all that pedaling puts mileage on their bodies.

"But you know what?" Adam said. "When it's raining out or snowing, delivery guys are happy."

"Why's that?"

"More people are going to stay in and eat. And the guilt tips increase."

As I talked to delivery people, they repeated widely different tipping outcomes. In Buffalo, Sandy said that she got tipped three to five bucks 70 percent of the time. She was paid $7.15 per hour whether she was in the shop or on the road, so she would make $40 or $50 a night in tips working a five-hour shift.

"Around here, people are assholes," Adam said, referring to his Virginia patrons. "You go to these rich neighborhoods and people will give you a dollar or two on a twenty-five-dollar order. That's less than ten percent."

If the rich customers are jerks, however, the poor aren't much better. Adam told me that 45 percent of customers living in subsidized housing projects never tip him, and 30 percent hand out only paltry gratuities. "Occasionally you'll get some people in the projects who'll tip well," Adam said. "But not often."

Not all delivery people are scraping by. At several pizzerias near my house in New Jersey, the owners told me, "We don't have delivery charges; just tip the guy." And the drivers told me they could make $80 in tips on a weeknight and $150 on a busy Friday. Some owners even adequately reimburse their drivers for mileage or provide a vehicle for them. So, not all pizzeria owners are jerks. But then again, pizza is a religion in Jersey.

"The worst kind of people are exact-changers," Sandy told me. These are the people who'll give you a twenty for a $19.60 order and say, "Keep the change."

"Have you ever confronted anyone about their bad tipping habits?"

"Once," Sandy said. "And the woman got so angry she physically assaulted me. I had to call the cops. But since I made the mistake of going into her home, the cops told me I could be arrested for trespassing if I pressed charges. So I let the whole matter drop." When Sandy told me this, I grinned. I once confronted a customer about his cheap tipping ways and he went ballistic on me. People do not like having their parsimony pointed out to them.

Be warned, though: not tipping the delivery driver brings its own set of problems.

"If I know a person's a bad tipper or an exact-changer," Sandy told me, "I'll always deliver their pizza *last*. Even if it makes geographic sense to go to the cheapskate's house first, I'll go out of the way to deliver to the good tippers first." Good tippers get their food hot and fresh. Bad tippers get cold cardboard.

Food delivery people have other ways to wreak vengeance on cheap tippers. "I'd just take the pizza out of the bag and let it get cold," Adam told me. "Or I'd tip it upside down once or twice and make all the cheese stick to the top of the box."

"I'd slam on the brakes and let everything shift around," Sandy said. "So when they got their pie it was a mess."

When I asked the delivery people what kinds of things they saw during their work, the glimpses of life they got when those front doors were cracked open, their answers were fascinating. "Well, you always had the pot smokers with the munchies," Missy said. "So I'd joke with them and say, 'Hey, I like your air freshener.'"

"You could tell a lot about people just from looking in their front door," Adam said. "You could see if their house was immaculate, if it was a mess. I had one lady—she was a really sad case. She'd always answer the door in her bathrobe, and her mail would be piled up in her mailbox. She'd always come to the door bright and cheery, but I could tell this lady never left her house. She worked at home. And she had a lot of cats."

"Sometimes what I see breaks my heart," Missy told me. "You see kids not being cared for, pets that are dirty or abused, couples fighting. It's just bad sometimes. Then you'd have the people who were just lovely to you. You never knew what was behind that door."

So, food delivery people often get a glimpse into your real life. And sometimes the lives they encounter belong to nasty people. Company policy at most places mandates that delivery people not enter a customer's home. That's for their protection and yours. Delivering food can be a very dangerous job. In 1997, teenagers in New Jersey gunned down two deliverymen as they delivered pizza to an isolated house in the boonies. In fact, according to the Bureau of Labor statistics, sales delivery personnel (which includes taxi drivers) have the *ninth most dangerous job in America*, accounting for 27 fatalities per 100,000 drivers. Many of these deaths come from traffic accidents, of course, but quite a few of them result from criminal assault and murder. In parts of the country where citizens are permitted to carry concealed weapons, food delivery drivers have taken to arming themselves.

"You ever get robbed?" I asked Pedro, a pizza driver in Lyndhurst, New Jersey.

"No," he said. "But one time a driver I knew got carjacked. Unfortunately for the 'jackers, the driver was the chief of police's son. They were caught in like ten minutes. They got the max."

Back in the Bronx, Liam and I are looking for an apartment. Despite the digitized prompts spilling out of his GPS-equipped iPhone, we're unable to find the place. The apartment complex is a warren of squat, weathered brick buildings that look relentlessly the same.

"This is the part of the job that sucks," Liam's other son, Michael, says. "Can you imagine trying to find this place at night?"

"It's got to be around here somewhere," I say, trying to make out the small signs denoting which building is which.

Liam decides to go around the block and find a back way in. But just as we coast through an amber traffic signal turning red, an NYPD cruiser lights us up.

"Oh, shit!" Liam mutters. A no-bullshit cop walks up to the driver's side looking visibly annoyed.

"Do you know why I pulled you over?"

"I'm sorry, officer," Liam says, his Irish voice modulated into a tone of soothing contrition. "I went through the yellow light as it turned red."

"You went through a *red* light," the officer says, correcting him. "I was right behind you. Didn't you see me?"

After giving the cop his license and registration, Liam calmly explains that he's a furniture deliveryman and he's looking for an apartment. "And if I slammed on the brakes to stop for that light," he explains, "I would have damaged the furniture I've got in the back." Not to mention probably mangling his two sons. The cop makes Liam open up the truck, and when he's satisfied he's telling the truth, he lets us off with a warning. Ah, the luck of the Irish.

Eventually, we find the right building and pull up to the front entrance. The complex looks like it's seen better days and seems to be overrun with feral cats. Liam's sons pull a couch and two wing chairs out of the van and cover them with protective blankets. Old pieces restored to their original condition, they're festooned with gaudy scenes of knights on horseback. Ugly as sin.

"Oh, man," I say. "That's what I call a busy couch."

"It's very matadorish," Liam says. "But Spanish people like that kind of stuff."

"But this stuff is so old! Why didn't they just get a new couch?"

"This furniture is actually very expensive," Liam says. "They spent like two grand getting it fixed. And it's worth far more than that."

"No way."

"The stuff you buy in furniture stores today is crap," Liam says. "It'll last you ten years at the most. If you want heirloom furniture, stuff that will last? The prices start at ten thousand dollars."

I treated myself to a new couch and an easy chair last year. Leather, very masculine, and sort of Art Deco–like. They cost me $2,000. Now Liam's telling me I bought crap. Then again, I didn't have $10,000 lying around.

"I delivered a dining room table and twelve chairs to a customer once." Liam says. "Cost forty-eight thousand. Their great-grandkids will be eating off of it when we're dead and gone." My new couch will have been composted into oblivion by then.

Luckily for Liam and me, his two sons are strong young men and they do all the heavy lifting. As I watch them gingerly work the couch through the building's drab concrete stairwells, I ask Liam what he thinks the tip is going to be.

"You can usually tell the moment they open the door," Liam says. "If they look like they're happy to see you and to get their furniture, you'll get something. But if they have a puss on their face you're probably out of luck."

When we get to the apartment, a small Hispanic lady opens the door and greets us warmly. Despite the housing project's dreary exterior, this woman's apartment is brightly lit and well cared for. Her wooden floor shines with polish, and nothing is out of place. Her living room is empty save for a china closet and a small desk with a laptop computer. I smile to myself. This lady may be elderly, but she's hooked into the electronic age.

As Liam's sons maneuver the furniture into the apartment, I snoop around a bit. Wedged into the china closet's doors are pictures of children, young and grown; photographs of graduations, marriages, honeymoons, vacations, and family and friends. A panorama of a long life filled with people.

As I talk to the old lady she tells me she's a widow and that her late husband was a furniture upholsterer. So she knows quality when she sees it, and she's very happy with her couch and chairs. As we leave she hands Liam thirty dollars. "Thank you very much," she says brightly. "I'm so glad the furniture got here today. I'm leaving to visit my family in Puerto Rico this week, so I was worried it'd never get here." I can see why the woman was anxious. Even though her furniture is "matador-ish," it fits her apartment perfectly. And now that it's inside, her modest home is complete.

Saying good-bye, we head off to our next delivery. "See that?" Liam says. "She was happy to see us. That's why she was a good tipper."

"Do you think your experience as a bartender and waiter helps you know when your deliveries are going to be good tip-pers?" I say. "When I was a waiter I had a sixth sense about these things."

"You know what's interesting about tipping," Liam tells me. "It's all about the relationship you make with the customer. In those brief moments at a table, tending bar, or even delivering furniture, you've only got a few seconds to make a bond with a patron. It's kind of like a microscopic relationship you see. And how you handle that relationship in the brief amount of time you have makes all the difference. Take that lady. She was happy to see us, we provided polite, good service, and she got her fur-niture. We had a good relationship. That's why she tipped us. And everyone's needs got met."

When Liam says the words *microscopic relationship*, a spark goes off in my brain. Like a name that's on the tip of your tongue, a half-formed idea tumbles around my mind. But I can't quite bring it to the surface.

We're delivering a beautiful leather recliner to our next stop: a larger, more foreboding housing project. When the tenant comes down and opens the door for us, he has a suspicious look on his face. I begin to wonder if Liam's crew will get a tip from this guy. Sadly we discover the elevator's a no-go. It's too small.

So Liam's sons have to haul the recliner up seven flights of stairs.

"Jesus," I say, watching them struggle with the heavy piece. "I'm glad I'm only observing."

"Ah, yes," Liam says. "I'm too old for this sort of thing myself." Liam's only forty-four.

"So, what do you think, Liam?" I ask. "Will we get a tip from that guy?"

"Not when I first saw him," Liam says. "But when he saw the boys had to carry his chair up the stairs, he softened a bit."

"Think he feels guilty?"

"Oh, yes." Thank God for guilt. It's the tippee's best friend.

By the time Liam's sons reach the third floor, I realize that if I were carrying this stuff I'd have been winded. By the fourth floor I'd have been in cardiac intensive care.

"Why don't you guys take a break?" Liam says. But the boys are young and in shape, and they refuse to stop. "Ah, there's that exuberance of youth thing I was telling you about," their father says to me.

"I'd be dead by now," I say, struggling to catch my breath.

When we finally get inside the apartment a small dog skitters across the linoleum floor and starts sniffing my pants. As I reach down to pet him I take a look around. The place is small, crowded, and full of cheap things. I get the sense that more than two people live here. The sagging fabric couch in the living room looks like it doubles for a bed—maybe a grown son or daughter lives here, too. A large plasma-screen television dominates the living room, and a Western starring the late, great Kirk Douglas is playing in hi-def. In front of the TV is an old, battered, cloth-covered recliner, which we're going to dispose of. This man probably sits in front of his big TV all day. Maybe it's his one great pleasure in life. Who knows?

"Now you've got a new chair to watch your Westerns in," I say.

"*Sí, sí,*" the old man says, smiling brightly.

"It's a beautiful chair," Liam says. "Enjoy it, sir."

And it *is* a beautiful chair, nicer than anything I own. Amid the old furniture crowded into the living room, it stands out like a new car in a junkyard.

"Sorry about the mess," the old man's wife says to me. "Our grandkids sometimes come here after work to sleep."

"Madam," I reply, "next to my apartment, yours looks like the Vatican."

The old man sits in his new chair, slaps the leather-covered armrests with glee, and, for a moment, turns into a little boy. As he and his wife chatter in Spanish about the new couch, I hear the word *propina*. That means tip.

While Liam has the old man sign some paperwork, I check out the apartment more closely. Just like the last one, it's filled with pictures. Children's artwork covers the refrigerator door, and photos of family and friends fill every available space on the wall—a tapestry of a life filled with people and events. As I look at the faces of people I'll never meet, I reflect on how few pictures I have in my own apartment. Sure, I've got pictures of my nephew, family, and friends. But I have no pictures of a wife and child of my own. And for a moment that absence fills me with sadness.

"There you go," the old man says, handing Liam twenty dollars. These people are living in a housing project in the Bronx and can probably ill afford a tip. But maybe Liam was right: We built a little relationship of guilt and flattery, and the man felt compelled to tip. Or maybe he's been the decent sort all along.

By the time we finish up in the Bronx the temperature is starting to drop and the sun has begun its afternoon dive toward the horizon. As we cross the George Washington Bridge again, I look at the skyscrapers glinting in the red-and-gold sunlight. For me, New York City is a place filled with memories—some good and some bad. I love the city, but I also hate it. And after visiting Portland, I've suddenly developed a yen to move west. I want to visit new places, meet new people, and create an entirely different life for myself. I'm forty-one years old and

I want to get some new pictures on *my* wall. But as I look at the sun-washed spires of the Big Apple, I wonder if I will ever truly leave.

"We're going to go to that lady's house again and try one more time," Liam says, interrupting my thoughts. "But let's have a spot to eat first. There's a dim sum place in Fort Lee I like."

"My treat," I say. "I didn't lift a thing today."

When we get to the dim sum place and dig into our food, I ask Liam what he thinks is an appropriate tip for delivering furniture.

"It's simple, really," he tells me. "One piece, ten minutes: ten bucks. Doesn't matter if two guys bring it or three. Ten is enough. If it's a two-man job—say, delivering a loveseat—then tip ten bucks a man. If two guys lug a sleep sofa up two flights of stairs, however, twenty bucks a guy is good."

"What about something more involved?" I ask. "Like four guys delivering a large bedroom or living room set?"

"A job involving six or seven pieces, including setup and takes an hour? Twenty bucks a guy."

"So, basically, it's ten bucks for something simple," I say. "But once it involves real effort we're looking at ten dollars a man for half an hour's work and twenty dollars a man for an hour."

"That's about right."

"So, when you delivered my bed and I tipped you thirty bucks, I was right on target."

Liam smiles. "Yes, you were."

After we finish our meal, we head back to Dumont and the troublesome lady. She and the store have worked something out, so we're cleared to bring her furniture inside. It's a small wooden kitchen table and two chairs, certainly not heirloom pieces. The apartment is on the ground floor, next to the laundry room. As Liam knocks on the door I can hear "Whip It," by Devo, blaring from behind the door. Hearing that music takes me back to a grammar school dance in 1981, when Reagan was president, Kathleen Turner was a sex symbol, and the cold war was still raging.

The door opens and a skinny woman in her midsixties with dyed red hair motions us in. The small studio apartment is a disaster. Clothes and makeup are strewn all over the place. A cheap exercise machine advertised on infomercials stands in for a clothesline, and the small twin bed wedged into the corner is a tangle of dirty sheets. The woman is dressed in black and has a name tag that reads "Sally" on her lapel. This woman's a waitress.

"Sorry about the mess," Sally says, her eyes nervously darting back and forth. "I've been working at the diner six nights a week. I don't have time to clean up." She's working the five-to-five shift and is running late.

"It's hard work," she tells me, her voice even. All traces of the harpy I overheard on Liam's cell phone are gone. "The tips ain't what they used to be."

As Liam and his sons bring the kitchen set into the apartment, I notice Sally's place is also filled with pictures. But not of family and friends—just movie stars dead and gone. A large poster of Ava Gardner is taped up over the unkempt bed, and Charlton Heston's face stares out at me from a picture frame on top of a rickety table. I see no evidence of family, friends, or lovers. The place is devoid of any signs of an outside life. It's a wasteland.

Liam and his sons place the kitchen table into a bare spot near Sally's tiny kitchenette. Just like the old man's recliner, its newness throws the cheapness of the woman's belongings into sharp relief.

"That looks very nice there," I tell her. "Now you have a nice place to eat when you come home from work." I can imagine this woman, tired after a long day slaving for tips, eating her lonely dinner out of a Styrofoam container. Maybe she watches old movies while she's eating.

"So, you're the boss?" Sally asks.

"No, ma'am," I say, pointing to Liam. "He's the boss. I'm only along for the ride."

"He's a trainee," Liam chortles.

I take a long look at Sally. I can tell she was once a very beautiful woman. Back in 1981 men were probably throwing themselves at her feet. Maybe that explains her musical choices.

"How long have you been a waitress?"

"Forever," she replies.

Being a deliveryman for a day has given me a glimpse into another person's life. And it's not a nice glimpse. Sally reminds me of all the times I wondered if I'd end up forgotten and alone in a small apartment devoid of life. The thought sends a shiver down my spine.

"There you go, ma'am," Liam says, handing Sally her receipt. "Just sign here."

After she signs the slip, she starts rummaging through her beat-up purse. "I need to tip you guys," she says. Liam looks mildly surprised when she hands him a crumpled ten, but I'm not. This woman's a waitress, and service people tend to be good tippers. The store was wrong about Sally. And just like that old man in the Bronx, this woman can hardly afford to tip. But as I look at her new kitchen table I realize we've done something good today. Her furniture may not last for a hundred years, but it has helped turn this mess into more of a home. And a home is something everyone deserves to have.

When we walk outside, I say to Liam's sons, "You guys are probably too young to realize this, but at one time that lady was a real beauty."

"Life's treated her pretty hard," Patrick says.

I turn to Liam. "Did you see what I saw?"

"All those pictures of film stars," he says, a sad smile playing on his thoughtful Irish face. "She probably wanted to be an actress when she was younger."

"The late seventies and early eighties were her time," I say.

"That's when she was young and lovely."

"Maybe some guy lured her to Hollywood years ago and she didn't make it. Now she has to work in a diner."

"I wonder what went wrong for her," I say, mostly to myself.

"Someone told her a story," Liam says. "And then stole all her glory."

Finished for the day, Liam and his sons drive me back to my apartment. After I say my good-byes, I let myself inside. My dog, Buster, runs up to greet me. I leash him up and take him outside for a walk. As Buster is doing his business, I look at the New York City skyline in the distance. The skyscrapers have lost their golden finery and now look dull and gray in the waning light. I think about Sally. I know in my bones I'll never end up like her. And that new life I want? Part of it has already happened for me. I just have a little more work to do.

Back inside I give my dog a treat, refill his water bowl, and grab myself a beer. Buster laps up his water, and I look at the pictures taped to my old refrigerator. As I take a long pull on my beer, the faces of children, family, and friends stare back at me.

At that moment I realize my home is an abode of riches.

CHAPTER 8

King George and the Flea
Casino Hosts, Card Dealers, and Cocktail Waitresses

There is a scene in the 1984 movie *Oh God! You Devil* that always rattles around my brain. The film's protagonist, a down-and-out musician named Bobby Shelton, abandons his pregnant wife and sells his soul to the devil in exchange for seven years of fame and wealth as a rock star. The only catch? At the end of his "contract," he has to give up his *immortal soul*. After unhealthy doses of fame, drugs, and groupie sex, Shelton realizes his life has become full of empty pleasures and he yearns to get his old one back. But since he's made a deal with the devil, only God almighty can get him out of it. After talking to several clergymen whose only response is to try locking him up in a psychiatric facility, Shelton runs into a mad street preacher and desperately asks, "Where can I find God?" The deranged holy man looks him straight in the eye and says, "If you want to find God you must go to the desert!" And what part of the desert would any self-respecting rock-and-roller in a George Burns movie go to? You guessed it: Las Vegas. Like the devil, God must like dry heat.

When I was a seminary student I was well acquainted with

the idea that you could commune with God in terrain with less-than-average rainfall. There's nothing like being in the silent and forbidding environs of a desert to free your mind from distractions and help you focus on the big picture. Before setting out on his public ministry, Jesus spent forty days and nights in the desert wrestling with Satan's temptations—a discipline many of his followers would later emulate. My godfather, a Catholic priest, used to tell me the story of one such devotee, St. Simeon of the Stylites. Like an ancient David Blaine, Simeon tried isolating himself from the world in the Syrian Desert by climbing on top of a pillar, known in Greek as a *style*, and living on a platform only a meter square for thirty-seven *years*! What did Blaine do: thirty-five *hours*? Pussy.

My quest to become a tipping guru is not a religious pilgrimage, thank God. My seminary days gave me a real distaste for austere surroundings, constant bad food, and the occasional pervert. But since I'm on a journey to understand the mysterious ways of tipping, I'm reminded of that cinematic holy man's words: "You must go to the desert!" So, like Bobby Shelton, I have to go to Vegas.

I don't know the first thing about Sin City. I've never been there. I have no contacts. Luckily, my accountant in New Jersey does a professional gambler's taxes, and after a few phone calls he hooks me up with a hotel on the Strip and a VIP manager at a high-end casino who will give me the inside scoop. Before you know it I'm white-knuckling my coach seat's armrest as the jet I'm traveling in rattles against the high-altitude winds on its way to Nevada. I'm journeying to a strange land to visit strange people. "Be careful in that town," a friend of mine said to me just before I left. "It can eat you up and spit you out." Part of me is afraid of what the Vegas desert will do to *my* immortal soul.

If tipping is a kind of religion, then Vegas is its Mecca, the Jerusalem of Gratuities, the Holy Land of the Quick Buck. When I get off the plane at McCarran International Airport my ears are immediately assaulted by the avaricious jingle emanating from the slot machines lining the terminal. Everywhere I look, there are signs promising huge casino jackpots and posters offering all-you-can-eat buffets that could sustain a small island nation. My fellow passengers' eyes glaze over like those of kids tempted by a sudden overabundance of candy. It's happening to me, too. As I walk to my limousine I feel my pulse quickening as if I'm about to get on a roller coaster. The city's seductive energy is already burrowing into my psyche. It's a weird, electric feeling. Dangerous, naughty, and oh so appealing. As the limo whisks me to my hotel, I spy several billboards featuring bikini-clad women in provocative poses beckoning me to visit strip clubs with names like the Sapphire, Olympic Garden, and the Peppermint Hippo. If St. Simeon ever came to Vegas, I'll wager good money that he'd hop off his pole to go watch those girls twirling around *theirs*.

After my limo deposits me at my hotel and the bellhop lets me into my room, I gasp. My gambler friend must've pulled more than a few strings, because the hotel has upgraded me to some high-roller digs. The far wall of the suite is comprised of massive floor-to-ceiling windows offering stunning views of the Las Vegas Strip. And the bathroom—complete with a hot tub, double vanities, and an enclosed rainwater shower—is twice the size of my apartment in Jersey. For the first time in my life I feel like I'm living large. As I sip some complimentary bottled water, I gaze out my bedroom window and admire the snowcaps still clinging to the beautiful Spring Mountains towering in the distance. I can't believe I'm really here. But when I see Donny and Marie Osmond's toothy smiles gleaming up at me from a huge billboard, I'm pulled back to reality. Yep, I'm in a crazy town. And it's my job to see how tipping makes it tick.

After a quick shower, I head down to the casino floor to meet a professional poker dealer named Ryan, who has agreed to explain to me what it's like to subsist on tips in Sin City. I find Ryan and his wife, Cassie, waiting for me near the casino's main entrance. A slim fellow with an ascetic face and a runner's physique, he's surveying the action on the gaming floor with a dispassionate, professional gaze. After we make our introductions, Cassie, a bubbly blonde with a winning smile, suggests we grab some lunch on the Strip.

"Why don't we go to Cheeseburger in Paradise?" she shouts over the roar of the casino. "It'll be a lot quieter over there. Easier to do an interview."

"Good idea," I say. "Let's go."

I clamber into the back of Ryan's small sports car, and soon we're traveling down the Strip. As we pass the Paris Hotel and Casino, I notice throngs of people underneath the fake Eiffel Tower drinking alcohol from open containers.

"My God, those people are drinking in public."

"Welcome to Vegas," Cassie says. "Just wait until you see someone having sex in the street."

"That happens here?"

"I have a saying," Cassie says. "You aren't a true Las Vegan until you've seen a casino getting blown up, Elvis driving down the street in a pink Cadillac, and a couple doing the nasty in public—all in the same day."

"I'll keep my eyes peeled, then."

As we drive to the restaurant, I get the lowdown on Cassie and Ryan's histories. Originally from New England, Cassie was a schoolteacher and Ryan worked for a company that made cash registers. Like many newly married couples, they encountered their share of economic difficulties. Unfortunately for them, theirs started almost on day one.

"We were living in a house with an attached apartment," Cassie explains as I watch her husband slalom through the busy traffic. "But our landlord's mother fell ill and he had to move her into our place to take care of her. On the day we got back from our honeymoon, he told us to get out. So we had to move in with my parents."

"Not an ideal situation for newlyweds," I say, wincing sympathetically. If I had to try enjoying marital bliss with my parents down the hall I'd probably have to consume mass quantities of vodka and Viagra.

"We tried finding a house, but the prices were ridiculous in New England back then," Ryan says, his eyes never leaving the road. "So, after one too many cold winters, I said, 'Hey, Cassie. How about Vegas?' My sister and parents were already out here. Cassie said, 'Why not?' When we got here, Cassie got a teaching job and I went to dealer's school. I started out dealing blackjack, but now I exclusively deal poker."

"Where do you work now?"

"I work at what's called a local casino," Ryan says. "We call them 'locals' because they're off the Strip and people who live in the area like to play in them."

"When you live in Vegas," Cassie explains, "the last place you want to be is on the Strip. Too much traffic. Too many tourists."

"Sort of like Manhattanites avoiding Times Square," I say.

"Exactly," Cassie says.

After battling the Strip's legendary traffic, we arrive at the restaurant and order some burgers and beers. After I take my first sip of Bass Ale, I pull out my notepad and get down to business.

"So, Ryan. How important are tips to Vegas dealers?"

"Being a dealer in Vegas, or anywhere for that matter," Ryan says, "is just like being a waiter. My casino only pays me $6.55 an hour, so I depend on the tips customers give me to survive. The hourly wage I get just covers the taxes on my tips."

"That's exactly like being a waiter," I say. "I heard before I came out here that tips in Vegas are called 'tokes' or 'zukes.'"

"That's right."

"So, what's the etiquette for 'toking' a dealer?"

"Dealers always prefer that you *bet* the tip for us," Ryan explains. "If you toss a guy a buck or two, that's nice. But say you bet a dollar for us while playing blackjack and you win. The dealer's made two bucks instead of one. And if you hit black-jack, you've made him two and a half bucks."

"But if I lose, the house gets your tip, correct?"

Ryan smiles. "That's why they call it gambling."

He goes on to explain how to toke a dealer when playing my favorite game, blackjack. Before you get your cards, you have to place your wager in the little betting circle in front of you. The bet *has* to be in the circle, not half in or out, or the dealer won't give you any cards. If you want to toke the dealer, you place a chip in front of your bet, outside the circle. That way the dealer knows it's for him or her.

"When should you toke a blackjack dealer?"

"You tip when you're up," Ryan says. "If you win two hands in a row, it's a good idea to tip the dealer."

"What's considered a good toke?"

"Never throw change at a dealer," Ryan says. "Never bet something like a fifty-cent chip. A dollar's considered good."

"What if I'm down?" I ask. "What if I'm on a losing streak?"

"Then they don't expect it," Ryan says. "But ask yourself, did you have fun? Was the dealer nice to you? When you leave you should still give them something."

"I went on a six-hour winning streak once," Cassie inter-jects. "And I must've pushed my dealer eighty dollars in tokes. But when I'm losing I'll always set five bucks aside so I can still lay a bet for the dealer if I run out of money."

"So, how about tipping on roulette?" I ask. "That game con-fuses me. How does that work?"

"Just ask the dealer what his favorite numbers are," Ryan says. "Say he tells you he likes seventeen, thirty-three, and forty-four and you lay a dollar on each for him. If he hits, he gets thirty-five bucks. Or you can just offset a chip on the numbers you're playing and tell the dealer it's for him."

"But everybody's stacking their chips on top of everybody else's. How does the dealer keep track of it all?"

"Each player gets different-colored chips," Ryan says patiently, as if explaining something simple to a small child. "That's how the dealer keeps track of everything."

"Got it. Now, you said you dealt poker. What's the deal there?"

"Tipping in poker is so much better than in blackjack, because there's a winner every hand. You're pushing a pot to a player every time. Typically they'll throw you a dollar when they rake in the pot. Sometimes more. It depends. The poker players in the local casinos tend to tip better. Because they're the same people, you see them all the time. You know them by name, and they tend to tip differently. You might get two or three dollars a pot instead of one. The problem with dealing blackjack is that you could get a cold deck and just be killing the players. Then they don't want to tip. They only want to tip when they're winning, and even then they often don't."

"You guys have a term for bad tippers?"

"Oh, yeah," Ryan says. "We call them stiffs. Sometimes we call them fleas."

"Fleas?"

"Yeah. They're like parasites."

"So, I guess there's a term for good tippers, too."

"Good tippers are called George," Ryan says. "And if they're really good they're called King George." When I hear this I wonder what dealers call a particularly bad tipper. Super flea?

"When I was a waiter I'd always warn my coworkers if a customer was a bad tipper," I say. "Do you guys do the same thing when you relieve one another?"

"Oh, yeah," Ryan says. "The dealer leaving will say, 'The lady in five's a George, but that kid on two's a real flea.'"

Cassie chimes in and explains that dealers can't hustle for tips. If they ask a patron for a toke, it's grounds for immediate termination. But that doesn't mean the dealer or other players can't shame a flea into tipping.

"Ryan was playing poker once, and every time he pushed the dealer a couple of bucks the dealer made it a point of thanking him *really* loudly. Well, another guy at the table said to the dealer, 'Hey, you keep pushing him pots! You two must have something going on.'"

"So, he accused you of cheating?"

"Yeah," Cassie says. "But I shouted, 'Hey, we're tipping him, so he's gonna be a lot nicer to us than to you, because you keep stiffing him!' Then the dealer gave me this wonderful 'Thank you very much!' look!"

In the old days, dealers used to keep all the tips they made at their tables. "You ate what you killed," Ryan says. But this system led to some serious inequities. You could be dealing high-stakes baccarat, for instance, working only two or three high-rollers, and make a couple of grand in tips doing little or no work. Now compare that to some poor slob dealing blackjack to newbie gamblers fresh off the bus from Iowa. He's constantly explaining the rules of the game, correcting mistakes, and making, if he's lucky, ten bucks an hour in tips. You don't need to be Johnny Vegas to realize that this can lead to some serious tension among the staff. I understand this dynamic completely. When I was a waiter, the servers who had the best sections always got the best customers and made the best tips. So, guess what happened. Waiters started greasing the manager's palm to get the best tables.

The same thing started happening in Vegas. Eventually the powers that be decided that in order to make things fairer and cut down on the chicanery, all the dealers' tokes over a twenty-four-hour period would be pooled. Now when a dealer gets a tip, instead of stuffing it in his shirt pocket, he puts it inside a "toke box." At the end of every shift all the toke boxes are collected, dumped on an empty table, and counted up by a "toke committee" comprised of three or four dealers. After they make the count, they take the chips to the cashier and get a receipt.

Then, when all the tokes are added up, they're divided evenly among all the dealers who worked that twenty-four-hour period and the monies are applied to their paycheck—after taxes are deducted, of course. So if you toss that cute dealer a hundred-dollar chip, she's not getting it! It's divvied up with everyone else working in the pits.

Casino dealers don't know what they're going to make on any given day. Say the casino has a great night—the Sultan of Brunei comes in and drops eighty grand in tokes or something. That money will be divided among the four hundred dealers working the floor during that period and they'll get two hundred bucks applied to their paychecks. *Ka-ching!* But if the casino has a *bad* twenty-four-hour period—say there's a freak snowstorm—the dealers could end up making only six bucks for the day.

What I found really cool was how dealers get paid for vacation time. Say you're a dealer and you work five shifts a week and you take a week off. You get paid out of the tokes for the week you're gone. So if you go on vacation during the convention season and your casino kicks ass, you could make thousands of dollars without doing a lick of work. Conversely, if the casino has a bad week—like after 9/11, for instance—you could end up getting very little.

"But poker's different," Ryan says to me. "In my case I keep all the tips I make."

"And because someone is usually toking you whenever they win a pot, you can potentially make more money than the dealers working in the pits."

"Some places are better than others," Ryan adds. "I average about a hundred and thirty bucks for an eight-hour shift. But if you're a poker dealer at the Big Three—The Palms, The Hard Rock, Planet Hollywood, the places where celebrities hang out—you can make a lot more. On New Year's Eve at The Hard Rock they were pulling down two to three thousand *each*."

"So I guess dealers really want to work in those places."

"But you're never gonna get hired by a Strip casino when you get out of dealing school," Ryan says. "You have to work in what's called a 'break-in' casino first. I had to work at a dump that was the boot camp of dealing. The dealers were okay, but the management was terrible."

I smile inwardly. When I was a waiter, my break-in restaurant was a hellhole called Amici's. Run by a dictatorial South American who terrorized his employees, it was indeed a boot camp for waiting tables. During my short time there I learned everything I needed to know about the trade. But the only thing the cooks wanted to "break in" was my ass.

"In fact," Cassie says, "you can't apply on the Strip unless you've had two years' dealing experience."

And you're pretty much guaranteed not to get a job unless you know someone. Ryan has been trying to break into the Strip for five years now. "There are waiting lists upon waiting lists. You start on what's called 'the extra board,' meaning they call you when they need you. That means you have to be on call and available, which makes having another job very difficult. Then you go to part time, then you get part time with benefits. Then, maybe, after three, four, five years, you might get full time."

"So, what do you make a year, Ryan?"

"What do I declare or what do I make?" he asks with a sly grin.

"Both."

"Well, I report I make twenty-four thousand dollars a year. But I really make forty-eight. But some dealers in this town make eighty thousand a year and up."

Forty-eight thousand dollars goes a long way in Las Vegas. Ryan explains that between his and his wife's salary they were finally able to achieve a life dream they couldn't realize at home—buying a house in the nearby suburb of Summerlin. Now they can get their groove on without their parents listening.

"When I was a waiter we always could peg people as bad tippers. Does that happen in Vegas?"

"Oh, man," Ryan says. "Canadians are the worst tippers! And they're proud of it! If we get a table of stiffs, we'll say, 'What the hell? Are half the people at this table Canadian?' "

As we finish our burgers I think about how similar waiters and casino dealers really are. Both are paid minimum wage, rely on tips and regulars, have to be "broken in," and are at the mercy of the customers' largesse and often victimized by their ignorance. Especially those pesky Canadians.

After I signal our waitress for the check, I ask Ryan, "If there's one thing you'd want people to know about tipping casino dealers, what would it be?"

"Don't make giving us a tip look like you're doing us a favor," Ryan says. "We're professionals doing a job."

After lunch, Ryan and Cassie take me down to visit the Fremont District in the "original" Las Vegas. Curiously enough, the casinos on the Strip aren't actually in the City of Las Vegas. They're located in an unincorporated patch of land in the towns of Winchester and Paradise, in Clark County, Nevada. But Fremont Street is where it all started. That's where you'll find some of the oldest casinos in Vegas: Binion's, the Golden Gate, Fitzgerald's, the Four Queens, and El Cortez.

When we reach the Fremont District I'm struck by the dichotomy between the "Old Vegas" and the new-fangled corporate theme park up the road. Whereas the resorts on the Strip try to pass themselves off as "family-friendly," Fremont throbs with a pleasant but slightly sleazy beat. In addition to finding blackjack tables with two-dollar minimums, the crowds milling in the streets seem more relaxed than their counterparts farther up the Strip. As I pass by the Golden Nugget, the casino where Steve Wynn began his gambling empire, I see a tired hooker with strong legs and lime-green high heels strutting her stuff outside the main entrance. If she tried doing that in the Disneyland atmosphere of the Strip, she'd be Hoovered up by the police in seconds.

I'm getting a real kick out of being here. Fremont Street is where the car chase in the 1971 James Bond film *Diamonds Are Forever* was filmed. Who could forget Sean Connery rocketing his Ford Mustang down these streets with the scrumptious Jill St. John at his side as he evaded the hapless Vegas police? Well, James Bond couldn't drive down this street now. In 1994 the street was closed to traffic and a colossal television screen stretching four blocks was built high above it. Originally powered by incandescent lightbulbs, the display is now comprised of 12.5 million LEDs controlled by large computers, making it the largest LED screen in the world. Every hour in the evening a free light and music show is put on for the public gathered underneath. After Ryan and Cassie help me pick up souvenirs, we grab some beers and stand under the electronic canopy to catch the first show.

Right on schedule the casino lights dim and a tricked-out rock video featuring George Thorogood and the Destroyers singing "Bad to the Bone" flares into life. As I watch computer-generated skeletons ride motorcycles across the giant screen with the bass from 220 speakers pushing 550,000 watts of sound into my chest, for the first time in a long time I smile like a little boy. My jet lag forgotten, I relax and start getting into the Vegas groove. But as I listen to the rock-and-roll extravaganza playing above me, I think back to what Cassie said to that stiff at the poker table who accused her husband of being in cahoots with the dealer he was handsomely toking. "Hey, we're tipping him, so he's gonna be a lot nicer to us than to you!" That makes me wonder. When I was a waiter, good tippers always got treated better than bad ones. How does it work in Vegas? What's the upside to being a George and the downside to being a flea?

At ten the next morning I meet Rick, the VIP casino host of an upscale casino and resort. With an open-collar blue silk shirt, polished brogues, and lightweight wool pants with a razor-sharp crease, Rick is a trim, tanned gentleman sporting a perfect set of white teeth and a welcoming demeanor. As he directs me toward the high-stakes enclave off the casino floor, I try to guess his age. A cross between Eddie Fisher and Joey Bishop, he could be anywhere between forty-five and sixty.

"Would you like a drink, Steve?" Rick asks as we settle into a plush booth.

Out of nowhere a statuesque blond waitress with sky blue eyes shows up to take our order. Rick gets a cranberry juice. I ask for a dirty vodka martini.

"Jesus," I say, looking my watch. "I just ordered hard liquor at ten in the morning."

"Welcome to Vegas," Rick says, laughing. "Enjoy."

The waitress returns with our drinks and sets them down in front of us. Rick pulls out a ten spot and hands it to her.

"Thanks, baby," he says.

"Wow," I say, watching the blonde's hips twitch suggestively as she departs. "That cocktail waitress is cute."

"Oh, Jennifer?" Rick says. "She's a great gal."

"I tried interviewing a cocktail waitress at my hotel earlier today," I say. "I thought wrapping my business card in a five-dollar bill and dropping it on her tray would do the trick. It didn't."

Rick laughs. "For never having been in Vegas you already seem to have a little bit of a handle on it."

"Yeah, just give out money."

"Nothing wrong with that," Rick says. "Listen, we thrive on that. It's our oil. Our gasoline. That's our *everything*."

A transplant from Brooklyn, Rick tells me he's been working in Las Vegas for almost forty years. Starting out as a blackjack dealer at a long-gone casino during the old Mafia days, he became a roulette dealer at the Golden Gate in Old Las Vegas before upscaling himself to deal baccarat at a tonier location.

"And making tips on all those jobs," Rick says, slinging me a toothy grin. I smile to myself. My estimate of Rick's age was wrong. He's over sixty. Man, I hope I look that good when I'm his age.

In 1985, Rick moved off the gaming floors to take a job as a casino host and has been one ever since. Basically the job of a casino host is to cultivate relationships with well-heeled players and encourage them to patronize his casino. Rick is the guy who hands out the goodies, the almighty comps. Depending on your level of play, he can comp you brunch, get you dinner at the best restaurant in town, secure hard-to-get show tickets, or ensconce you in a macked-out hotel suite with a swimming pool and a basketball court. After talking to him and listening to his encyclopedic knowledge of Vegas facts, figures, and stories, I realize that I'm talking to the right man.

"So, Rick," I say, "I've discovered in this town a good tipper is a George and a bad tipper is a flea."

"You're a quick learner," he says. "Top marks."

"How can being a George help you in Las Vegas? How can it enhance your stay?"

His face brightens. "I'll tell you several ways," he says. "Probably the most important one is that errors on gambling games do happen. You know, disputes. The dealer makes an error, customers make a mistake when signaling whether they want a hit or not. Say you're playing blackjack. You have a fifteen and the dealer has a five. Basic strategy calls for you to stand on that hand. Now let's just say you make a motion which the dealer thought was you signaling for another card and he deals you a ten—busting you. But if you didn't want that card and you're a George, when the dealer calls the floor man over he's more than likely to sell him your side of the story, so you get the benefit of the decision. In many cases you won't have to take the card."

"So the dealer will be your advocate."

"But here's the contrast," Rick says. "If you're a flea and this happens to you, the dealer's going to call out to the floor man,

'Hey, Sam, I need to see you for a minute. This gentleman says he didn't ask for a hit, but I saw a clear motion.' Now, the floor man can't let his dealers' getting tipped or not influence his decision. But for whatever reason, if he's not on his game, whatever, and he's relying on his dealer's information and vibe, he'll just say, 'Sorry, sir. I can have the manager check the videotape, and that will conclusively show whether or not you signaled for a card.'"

"The flea's out of luck. So good tipping is good karma."

"You took the words right out of my mouth," Rick says. "Here's another example of how being a George helps you. You're a real George. You're by yourself. You say to the dealer, 'Man, I've never seen so many beautiful girls around here. I don't know if I'm being out of line, but how does one get hooked up with one of them?'"

"So a dealer could set you up with a hooker if you're a George?"

"If they're so inclined," Rick says, "a dealer will tell you where to go."

"And if you're a flea?"

"They'll throw up their hands and say, 'I don't know what you're talking about, pal. Sorry.'"

"Or they can send you to a transvestite bar."

Rick roars. "Readers, I doubt the veracity of the author's statement that he's a Vegas virgin. He knows too much for being here only twenty-four hours."

"Like you said: I'm a quick learner."

"Now here's another thing dealers used to do to fleas," Rick says. "There was this casino—I swear to God it was called Honest John's. You know what they'd do?"

"I'm afraid to ask."

"They'd fuck 'em!" he almost shouts. "Some of these dealers were cardsharps—mechanics, they used to call 'em. And they'd deal from the bottom of the deck and give a stiff a losing card."

"Does that still happen today?"

"Not with the eye in the sky." He points to the omnipresent video cameras in the ceiling. "But it used to happen."

I finish my martini and, like magic, the beautiful Jennifer materializes and asks if I want another one. I order a Diet Coke instead. High-proof alcohol this early in the morning is deleterious to my interviewing skills.

"And if you're a George," Rick says, continuing his tutorial, "you can hook up with someone like me, a host. Say you come in and play five thousand dollars on the baccarat tables. The floor supervisor's going to call me and I'm gonna run out and give you my card. Depending on your level of play I'm going to ask, 'Would you like a room? Would you like dinner? Lunch? Where are you staying? I can move you into a suite right now. I'll give you a room with a pool table.' Maybe you tell me, 'Rick, I heard you've got a great steakhouse here.' If you're playing well, I'll set you up."

"How much does a player have to be wagering to get your attention?"

"About five grand."

"And comps are awarded how?"

"Well, we have a formula. If you lose a hundred, you're not getting anything. But if you drop a thousand, we might comp you ten percent of the loss—a hundred bucks or something. But if you're playing with lots of money, we're going to treat you like a king."

"What do you say to patrons who don't play with that kind of money and are resentful they don't get the same level of service?"

"Listen," Rick says, "realistically and theoretically every customer who walks through that door deserves great service. Georges and stiffs alike. But there's a pecking order. When you're a frequent flyer on an airline, there're twelve seats in first class. The most loyal people are going to get upgraded. If you fly once a year you're gonna sit in 26A. If you fly once a month? You're gonna sit in 2D. Same thing here. There's a pecking order."

"What do you say to people who think that's unfair?"

"Spend more money."

"Do you run into people who expect your services but don't want to pay for them?"

"Oy vey, yes," Rick says. "We have a word for them. It's a Yiddish term. We call them *schnorers*."

"*Schnorers?*"

Suddenly a tinny rendition of the theme song from the 1973 movie *The Sting* interrupts our conversation. It's Rick's cell phone. How appropriate.

"Hang on a sec," he says, glancing at the number on the phone's display. "It's a high-roller. I've got to take this."

As I leave Rick to schmooze his high-roller, I look around the high-stakes room. Richly appointed with gilt-edged tables and plush red leather chairs, the room is used for games such as baccarat and poker with a minimum table bet of $100 and a maximum bet of $10,000. Despite the opulence of the surroundings, there's only one player in the vast room: a young guy dressed in jeans, a denim shirt, and a John Deere baseball cap. He might look like a truck driver, but he's playing baccarat for as much as $10,000 a hand. As I look at the vast pile of chips arranged before him, I realize this guy's playing with more money than I've ever made in my entire life. The funny thing is he doesn't look happy or sad. Instead, his face is a curious mixture of boredom and seriousness. The dealers in the room don't look thrilled either. Guarding their empty tables like silent sentinels, they all look like they'd rather be somewhere, anywhere else. I feel a sudden kinship with them. I guess it doesn't matter whether you work in a restaurant or a casino. When the tables are dead and you're not making money, all you want to do is go home.

"Sorry about that, Steve," Rick says, flipping his phone shut. "Now, where were we?"

"We were talking about *schnorers*."

"Oh, yeah. A *schnorer* is not so much a stiff, but they hardly tip at all, and when they do it's real small," he says. "But they ask for *everything*. And I mean everything. They might be wagering twenty bucks, but they'll ask me, 'Can I go to the café or go bowling? Do you have a line on tickets for the Celine Dion show?' After a few minutes dealing with these kinds of people, my colleagues will say, 'Rick, what's the matter? You look beat up.' And I'll be like, 'Man, I've got this fucking *schnorer* on seat five and she's driving me fucking crazy.' "

I think back to that old lady at the car wash who was looking for a thirteen-dollar miracle and the cheap people who wanted to jump the car valet line without tipping a cent. If those people weren't *schnorers*, I don't know who is.

"The stiff will make you angry," Rick continues, "but the *schnorer* will drive you the most crazy. When I was a dealer I'd rather deal to a stiff than a *schnorer*. At least the stiff kept his fucking mouth shut."

"But does the squeaky wheel sometimes get the grease?"

"Oh, yeah," he says. "I had this one lady who broke me down after thirty years in the business. I told her, 'Lady, you're flat fucking killing me.' But I wrote her the comp just to get her to leave me alone."

As I listen to him talk about his hatred of *schnorers* and fleas, I direct the conversation to some of the more basic forms of Vegas tipping. He tells me that he considers two bucks to be the absolute minimum Vegas tip. A doorman gets two bucks. A cocktail waitress gets five. Since valet parking is free in Vegas there's usually a long line to get your car at the end of the evening. But if you tip the valet a ten spot when you hand him your keys and another when you're ready to pick up your ride, you'll get your car lickety-split.

Curiously enough, Rick doesn't get cash tips himself. According to him, the hard hustle won't do, and he claims he's well compensated and can pay his own way. But over the years his customers have "toked" him in different and substantial ways: first-class plane tickets, sky boxes at hockey games, front-row seats at Yankee Stadium. For several years he never paid to go to Disneyland. In addition to the goodies he's gotten for himself, his customers have lavished gifts on his young daughter. "You should see the scores I've made for my daughter," Rick says. "More princess bags than I can count. Dolls, toys, you name it."

"So, who's the greatest tipper you've ever met?"

"Hands down it was a guy called Kerry Packer," Rick says. "He's a legend in this town. One night he's dealing baccarat at two hundred and fifty thousand a hand. He calls the cocktail waitress over and asks, 'How much is your mortgage?' The waitress goes, 'I don't know, Mr. Packer. I'd have to call my husband and find out.' So Packer says, 'Well, call him.' When the waitress returns, she says she and her husband owe eighty grand on the house. So Packer just handed her eighty thousand in chips.

"Let me tell ya, Steve, there are some great tippers in this town. Charles Barkley. He's aces. Matt Damon, Ben Affleck, Wayne Gretzky, Dennis Rodman. They're all great tippers."

"Dennis Rodman?" I say. "I wouldn't have figured that."

"He might be crazy," Rick says, "but he's a great tipper."

"And what about the bad tippers? Anyone famous?"

Rick gives me a sly smile. "The worst tippers I've met in this town are Tiger Woods, Michael Jordan, and Diana Ross. And Telly Savalas, God rest him, he was a pure terror."

"And they're loaded."

"Just remember, Steve, if you act like a George, even on a budget, the people who work in this town will know it and you'll optimize your experience."

When I arrive back at my casino I head for the blackjack tables. I want to put Ryan and Rick's words into action and see if I can get someone to call me a George. Since I'm not rich, I try looking for a blackjack table with a five-dollar minimum. Good luck. At the casino where I'm staying that's like trying to find an honest car salesman. But I'm here to do a job, so I sit down at an empty table with a placard advertising a fifteen-dollar minimum.

"Hello, sir," the dealer, a friendly, open-faced kid with a Midwestern accent, says. "Ready to play some blackjack?"

"Yes, sir," I say, sliding five Benjamins across the felt table.

"Changing five hundred!" the dealer shouts, and in seconds my money is converted into a pile of clay chips. I place fifteen on the betting circle and wait for my cards. I toke him a five.

"Good luck, sir," the dealer says cheerily, dealing me a five and a six. The dealer's got a four showing. Since I've got eleven, the smart play is to double down. I take a hit and get an eight. Nineteen. The dealer flips up his card. It's a six. Then he deals himself a king. Twenty. I lose. Shit. But I'm not here to win. I'm here to redeem myself.

I never knew it was customary to tip a card dealer. When I learned that tidbit, I cringed at the thought of all the dealers I'd stiffed over the years. In my defense I don't gamble often, but for me that's a sin akin to not tipping a fellow waiter. This time, however, I want to set things right. And part of my journey to the desert is to purge myself of my gratuity sins.

I place thirty in the circle and toke the dealer five bucks again. "Thank you very much, sir," the dealer says. "Good luck." Of course he hits blackjack.

"Well, that sucks," I say.

"That's the way it goes, sir," the dealer replies, his face a study in friendly impassivity. "Care to go again?"

"Sure." And as the cards go back and forth, I put down a five-dollar bet for the dealer each time.

While we're playing, a pretty cocktail waitress asks me if I want a drink. I order a dirty martini. I slip her a five, and

the drink comes out almost immediately. But before I've finished drinking it, all the bad energy I've accumulated from stiffing dealers in the past catches up with me. I'm wiped out. Five
hundred dollars gone. And because I lost almost every wager I
made, the dealer made very little off the tokes I bet for him.

"I can't believe I lost all that money that fast."

"It happens, sir," the dealer says. "But thanks for trying to
toke me."

"No problem," I say, grinning. "Besides, I've never had a
five-hundred-dollar martini before."

"I'll get the girl to bring you another one," the dealer says.

"Thanks, man."

"Sure," the dealer says. "Anything for a George."

CHAPTER 9

Sex Tips
Dominatrixes, Phone Sex Operators,
and Prostitutes

Don't get excited. This chapter isn't about spicing up the ol' missionary position or teaching you how to have sex while hanging upside down from a chandelier. If you're looking to read about that kind of stuff, pick up a copy of *Cosmo* or log on to the greatest source of half-baked sexual information the world has ever known: the Internet.

What I *am* going to do is offer some guidance on tipping while *purchasing* sexual activity. Now, don't go all prudish on me. Sex is big business in America. We spend something like $10 billion a year on pornography, and plunk down more cash in strip clubs than we do for Broadway shows. Prostitution is a huge enterprise, and advertisements for escorts, full-body massages, and steamy invitations to "role play with Inga" can be found in the back of mainstream magazines, the local phone book, and, if you don't sweat the serial killers, Craigslist. There are sex clubs and red-light districts in every major American city. Make no mistake about it, sex is a multibillion-dollar service industry in the United States. And with millions of people paying good money to get their rocks off, someone has to be getting tipped somewhere. So I decided to focus my research on sex tipping in a city that has been producing and packaging carnality for almost one hundred years: Los Angeles. That's right, I'm going to Tinseltown.

As soon as my flight lands at LAX, I'm struck by the eerie sensation that everything in L.A. seems familiar. After I check into my hotel at the base of Beverly Hills, I drive my rental car down Sunset and stop to have a late lunch at Pinches Tacos, a Mexican joint across the street from the Chateau Marmont. As I munch on my chorizo taco and look at the storied hotel where John Belushi died of an overdose, I suddenly realize the source of my déjà vu. I *have* been to L.A. before—through movies and television. Because no part of this town *hasn't* been used as a film set or backdrop, the city has been imprinted on my memory like images on celluloid. I'm in Hollyweird.

I return to my hotel to sleep off the jet lag seeping into my bones. When I awake at 7:00 p.m., I shower, dress, and ask the hotel's car valet to retrieve my car.

"Where you going, boss?" the valet asks.

"Inglewood."

"Why you going there?" he asks. When I tell him, his eyes widen in disbelief.

Soon I'm driving down South La Cienega Boulevard back toward LAX. The sun has almost set and the day's heat is retreating into the darkening sky. As I move from L.A. into Culver City, the landscape begins taking on a foreboding, industrial edge. Beads of nervous sweat start rolling down my back and I grip the steering wheel tightly. Through my driver's-side window, I watch as the horsehead pumps on top of the oil derricks lining the highway rise and fall against the jaundiced Southern California twilight. As the derricks plunge their shafts in and out of the soil I'm reminded of a more carnal type of pumping. Now, you might think I'm being sophomoric, but my free-associating sexual congress with the rhythmic motion of metal structures doesn't surprise me. That's probably because the people who work at the place I'm driving toward routinely meld sexuality with iron and steel—plus leather, whips, and chains. That's right. I'm headed for a sex dungeon.

After some illegal U-turns and cursing out my GPS system, I finally find the dungeon, near a row of warehouses close to the airport. The outside of the building doesn't give the slightest inkling as to what's hidden inside. Even the nameplate on the door, "Passive Arts Studio," is small, unobtrusive, and really doesn't tell you much. For all I know it could be a yoga studio. But when I walk into the darkly lit reception area, the first thing I see is a tall blond woman sitting on a desk wearing stiletto heels, garters, a severe bustier, and a crushed-leather German officer's cap. Something tells me I'm in the right place.

"Hello," she says. "Welcome to Passive Arts. Can I help you?"

As my rods and cones start adjusting to the dim light I realize that the lady in fascist lingerie and I are not alone. A pale redhead wearing sweatpants and a long-sleeve T-shirt is sitting in a plush chair to my left. In the background a television set plays softly. The two women look at me intently.

"My name's Steve. I have an appointment with Dana."

"Oh," the woman with the leather cap says, "so *you're* the writer guy."

"In the flesh."

"Hi, Steve," the redhead says, getting up from her chair. "I'm Dana."

"A pleasure to finally meet you," I say, shaking her hand. "Thanks for offering to show me around."

"Is this your first time in a place like this?"

"Yep," I say nervously.

"Would you like to start with a tour? Or would you like to speak to the girls first?"

"A tour would be great."

She leads me into a small, neat room just off the reception area. A low set of drawers lies snug against the left wall and a variety of whips, paddles, and canes of various sizes and levels of ferocity lines the walls.

"This is the playroom," she says. "This is where we keep the toys that our customers may want to use during their visit here. Of course some of the heavy players who come here bring their own equipment." My eyes widen as I look at the implements of torture surrounding me.

"People bring their own equipment?"

"Sure."

"Sort of like bringing your own bottle to a restaurant?" I say. "Bring your own whip?"

She ignores my attempt at humor and plucks a large wooden paddle off the wall. "Now, this," she says, "is a heavy paddle for spanking."

"Do customers ever use that paddle on you?"

"I'm what's called a 'light submissive,'" Dana replies. "I'm not into receiving too much pain. And look at me," she says, pointing to her pale, lightly freckled face. "I bruise easily."

"But there are other girls who are on the receiving end of that thing?"

She explains that there are two kinds of workers at Passive Arts. To grossly oversimplify: The women who dish out punishment, give orders, and treat customers like slaves are called "tops." The girls who take a more submissive role in the proceedings are called "bottoms." "Some girls are heavy submissives," Dana says, hefting the paddle. "They like or don't mind the pain. And if a customer's going to leave bruises, the girls can charge what's called a 'marking fee.'"

"Marking fee?"

"If a girl knows a session's going to leave her with bruises that'll take time to heal," Dana says, "then she can charge additional money on top of her fee."

"How much do those marking fees run?"

"Usually from a hundred to two hundred dollars. Sometimes as high as five hundred."

I shudder to imagine what it takes to earn that five hundred.

As we talk further, Dana explains the dungeon's fee structure.

Customers pay $180 for an hour or $90 for a half hour. The girls give half the fee to the house but get to keep all of the tips and marking fees they earn. And while the girls get paid in cash, Passive Arts is aboveboard as far as taxes are concerned. Its employees are considered independent contractors and receive 1099s that accurately reflect their earnings, so Uncle Sam gets his cut. Passive Arts also operates as a legal establishment because the girls have to wear a G-string, and nudity is restricted to their being topless. The workers are also forbidden to touch a client sexually. "Besides," Dana tells me, "fifty percent of the guys who come here ejaculate on their own."

"So, what do you consider a good tip?"

"At least twenty dollars," she says. "When we're done touring the facility I'll introduce you to the girls. They'll probably be happy to tell you what they think is a good tip or a bad tip."

As she continues showing me the whips, horse bridles, pinwheels, surgical clamps, mousetraps, and other assorted goodies inside the drawer, my attention is drawn to several iron balls with handles.

"What are these for?" I ask, holding one in my hand. It must weigh close to twenty pounds.

"Those are for cock-and-ball torture," she says. "Men hang them from their balls."

"Are you serious? This thing looks like a shot put from track and field!"

"Guys will only have them attached for five minutes or so," she says. "But we also have guys whose fetish is to get kicked in the balls. Sometimes they dare us to kick them as hard as we can."

I place the iron weight back in the drawer. If some guys want their scrotums touching the floor or their 'nads turned into peanut butter, who am I to argue?

"We also have a few other devices for cock-and-ball torture here," she says, rummaging through the drawer. "Locking cock cages, rubber penis prisons, ball stretchers, wooden nutcrackers." She pulls out a catalog for a company that sells S&M equipment and opens to a page advertising stainless-steel-toothed cock rings. "And some customers like to use these things," she says. "It's a chastity device."

Normal cock rings are designed to be fitted around the base of a man's penis to trap the blood flow and keep his erection firm. But this cock ring's purpose is exactly the opposite: it's fitted with shiny pointed teeth on the *inside*. If you get erect while wearing one of these things, you're in for some serious discomfort.

"That would certainly keep *me* chaste," I say.

"And that's the whole point. We call it cock control." After seeing that spiky deterrent, I'm surprised every woman in the world doesn't keep one of them in her handbag.

"Shall we see the rest of the dungeon?" Dana asks brightly.

"I'm game if you are."

Passive Arts is a big place. Housed in a refurbished ware-house, the studio offers several theme rooms where custom-ers can indulge in whatever sadomasochistic activity they can think of. As I expected, there are rooms with cells, stockades, whipping posts, hanging cages, suspension devices, and even an honest-to-goodness rack straight out of an auto-da-fé. But some of the theme rooms cater to different tastes.

"This," Dana says, leading me into a very feminine-looking suite, "is the Mae West Room."

Looking like a backstage dressing room you'd see in an old movie, the Mae West Room is painted pink and has a large yellow table with a triptych makeup mirror as its focal point. Several mannequin heads wearing wigs stare up from a low table under which an assortment of high-heel shoes lie ready for use. Frilly ladies' garments hang on a coat rack, and a large Oriental rug is spread out on the floor. A couple of tasteful prints adorn the walls, and there are overstuffed chairs and a red slip-covered couch to sit on.

"What's this room used for?"

"This is for guys who like to play dress-up," Dana says. "They come in here and put on makeup, wear wigs, high heels—stuff like that. They're sometimes called sissy boys."

"Cross-dressers?"

"Sometimes, but not always."

"And this," she says, opening the door to another room, "is the medical suite."

When I look inside, my jaw drops. So far I've seen whips, chains, latex wraps, even dog cages for customers who indulge in "puppy play," and so far nothing's shocked me. But what I'm seeing now sends a chill down my spine. I'm looking at a dentist's chair.

"Oh, God!" I yelp, painfully recalling whirring drills and the smell of vaporized enamel. "This is a dentist's office!"

"And a doctor's office, too," Dana says, pointing to an examination table on the other side of the room.

I hate going to the dentist. Don't get me wrong—my dentist is a wonderful man and a skilled practitioner. But I need to be loaded on benzodiazepine just to get a simple cleaning.

"This place doesn't do it for you?" Dana asks, grinning.

"Honestly? It creeps me out. But what's really interesting is what turns some people on. What would you say the majority of your clients are looking for when they come here?"

"Actually, thirty percent of our clients are tickle fetishists."

"People come here just to get tickled?"

"And they're usually super nice guys," she says. "The tickling fetish is also very nonsexual. It's easy money, and the guys are friendly, funny, and good tippers."

"What's the next most popular fetish your customers subscribe to?"

"Foot fetishes are big," she says. "I'd say twenty percent of guys are into that. Some guys are really into feet. Some of my customers get so focused looking at my feet it's like I don't exist from the ankles up."

"Are there any fetishes you find disturbing?"

She thinks about that for a moment. "One time I saw something in a catalog that disturbed me: a rubber foot for foot fetishists."

"What makes that unusual?"

"Foot fetishes aren't unusual in and of themselves," she says. "We have guys who bring their own props all the time. But the thing in the catalog was a rubber foot with a bone sticking out of it." She pauses for a moment, as if she's just thought of something. "You're not going to make fun of the guys who come in here, are you?" she asks. "I wouldn't like that. They're people, you know."

"Don't worry, Dana. I'm not here to make any judgments."

"Well, most of the guys who come in here are harmless," she continues. "But sometimes we get someone who makes us uncomfortable. We had one guy who liked to beat on women. I mean really whale on them. Only a few of the heavy submissives could deal with him. But there was something about him that was scary, so we told him to stop coming."

"Are guys like that a rare occurrence?"

"They are," she says. "But we have ways of keeping ourselves safe here. We have security in place, and the girls are free to refuse to work with any customer for any reason."

As we talk, I ask if supplying a safe and controlled environment for men to explore their violent fantasies might keep them from harming women in the real world. "Do you think you've ever stopped a guy from developing into a full-blown serial killer?"

"I think on occasion we might have," she says. "But, like I said, most fetishes are benign. There are guys who like to give girls piggyback rides and even be hit in the face with pies."

"You're kidding."

"No. I'm serious. Guys will bring in pie tins full of whipped cream and they throw them at us or we throw it at them. It's called sploshing."

"I guess that's the Soupy Sales version of fetishism." For the first time, I get a laugh out of my tour guide. I ask Dana how she thinks fetishes, whether for whips, dentist work, or pies, develop.

"Fetishes are primarily found in men," she says. "And I think they're formed at some critical point in their psychosocial development—like twelve or thirteen. Have you ever heard of a website called Savage Love?" She mentions Dan Savage, a sex columnist in Seattle. One day a guy wrote in to his column concerned that his new girlfriend would freak out when he told her about his fetish: having her wear scuba flippers during sex. I can see how that might not go over well.

"But what's really interesting," Dana says, "was Savage's take on how this guy's fetish started in the first place. The guy who wrote in thought his fixation started because his earliest sexual fantasies revolved around a woman he saw in the movie *The Deep* as a kid."

"Jacqueline Bisset," I reply. "Nineteen seventy-seven. She was a knockout back then."

"Well, Savage said that seeing a beautiful woman wearing swim fins at that sensitive time in the guy's psychosexual development must've put that fetish in his head."

As Dana leads me to the staff room to talk to the girls about tipping, I think about my own sexual life and the preferences I've acquired. Did I develop any fetishes during my impressionable years? When I think of that young man who got hot and bothered by Jacqueline Bisset's shapely fins, I think the answer might be yes. When I turned thirteen, the James Bond film *For Your Eyes Only* had just come out. The poster for the movie featured the bottom half of a crossbow-wielding woman wearing a skimpy bikini. She was facing Roger Moore and framing him between her spectacularly outstretched legs. Old Roger never looked so happy. And let me tell you, I stared at that picture for *months*. No, I don't get a woody looking at crossbows now. But remember how that stripper in Vegas figured out my gluteal predilection in three seconds? I'm an ass man. Blame it on 007.

Dana takes me into the staff room. It's a small, comfortable space with couches, a fridge, a coffeemaker, and a television. As I walk in, the girls are watching *American Idol*, which so far has been the most torturous thing I've experienced in this place. After the introductions are made, I get down to the real reason for my visit: discussing the tip.

The girls quickly explain that because half of their fee goes to the house, a tip that makes up for that deduction is the most appreciated. But since the economy is down, so is business at the dungeon. Girls who used to make three thousand a month are now pulling down two. Customers are ratcheting back on their visits, buying a half hour's worth of time instead of an hour, and tipping less.

"Some guys are still good tippers," says Giselle, a raven-haired Latina wearing a lacy corset and garters. "But others? Yuck."

"If I get forty dollars," says Sandy, a pretty girl with pink streaks in her hair, "then I know the guy's a good tipper."

"What percentage of your customers tip?"

"I'd say fifty to sixty percent of customers tip," Giselle says. "But usually they just give us twenty bucks."

"But not all tips are monetary," Allison, a curvy brunette in a baby-doll nightie, chimes in. "Sometimes we get gifts. Candy, gift cards, lingerie, shoes . . ."

"And then there's the slave thing," Sandy says. "Sometimes we get tipped that way."

"Slave thing?"

She explains that men who are submissives love hanging around their whip-cracking dominatrixes. But having a guy just loitering about is boring and has no utility. What the girls really love is when the men tip them by offering to be their personal slave, providing them with services outside the dungeon, such as babysitting their dogs, doing their grocery shopping, fixing their cars, painting their bathrooms, and even chauffeuring them to the airport. I like this idea of servitude as a tip. The thought of my old restaurant patrons scrubbing my toilet makes me smile.

The girls go on to tell me that, slave labor aside, monetary tips make up 20 percent of their income. "And the marking fees?" I ask. "They run from a hundred to two hundred dollars, sometimes as high as five hundred. Right?"

"It depends on what the customer wants to do," Allison says, brushing a heavy lock of dark hair away from her face. "If the customer's a heavy hitter and is going to leave bruises, he's got to pay. We'll sit down with the guy in advance to find out exactly what he's into and negotiate the fee. But sometimes guys come in here wanting to really beat on a girl and no one's around who's willing to do it."

"Do you want a tip on top of the marking fee?"

"If a guy's really into giving pain, he'd better be a good tipper," she says. "If he isn't, no one will want to work with him."

Tipping in a dungeon is just like tipping in a restaurant. If you want the best table in the house, you pay. If you want to indulge in sadism, you pay. Come to think of it, lots of my old customers were emotional sadists.

"One last question," I say. "How does one get into this business?"

"I knew I was into this years ago," Sandy says. "When I was younger I'd beat myself with spoons and took turns with the other kids in my neighborhood tying each other up. I liked it."

"I found out I was into being submissive later in life," Dana adds. "After my divorce, I was dating this guy who I didn't know was a dom. Well, one night when we're in bed he tells me to go on all fours. When I turned around to look at him he spanked me *hard*, saying, 'Did I tell you that you could turn around?' To my surprise I enjoyed it. It was then I knew."

"And what does this work do for you personally?" I ask. "It can't just be the money."

"I used to be the type of person who had trouble saying no to people," Dana says. "I have a more submissive personality;

that's why I'm a bottom. But when you're in this line of work you have to be able to set boundaries to keep you safe. We have code words to tell a client when he's going too far. If a guy's getting too rough I'll say 'yellow.' If he's crossed the line and I'm uncomfortable, I'll say 'red.' And if he doesn't listen he gets kicked out. This work has taught me to say *no*."

"So, being a submissive taught you how to be more assertive? Kind of paradoxical."

"Oh my God," Sandy says. "This place totally helped me get stronger. My friends who knew me before I started working here don't even recognize me anymore. I used to be a doormat. Not anymore."

When I first walked into Passive Arts, I was worried the girls here would be a bunch of strange, dysfunctional people. But as I talk to these sex workers, I feel no impulse to judge, much less feel nervous. In fact, I feel quite comfortable around them. That's probably because I can sense that they have their heads screwed on straight and are conscious of what drives them to do what they do. Over the course of my life I've encountered many "normal" people who, despite their polished outward appearance, were damaged, self-destructive humans with little or no insight into their own behavior. Like the old saying goes, "You can't always judge a book by its cover." You may not approve of what these girls do for a living, but I guarantee there's someone in your church or cubicle farm who's more screwed up than these girls ever could be.

So if you avail yourself of these girls' services, tip them well.

Back at my hotel, the car valet comes to get my keys with a mirthful smirk on his face.

"So, how'd it go, boss?"

"My man," I reply. "Everybody's got a little bit of kink."

To indulge their kinkiness, most people don't visit sex dungeons. Most people surf online porn, rent dirty movies, or go to strip clubs. But if you want to explore your sexual desires with a real, live person, without the complications of face-to-face contact, then phone sex is for you. And guess what? Phone sex operators like tips, too.

My one and only encounter with phone sex ended in embarrassing disaster. When I was a freshman in high school one of my more perverted classmates stuck a crumpled piece of paper into my hands and whispered, "Hey, Dublanica. If you call this number a hot girl will talk dirty to you." Of course, I called the number as soon as I got home. And let me tell you, the breathy, erotic words that seeped out of the earpiece and slithered into my teenage lizard brain made me very happy. And since fourteen-year-old boys are basically Portnoyesque masturbation machines, I called that number over and over and *over* again.

But because my hormone-laden blood was being drawn away from my cerebral cortex, it didn't dawn on me that these calls *cost money.* So when my mom opened the phone bill, the shit hit the fan. Seeing hundreds of dollars in charges, she called the mysterious number to find out what was going on. She found out all right. I don't know what's more embarrassing: that my mother knew I was spanking it to bad phone porn or that she had listened to some disembodied woman squealing in mock orgasmic pleasure. Before you knew it, my dad and I were having an ice-cream cone while talking about the birds and the bees. "Let me tell you about sex, son," my dad said. "And don't ever call that number again." To say I was mortified would be an understatement of galactic proportions, cubed.

But now, since I want to be a tipping guru, I push my adolescent trauma aside and call a phone sex operator named Mona who has offered to talk to me. As the phone rings, I remind myself not to breathe heavy.

When Mona answers, I immediately notice she has a deep, smoky voice—custom-made for her line of work. To break the ice I tell her about my phone sex escapade.

"So, after that, I was done with phone sex," I say in conclusion.

"Oh, yeah," Mona says. "In the early eighties those nine hundred numbers were big."

"You're not charging me for this call, are you?" I say, flashing back to the look on my mom's face.

"No, honey," Mona says. "This call's free. But you'd be surprised how many stories like yours are out there. Guys call my number saying, 'I want to call you. I'm really horny and I want to get off.' And then they go, 'Oh! You mean I have to pay?' And I'm like, 'Um . . . hello? Did you read the website?' So sorry. This is how I pay my bills."

Mona works for a website that serves as a dispatch company, and customers pay by credit card or money order for calls costing between $1.99 and $2.50 a minute with a ten-minute minimum. Their service offers a rate for international calls as well. (Don't they have phone sex in France?) I also learn that in the phone sex business, how much you make is a combination of two things: the rate you're paid per minute and how much time you spend on the phone. Mona tells me that her boss pays well for a dispatch company and that girls start out at $0.40 a minute, eventually working their way up to $0.80 per minute. Since Mona's been in the biz for a while, she commands $0.90 a minute and spends roughly 750 minutes on the phone per week—which yields $2,700 a month before taxes. But Mona is a mute slacker compared to some of her comrades, who clock in 33 hours a week—nearly 2,000 minutes!—helping men get off. I sure hope those aural sex kittens don't use cell phones. That much radio wattage could cause unwanted appendages to grow out of your head.

Mona tells me that one of the great things about the phone sex industry is the ability to work out of your house as an independent contractor. Through the miracle of digital telephony, the bad old days of being cooped up in a small room with dozens of women droning, "Oh, yeah, baby. Do it to me," have been replaced by the comfort and privacy of working from home. According to Mona, the only drawbacks are that she has to buy her own health insurance and pay an accountant to do her taxes. Just like the girls at the dungeon, she has to file those pesky 1099 forms.

"So, what does a buck ninety-nine get you?" I ask her.

"Well, . . . guys can really talk about anything they want. A lot of guys think they want to talk about one thing, but things really blend together—cuckold fantasies; that's when guys want to see their girlfriends or wives with another man. That ties into orgasm denial, sensuous teasing, cock control, small penis humiliation . . .

"Before I started working for a fem-dom service," she says, reading my mind, "I had *no* idea this stuff was out there. I was working a vanilla site and, you know, it was all just straight sex. Now I work for a website that offers a lot of feminization and forced bi. Take It All. That's our forced bi site. It's for men who fantasize about being forced into bisexual acts. Although sometimes there's very little forcing going on. All they have to hear is 'All right, slut! Get on your knees!' and they're like, 'Yes, Mistress! Can I suck it now?' "

From what I'm hearing, Mona's website offers the telephonic version of Passive Arts's dungeon.

"And what does two-fifty a minute get you?" I ask.

"Well, we have our Giantess Alley site," she says. "That's where we charge a premium."

"The *what* site?" I ask, not sure I heard her correctly. "*Gigantic Alley* site?"

"Giantess Alley," she says. "That's where we shrink the guys. It's for men who like giant women."

"You're gonna have to explain that one to me."

"For Giantess Alley," she says, "I have one caller who likes the idea of me *growing* inside his apartment. For some reason I start growing and smash my way out of his building and start chasing him. Sometimes I find him with another girl and I drop-kick her."

"So it's like *Attack of the 50 Ft. Woman*," I say, referring to the classic 1958 sci-fi film.

"Oh, yeah," she says. "Sometimes the guy lives; sometimes he doesn't. Sometimes he likes to imagine he's been captured by Amazons and I'm their huge deity and he's my sacrifice. Then there are guys who want to be stomped. They want you to squish them between your toes. Some guys even want to be eaten alive. There's a technical term for that, but I call it 'gold-fishing.'"

After my conversation with Dana about how sexual fetishes take hold in the male psyche, I'm not surprised Giantess Alley exists. Maybe some thirteen-year-old kid got his first woody watching the curvaceous Allison Hayes wreak her Brobding-nagian havoc and now has a thing for chicks who can turn him into jelly between their toes or swallow him whole. I see how it could happen.

"Now, you girls get tips, right?"

"I don't get tips often," she says. "But we've had girls get tipped thousands in a weekend by one guy."

She tells me most of her customers don't tip, and the bulk of her income comes from the ninety cents a minute she earns. But if a patron wishes to leave a gratuity they can charge it to a credit card or debit it from a prepaid account. The appropriate tip, though the phone sex operators often don't get it, is 20 percent. "It's also nice to leave the dispatcher a tip, too," Mona says. "But a very popular way for clients to give tips is to give us presents."

This sounds just like the dungeon. Mona directs me to her company's website and tells me to look up the pictures of the available mistresses. "Click on Amber's pic," she says. "She's always a princess."

I click on a sultry blonde's picture and read her profile aloud. "Hi! I'm Amber! I'm a spoiled little tease."

"See the little gift-wrapped package in the corner of the screen?"

When I click on the gift box icon, I'm taken to a "wish list" on Amazon.com. On it I find a bunch of gifts Amber would like to receive from her gentlemen callers. Judging from the four-thousand-dollar necklace, two-thousand-dollar laptop, and the other pricey items, this girl has expensive tastes. But when I tab over to the "Purchased" list and examine the goodies Amber's admirers have already bought her, my mouth drops open. This girl's gotten a Movado watch, a thirty-two-inch plasma-screen television, five-hundred-dollar earrings, two-hundred-dollar sandals, and a stainless-steel Kitchen Aid mixer. Man, I'm in the wrong business.

"Do you have a gift list?"

"Sure," Mona says. "Click on the picture labeled 'Wank Mistress.' That's me."

I click on a photo icon of a brunette in a swimsuit and tab over to Mona's wish list. Among the desirable goodies listed are DVDs, modest pieces of jewelry, high-thread-count sheets, and there, shining in all its glory, a link to my book.

"Hey, *Waiter Rant*!" I hoot. "That's hysterical."

"One of the ladies I work with got me that as a birthday present," Mona says. "That was on my gift list as one of the first things I wanted." Phone sex girls want my book as a tip. *I have arrived.*

"So, Mona," I ask, "when you get a tip, what does it mean to you?"

"A tip for me means that somebody thinks that I've done something really special for them," she says. "They're showing me real above-and-beyond appreciation. Whenever a guy tips me or takes time to write a nice email to my boss, it really means a lot to me. It lets me know whatever I'm doing I must be doing it well."

"What's the one thing about phone sex operators that you'd want the general public to know that you don't think they know?"

"That we do care about our callers," she says. "I get very protective of my guys. When somebody says, 'How can you stand to talk to those freaks?' I'm like, these are real people who trust us with some very scary stuff in their lives sometimes. We care about our callers. And we want to do right by them. We want to do a good job, just like everybody else."

I like Mona. Her tolerant attitude and the dedication she shows to her job, albeit a strange one, touches me. After we hang up, I reconsider my relationship with phone sex. Who knows? One day I might find a girlfriend who likes dirty phone talk. Maybe I'll ask her to pretend she's a fifty-foot goddess with a jones to drop-kick me.

When it comes to talking about tipping and sex, I'd be remiss in my duties if I didn't investigate the relationship between gratuities and the oldest profession the world: prostitution. Do hookers expect tips? If so, how much? Does tipping get you a more enthusiastic performance? A little something extra? What's a good tip on a blow job? I hit the streets to find out.

This might not come as a shock to you, but prostitution is *everywhere*. There are ads for escort agencies in the phonebook, and you'll find hookers operating in casinos, nightclubs, truck stops, massage parlors, even college campuses. And while some antediluvian prostitutes still work street corners, the vast majority of the sex trade has moved online. When you think about it, the Internet has become the biggest, baddest pimp on the planet. Part-time escorts use the Web to turn a trick or two out of their homes, while seasoned operators use travel websites to book discounted hotel rooms and service up to twenty guys on a weekend. And if you don't like to travel, you can log on to websites such as Backpage or Craigslist and have an escort come to your house right now! But be careful. The cops monitor those websites.

Just because you can find prostitutes everywhere doesn't mean it's easy to interview them. My initial forays into this underground world were met with outright rejection and hostility. I didn't take it personally. Prostitutes always have to be on the lookout for sociopaths and freaks. Besides, in most localities, the exchange of money for sex is a crime. Since I'm talking to these women about tipping while providing sexual services, I'm basically asking them to incriminate themselves. But after months of trolling the Internet, I found some women who were willing to talk to me over the telephone. During those interviews I discovered something surprising: prostitutes usually don't get tips. I also learned that if a customer wants something extra, that's arranged when negotiating the upfront fee.

"Tipping's appreciated," one call girl told me, "but not expected. We make such an insane amount of money, it's like, what are they tipping me for?" Other working girls told me they'd get clothing, liquor, and even marijuana as gratuities. But for many johns, tipping is a city in China.

Now, talking to prostitutes on the phone is nice and all, but I knew that to ensure my bona fides as a tipping guru, sooner or later I'd have to talk to a working girl in person. So when I return from my trip to the dungeon, I call Thalia, an L.A. prostitute I'd struck up an email correspondence with, and invite her to dinner.

Driving a little sports car, Thalia arrives promptly at my hotel at seven o'clock. One of the first questions she asks me is, "How do you feel about meat?"

"Beg your pardon?"

"I want to go to this restaurant that only serves meat," she says. "I just want to make sure you're not a vegetarian."

This is the second time since I've been to California that someone has asked me that question in that particular way. I don't feel any which way about meat. I just eat it.

The restaurant turns out to be very popular and we can't get a reservation until nine o'clock. Faced with this delay, Thalia suggests we find a bar at the Grove, a shopping center on Fairfax, and indulge in some libations. After a white-knuckle car drive through L.A. traffic, Thalia and I get to the shopping center and make a beeline for the Cheesecake Factory. I have a hankering for one of their dirty vodka martinis with blue-cheese-stuffed olives. But before we get ten feet from the car, craziness explodes in front of us. Two women, a skinny redhead in a miniskirt and a shapely Asian girl in an expensive sheath dress, begin screaming at each other.

"You fucking slut!" the obviously inebriated redhead screams. "Give me back my fucking keys!"

"You're drunk," the Asian girl says. "No way."

"You slope cunt!" the redhead screams, grabbing a chunk of the Asian girl's hair. "You can't do this to me. Give me back my keys!"

The redhead lunges at the Asian woman. Soon they're slapping the shit out of each other in the parking lot. Welcome to L.A.

"Oh my God!" Thalia yelps.

To my surprise, she walks over to the belligerent redhead and tries talking to her in soothing tones. But the Asian woman looks like she's going to murder someone. Uh-oh. If this thing goes south, there goes my interview. For the sake of my quest, I decide to get involved. The first order of business is to separate the combatants. Since Thalia's got the redhead, I focus my attentions on the Asian woman. "You there," I bark in my best command voice. "Come over here this instant!" The Asian woman complies.

It turns out that they are spoiled rich kids who have just gotten out of a tony rehab program and decided to celebrate by drinking and getting high as kites. As running buddies are wont to do, they turned on each other when the redhead, much too drunk to drive, agreed to let a shady character she met in the bar drive her back to his place in her expensive BMW. The Asian girl, fearing the man's intentions were less than pure, but probably more upset she was being left in the lurch, took the redhead's car keys and hilarity ensued.

After an hour of our trying to keep things under control, the LAPD finally arrive and bring rapid closure to the situation. They give the girls a simple choice. They can both walk away from the situation or file assault charges against each other and spend the night in a lovely cell in South Central. The girls wisely take separate cabs home.

When Thalia and I finally get to our restaurant and order drinks, I say, "I'm surprised you stepped into that mess."

"Why?"

"Well, you're an escort. I thought avoiding the police was a priority."

"Only when I'm working," she says, winking. "Otherwise I try and help whenever I can."

Thalia is a voluptuous blonde with a sexy deep voice that would've put Lauren Bacall's to shame. When she tells me a recent vice squad crackdown has been putting a dent in her business, I suggest she give Mona a call. "Don't think I haven't thought of doing the phone sex thing," she says, grinning. "I've been told my voice gives men instant hard-ons."

After we place our order we get straight to business. Thalia is in her early forties, divorced, works a professional job by day, and has been a part-time independent escort for over a year. She charges three hundred dollars an hour and provides what's called the Girlfriend Experience, or GFE. She explains that the focus of a GFE encounter isn't just the sexual act itself but also creating an illusion that an intimate relationship exists between the customer and the provider. A sexual act with a non-GFE provider is crudely akin to using another human being as a masturbation tool. Traditional providers often eschew kissing on the grounds that it's too intimate, they won't let the customer pleasure them, and they focus on getting the man to climax quickly, turning the contracted hour into a quickie and maximizing the earning potential of their time. GFEs, on the other hand, will spend the full advertised time with the customer and engage in unrushed sex complete with French kissing, mutual pleasuring, and lots of talking. Thalia explains that a GFE encounter is charged with feeling, so the provider needs to possess a highly developed set of emotional and communication skills to pull off the illusion. Unlike traditional providers, who treat the sexual act like a handshake, a GFE tries to make the customer seem like the center of her universe. "In many ways what I do is therapy."

"So, how'd you get into this business?"

"I was divorced and suffered through, like, two hundred bad dates afterward," Thalia says. "But I enjoy sex. And since enough people said I was good at it, I decided to cut out the dating middleman and make money while doing it. That's how I got started. Odd as this may sound, it restored my self-confidence."

When I ask her about gratuities, she tells me that only 5 percent of her customers tip. The vast majority of her income is derived from the three hundred dollars she charges. "Sometimes the guys do nice things like bring me flowers, wine, a good bottle of scotch, or even a six-pack of beer. I like when they do that, that someone made an effort to see me as a person."

"But have you gotten cash tips?"

"Occasionally someone will give me double my fee. But you know what? I'd rather spend my time with a nice guy who doesn't tip than an asshole who does."

She then tells me something that surprises me. "I [won't take on] married men as customers."

"Why not?" I ask. "I thought they'd be your bread and butter."

"I was married once," she says. "I know the pain cheating causes. It's just wrong."

"But how do you know a guy's married?" I ask. "He could lie and say he's single."

"I screen my clients," she says. "I can usually tell if they're married or not. Occasionally one slips by me, but I'll never see him again."

"How do you catch them?"

She smiles sadly. "Because married men are almost unfailingly miserable when we're finished."

After our dinner plates are cleared we order dessert and I ask her about the pitfalls of being a GFE provider.

"I don't like having to set the boundaries after the time is over," she says. "Some guys have a hard time when they realize the connection's over, and get depressed. They think what we've shared is going to fix their lives. But I just can't do that."

"You can never fix another person," I say. "That's something I know from bitter experience."

"It's just so hard," she says. "I hate it when I sense a customer's going to feel lonelier when they leave than when they came in. That's when I feel like I've failed."

"Do you remember the movie *Frankie and Johnny*?"

"Yeah, why?"

"Pacino's got a great line in the movie concerning one-night stands," I say. "He calls them a 'Band-Aid on loneliness.'"

"Well," she says, "then I'm a Band-Aid when these people need a tourniquet."

We spend the rest of the night talking about the pros and cons of legalizing prostitution, the nature of God, and the problem of evil in the world. Not the kind of stuff you'd expect to talk about with a sex worker. But Thalia is much more than her night job. She's a well-educated woman with interests in science, theology, and Eastern philosophies. Some people might look askance at what she does. But as evidenced by her intervention at the Grove and the protective feelings she harbors for her customers, I can tell she's a good person. When our time together ends I'm sorry to see her go.

Back at my hotel, I ponder tipping and sex work. The first thing I noticed was that sex workers like tips because they demonstrate that the customer values them as people and appreciates the work they do. I guess it doesn't matter if you cut hair, deliver food, or give head—people like to know they're doing a good job. But while it's a basic societal rule in America that restaurant servers get tipped 15 to 20 percent, my research showed that there's no equivalent standard for sex workers. While the amounts weren't staggering, the girls at Passive Arts seem to get the most in cash tips, followed by phone sex operators and then prostitutes, who usually get nothing. And in all these professions, gifts figure as prominently as gratuities. What's going on here?

First, let me focus on why the consumers of sexual services usually don't tip prostitutes.

When you peruse the Internet forums frequented by men who patronize prostitutes, tipping is often considered unnecessary, even stupid. While some of these "hobbyists" write that a tip of 20 percent is reasonable and polite, they are in a distinct minority. "If the service is all-inclusive," one poster counters, "why should you tip? I can understand a waitress at a food establishment because they are paid nearly nothing per hour and depend on tips, but a provider makes damn good money per hour . . . She's already getting a lot as it is!" One wag even writes, "I would give her this as a tip: 'Get into a healthier occupation.'"

Most men on the forums state that they don't leave tips. And when they do leave a gratuity, the most common explanation is that they found a sex worker they liked and tipped so she'd remember them. As one hobbyist writes, "I am much more likely to tip a lady that I am likely to see again. Often the extra $10 or $20 invested in a tip one visit ensures an eager provider next visit." Men also say they give tips if the service was exceptional, but those amounts tend to be small.

Just like waiters, hotel workers, hairstylists, doormen, bartenders and baristas, prostitutes work in a service occupation. But why did tipping take hold in those professions and not the oldest one in the world? I think there are a few reasons:

THE PRICE

The fees prostitutes charge can range from $50 for a back-alley blow job to $30,000 for a weekend romp with a high-end call girl. But no matter what the extreme, fees have usually been considered all-inclusive and are paid in advance. And most men think the amount of money they're spending is enough, which lessens the impulse to leave a gratuity.

DODGY CUSTOMER BASE

Let's face it, guys who patronize prostitutes aren't choirboys, so the odds are good they'll be bad tippers. Sex workers are in this business to make money. If they depended on the tipping largesse of their customer base for a significant chunk of their income, they'd go broke. That's why sex providers, whether they are dungeon mistresses, phone sex operators, or prostitutes, use the up-front business model. They want to get paid.

PSYCHOLOGY

Men who frequent prostitutes want to have sex. Thinking, "Do I have to tip this girl?" while doing the horizontal mambo might lead to deflationary side effects. Doing math in your head is like thinking about old nuns. Men want to pay, get what they came for, and leave. And this is sex we're talking about. In the best of all worlds it should be free. For some johns there's a sense of shame in having to pay for sex. They don't want to feel compelled to tip on top of it.

ANONYMITY

By its very nature, prostitution is a secretive and discreet transaction, and the customer usually knows nothing about the sex worker as a human being. Dr. P. M. Forni states in his book *Choosing Civility* that anonymity is one of the major causes of rude behavior. Basically, we treat strangers like shit. Because of anonymity, Forni writes, "we know that our crudeness and boorishness will go unreported—that we can get away with it." Many johns see prostitutes as anonymous, so they're less likely to care if the girls feel slighted about not getting tipped. Sadly, this "rudeness" isn't limited to poor gratuities but can include mental and physical abuse.

PIMPS

While many prostitutes today are independent contractors, others are in the employ of pimps, madams, and escort agencies. All of these entities take a share of the sex worker's dollar—some more than others. And as one Internet poster had it, "If you tip her, that's just that much more she has to pay her pimp. Don't bother."

HISTORY

As noted earlier with regard to flight attendants, if tipping doesn't become firmly entrenched in a profession at its inception, it seldom becomes the norm. Well, prostitution has been around since before there was even money to tip with! In prehistory, sex was traded for furs, protection, shelter, and food. This probably explains why today's prostitutes and other sex workers are often tipped with small gifts, booze, clothes, drugs, and restaurant meals. The concept of cash tipping came eons later, so prostitutes missed out on what their counterparts in more modern service industries enjoy today.

My theory is that dungeon mistresses and phone sex operators make more in tips than their prostitute sisters because they are a more modern incarnation of sexual activity. Because they're the new kids on the sex block, they got partially absorbed into the American system of tipping. And the reason modern prostitutes get any tips at all is due to "tip creep"— the phenomenon where tipping starts to appear in occupations where it didn't exist before. Look at it this way: customers who patronize prostitutes tip service workers in other professions. So it's only natural for them to wonder if they should tip sex workers, too. Some will, some won't. But America is the land of the tip. And the more a population gets habituated to a practice, the more likely it is to spread. I'll go out on a limb here and make a prediction: in twenty years, prostitution and other forms of sex work will get absorbed into the American tipping paradigm and gratuities of 15 to 20 percent will become the norm. I hope I'm around to be proved right, and that the girls in the dungeon, the phone sex operators, and the prostitutes make a nice buck out of it.

And I have a sneaking suspicion that pimps and hustlers not yet born will figure out a way to steal it from them.

CHAPTER 10

Shake It, Baby, Shake It!
Strippers and Exotic Dancers

S ince we've just discussed sex workers and gratuities, let's head back to Vegas to find out how tipping works with other kinds of scantily clad women. So to all you guys who skipped ahead to this chapter: that's right, I'm going to talk about strippers. Boy, do they *love* tips. And with over forty gentlemen's clubs to choose from, Las Vegas is the strip club capital of the United States. Hang on to your wallets, guys. It's going to be a bumpy ride.

Of course, I'd be nuts to head off to Sin City without doing a little "stripper recon first." You can't just walk up to a naked woman in a strip club and say, "Hey, I'm writing a book. Wanna talk?" They've heard that line from perverted amateur sociologists before, and it's a good way to get beaten up by some steroid-raging bouncer to boot. Since I bruise easily, I decided to learn as much as I could about the strip club business before setting foot in this town. So I went to the Internet forums where women who take their clothes off for a living commiserate online— StripperWeb.com and ExoticDancer.net. Oh, man, did I take a beating.

I naïvely thought that interviewing strippers would be fun.

On every heroic journey your average hairy-chested protagonist is tempted by all manner of slinky females trying to waylay him from his quest. Ulysses had the Sirens, Aeneas had Dido, and Beowulf got a naked, dripping-wet Angelina Jolie with a computer-generated tail. Hot, hot, hot. Sadly, my initial encounters with the exotic dancers on the forums had less to do with temptation than with humiliation. Many of the women online were convinced I was just a peeper looking to get a free show. Others were just looking for money. "I'd be happy to share my story as long as you pay me," one stripper wrote. But when I replied that paying for interviews was unethical, and the best I could do was buy her lunch, the shit really hit the fan.

"Excuse the fuck outta me," the aggrieved dancer wrote. "But what journalism/creative writing/ethics course did you take that says that compensating a person for their intellectual property is 'unethical'? If you have every intention of profiting from strippers' anecdotes, stories, and experiences you should pay them! Imagine if your publisher started paying you royalties in dinners and lunches . . . Would you be happy about it?" Then after we slugged it out in the forum the stripper posted the most unflattering picture of me she could find on the Internet—the one that makes me look like the waiter who ate Cleveland.

"Oh, wait . . . is that how you get paid . . . Chubsy?" the photo's caption read. Ouch.

I thought my quest had hit a dead end. But after a while, several dancers from the forums who didn't share their comrades' mercenary attitudes agreed to talk with me. And after many hours of interviews, they told me everything I'd ever wanted to know about the business of the bump and grind: how strip clubs operate, how to tip dancers, and—yes, guys—whether or not there really is sex in the Champagne Room. So let's pop open that bottle of Cristal and get started.

*   *   *

At eleven o'clock on Friday night, I walk out of my hotel room freshly showered and shaved and take the elevator down to the casino floor. I'm wearing dress slacks, shiny new shoes, an expensive wide-lapel cotton shirt open to the third button, and a blazer a little too flashy for my taste. As I admire my reflection in the elevator mirror, I wonder if adding a few gold chains to my ensemble would be over the top. Yeah, probably. When I reach the casino floor, I walk past the crowded gaming tables and jangling slot machines and march straight toward the main entrance. No time for gambling tonight. I'm going to one of the most famous strip clubs in the world: the Peppermint Hippo at Las Vegas.

"Can I call you a cab, sir?" the doorman asks as I walk to the curb.

"No, thanks," I say, slipping him a buck anyway. "I'm waiting for a limo from the Hippo."

"Out for some fun tonight, sir?"

"Oh, yeah," I reply, savoring the cooling desert air.

Most strip clubs in the United States have entrance fees of one kind or another. This is the *first* point of contact, where they begin the process of separating you from your money. The Peppermint Hippo's entrance fee is ten dollars if you're a Vegas resident and thirty if you're from out of town. But if you call the Hippo and ask for their limo to pick you up at your hotel, they'll waive the fee. Most of the Hippo's worthy competitors have the same policy. And why do strip clubs shell out for this expense? As we'll learn later, sending a limo to pick customers up *saves* them money.

The limo from the Hippo pulls up, and soon I arrive in style at the VIP entrance in the back. When you use the limo service, not only do you avoid the entrance fee, but you also bypass the line of horny guys snaking up to the front door. After I tip the limo guy twenty bucks, I've saved myself ten whole dollars. That will be the *only* money I'll save all night.

As I walk toward the VIP entrance I can feel the music from

inside the club vibrating up through the parking lot's pavement and into my legs. Despite my "VIP" status, I'm still frisked and metal-wanded by the Hippo's security staff. In Nevada, citizens are allowed to carry concealed handguns, so the security staff is taking no chances. And while they're gentle, they're very, very thorough.

"That's probably the only time I'm going to get felt up tonight," I quip to the very large man doing the frisking. He does not laugh at my joke.

"Yes, sir," the man says crisply. "You have yourself a nice time."

As I walk inside the Hippo, the pounding bass emanating from the club's impressive sound system immediately assaults my ears. In the lobby the raucous laughter of men intermingled with the crystalline giggles of women rises and falls below the heavy flow of music. It takes a while for my eyes to adjust to the dim light. In the meantime, several scantily clad women dart out of a service door and disappear into the darkness. The air is filled with the odor of liquor, cologne, perfume, and the musky scent of male lust. My heart pounds inside my chest. I'm not sure my sudden cardiac surge is from excitement, sensory overload, or a vibrato assist from all the acoustic megawattage.

"Hello, sir!" A fit young man in a black suit, white shirt, and black tie is offering me his hand. "Welcome to the Peppermint Hippo. I'm Ben and I'll be your host tonight."

As I shake Ben's hand, I'm immediately impressed by his strong grip. In that little mental evaluation all men do upon meeting one another, I instantly ascertain that Ben could kick my ass without breaking a sweat. All strip clubs have bouncers. Whenever you mix men with naked women, money, and booze, testosterone levels are sure to spike, and trouble is inevitable. And while a VIP host may act as a bouncer, not all bouncers, especially at a club like the Hippo, are hosts. A VIP host at a high-end strip club is like a maître d' in a restaurant. It's his job to welcome you, escort you to a table, tell you about the menu, and begin the process of vacuuming the money out of your wallet. And he's only the first hustler you'll meet in the tipping gladiator pit.

Inside a strip club everybody tips *everybody*. The first workers a stripper has to tip out are VIP hosts like Ben. "Social capital is big," a gorgeous brunette dancer named Victoria explained to me. "If you don't tip the hosts, you'll get 'cock-blocked.' The hosts will shut you out of the VIP room, saying, 'We're full,' or undersell you." (Meaning they won't give the dancer access to wild spenders or they'll pawn them off on cheaper clientele.) "One girl I know made three thousand dollars one night and didn't tip out, so she lost her shifts. They didn't extort her or anything. They told her she had to lose weight."

I smiled when Victoria said that. When I was a waiter, if you were on the outs with the manager or maître d', you could end up getting your shifts cut or languishing in a bad section handing out kiddie menus all night. So if a host sets up a girl with a "big baller"—stripper parlance for a big spender—she has to kick back something in the ballpark of 20 percent. And some dancers have told me they made as much as $5,500 in a night from customers they got hooked up with by the VIP host.

In addition to the VIP hosts dipping their beaks, strippers sometimes have to tip out to the "house moms," the ladies who wrangle the strippers and keep the G-strings in order—usually fifteen dollars. At the Hippo, the bouncers can get anywhere from five to ten dollars apiece from the strippers, and the guy collecting the entrance fee usually gets a five. Cocktail waitresses who set dancers up with a score also get a cut. But the most important person a dancer has to tip out to is the DJ— around 10 percent of a girl's sales. "Never stiff the DJ," one stripper told me. She reminded me that a lap dance is the *length* of a song. And if you're grinding away on some smelly fat guy's lap and the DJ's pissed at you, he can keep you glued to that olfactory-challenging patron by playing "Freebird" or "Bohemian Rhapsody."

In a strip club everyone's out for a piece of the action. It's the land of quid pro quo. I set you up, you set me up. If a dancer tips generously she has access to the customer money trough. If she doesn't, she can find herself shut out. And in a place where everyone is keeping track of who's tipping whom, you can cut the atmosphere of greed with a knife. (Is it just me or does that sound a bit like Washington, D.C.?) It's in a strip club that you'll find all five kinds of tipping that economist Ofer Azar wrote about. "So tell me, Ben," I ask my host as I reach for my wallet. "How do things work here?" What he doesn't realize is that I already know how things work here. For a strip club customer, knowledge is power.

"Well, sir," Ben says. "We have a section where you can get three dances for a hundred dollars."

"How long does that last?"

"About ten minutes."

"And if I want something a little more, uh, private?"

"We have two excellent VIP lounges, sir," he says. "We have a half-hour option for two hundred dollars and an hour option for four hundred. We also have an excellent champagne room for four hundred dollars an hour with a three-seventy-five minimum on the bottle."

Most VIP lounges at fancy strip clubs throughout the country have similar setups. But Ben isn't telling me the whole story. First off, there are "drink minimums" in most VIP rooms. And while the Hippo has some of the lowest drink minimums in town, a customer getting the half-hour VIP treatment has to buy two drinks at fifteen dollars a pop. For the hour session he has to buy four. So now you're out another thirty or sixty dollars. Then you have to tip the cocktail waitress. If you're a good sport and tip 20 percent, you're now out another six or twelve bucks. You also have to tip the bouncer guarding the VIP room twenty dollars for every half hour you're in there, and then you have to tip the stripper on top of that. While some strip club "Georges" will tip scads of cash, and the "fleas" won't tip anything, all the strippers I interviewed said the minimally acceptable tip for VIP attention is 20 percent. So now you're out another forty or eighty bucks. Sound complicated? Let me break it down for you.

Half-hour VIP dance	$200
Two-drink minimum	$ 30
Tip for cocktail waitress	$ 6
Tip for bouncer	$ 20
Tip for dancer	$ 40
Total	$296

That $200 VIP room just got a lot more expensive, no? Ah, the devil's in the details. The money hemorrhage gets even worse if you pay by credit card. When you use plastic, there's a 10 percent surcharge on the dance and the dancer's tip. Now that $240 you pay the dancer becomes $264. Luckily there's no surcharge added for the drinks or the bouncer and waitress's tips. So if you use a credit card, you're now out a grand total of $320 for the half hour. Adds up, doesn't it?

You might think that strippers always prefer cash. They don't. Why? Because if you come with only cash, you can get tapped out. But if you have a credit card with a $10,000 limit, then you can have that much more fun. "Guys spend more and tip more on credit cards," one stripper told me. "They get all macho about showing a girl how much money [they have]. So when I see a guy whip out a credit card, I go, *ka-ching*!" And if your credit card company questions your charging three grand at the strip club and seeks your approval, the dancers will be happy to take your phone out of your drunken hands and dial American Express for you. Now, that's service! The lesson here? It's always cheaper if you go to a strip club with plenty of cash. And for God's sake, don't use the ATM in a strip club. The scam with these machines is that they usually charge you $10 to $15 for every $100 you take out. And some of the more unscrupulous places will charge a percentage on top of that!

As Ben is explaining the club's offerings, we walk into the main room. The Peppermint Hippo is a big place. At twenty thousand square feet, it's one of the largest strip joints in Vegas. The main room features a dramatically backlit stage, and there are two smaller go-go stages in the back. In addition to two large VIP lounges there are several alcoves where patrons can view the action on the main floor or draw a curtain for more privacy. Throughout the club are plush chairs and couches where the guests can mingle, drink, get lap dances, talk to strippers, and gawk like high school freshmen. There's only one problem. It's Friday night and the Hippo's *packed*. There's no place for me to sit.

"What I think I'd like now, Ben," I say, slipping my host a fifty, "is a place to sit down and get a drink." *The bribe tip.*

"Yes, sir," he says. "Thank you very much, sir. Give me a moment."

I sit back and watch as Ben calls over several bouncers and proceeds to eject four men from their comfy couch. As I learned during my research, if strip club patrons aren't spending money, the management has no qualms about moving them out for someone who will.

"There you go, sir," Ben says, ushering me into my new digs. "I'll send the cocktail waitress right over."

"Thanks, Ben," I say, handing him another fifty. *The gift*, or *thank-you, tip.*

"Thank you, sir. Thank you very much."

The cocktail waitress comes over and I order a dirty martini. The drink costs fifteen dollars. I give the waitress a twenty.

"Keep it," I say. *The reward tip.*

As I sip my martini, I make a running tally of my costs. Twenty for the limo driver, $20 for the drink, and $100 for Ben. I've spent $140 in five minutes and haven't talked to a single girl yet.

Suddenly a hand with French-manicured nails slinks over

my shoulder and runs down my chest. It has begun. Ben's probably sent over one of the girls with whom he's developed "social capital." Maybe he thinks I'm a "big baller."

"Hey, baby," a voice whispers hotly in my ear. "Why are you here all by your lonesome?"

When the dancer comes into view I have to force myself from choking on my martini olive. A California blonde with a blue bikini framing a spectacular body, this woman has a flawless face, pearly white teeth, and breasts like ripe pomegranates. Instantly a line from Raymond Chandler's *Farewell My Lovely* floats into my testosterone-addled brain. "It was a blonde. A blonde to make a bishop kick a hole in a stained-glass window." If only my former seminary professors could see me now.

"Well," I say, taking the woman's hand into my own. "Why don't you keep me company?"

"Well, hell yes, sugar," the girl says, flashing me a smile I can feel in my corpora cavernosa.

The young woman hops into my lap, tells me her name is Caleigh, and rapidly informs me that she's from Southern California and likes surfing, dogs, partying, and "sweet-looking" guys like me. Of course I know that Caleigh wouldn't give me the time of day in normal circumstances. But her job is to sell me on herself and get me to spend money on her in the VIP room. To accomplish this task, she employs what strippers call "the hustle."

Like waiters, a good stripper has to be a social chameleon and a world-class seducer. When I was serving tables, I had to quickly adjust my personality to suit the expectations of the table I was working. Did my customers want a server who was reserved? A joke teller? A flirt? And once I established what role to play, I'd mine my customer's personality to sell them as much shit as I could. Is this guy a wine snob? I'll sell him the most expensive bottle. Is she a foodie? I'll turn her on to the braised short ribs with the white truffles. And by increasing the bill, I increased my tip. A stripper also has to instantly size up a customer's tastes and sell him the most expensive thing she can. Does he want a coquette? A dirty vamp? The girl next door who'll stick her boobs in his face? Can she get this guy to blow $1,000 on her in the Champagne Lounge? This is where the hustle comes into play. And while they come in all shapes and sizes, all hustles share common characteristics: get down to the customer's eye level, express interest in his life and career, and employ plenty of touching. A few years ago Dr. Lynn from Cornell performed a study that showed that waiters who knelt down at the table to make eye contact with the customers and lightly touched them made better tips than waiters who did not. He also did another study that claimed blond waitresses with big busts and slim hips made more money than their less physically endowed counterparts. Hmm. Am I beginning to detect a pattern here? Dr. Lynn could just as easily have been talking about strip clubs. And here's another interesting tidbit. According to *Psychology Today*, strippers make more in tips when they're ovulating!

Caleigh follows the predictable stripper hustle pattern. As she looks at me wonderingly with her baby blue eyes, she asks why I'm in Vegas, where I'm staying, and what I do for a living. I tell her I'm from New York City and that I'm in town on business. I keep the "business" part purposefully vague. But Caleigh's very good at her job. While she's sitting on my lap she gives me the impression that I'm the most important person in the universe.

"So, what are you looking for, sugar?" she asks.

"I'm just here to relax and look at beautiful women."

"Mmm," she says. "Do you think I'm beautiful?"

"That would be an understatement."

My eyes wander down her body and take in the sights. Sensing my gaze, she gets up, turns around, and sinuously starts waving her perfectly formed rear end two inches in front of my face. "Oh, baby," she says. "I think I know what you're looking for." Within seconds of meeting me, Caleigh has mined *my* personality and figured out what to sell me.

"You wanna go in the back?" she asks, looking at me over her shoulder. "I'll show you the time of your life."

Every part of my being wants to race off to the VIP lounge and let her have her way with me. But I've been in the Hippo all of ten minutes. If I go with her now I'll blow my budget within forty-five minutes. I remind myself that I'm not here for my own personal enjoyment. I have a job to do. So, like Ulysses, I resist this siren's call and decline her offer.

"Baby, I just got here," I say. "But I'll keep you in mind. How about a lap dance for now?"

A small flicker of disappointment ripples across her face, but quickly disappears. "Sure thing, baby," she says, straddling me with her long legs. "Mmm, you're so cute."

With Caleigh wiggling her butt in my lap, now would be a good time to talk about tipping on lap dances. The price of lap dances, when you think about it, is a pretty good value. When I went to Delilah's Den in Philadelphia for a bachelor party back in the early nineties, lap dances cost twenty bucks. Twenty years later, lap dances in most strip clubs are still the same price. Some places in L.A. are now charging thirty, while Phoenix is the land of the ten-dollar lap dance. Overall, though, the price of lap dances hasn't risen with inflation. So, what's a good tip on a lap dance? Five bucks per dance seems to be the acceptable amount. So if you have two lap dances, you pay forty bucks and tip the girl ten. Of course in a strip club, the sky can be the limit as far as tipping's concerned. "Some guys buy these girls cars!" one stripper told me.

One of the reasons strippers want tips on lap dances is because very often a dancer has to kick back to the house part of what she makes. And while these fees vary wildly from place to place, generally the girl has to give management anywhere from a quarter to a third of the price of a dance. So if she makes only fifteen dollars on a twenty-dollar lap dance, your tip helps replace the percentage siphoned off by the house.

The song ends, and Caleigh asks if I want another one. That's good. A hustle some strippers employ is "stacking dances."

That's when a girl, knowing her customer is horny, inebriated, or overloaded with lust, just keeps grinding away for one song after another. Then, when she's done, she turns around and tells the unsuspecting mark, "That'll be two hundred dollars." Caleigh's not playing that game.

"No thanks, honey," I say, handing her two twenties. "But maybe I'll look for you later." The *service tip* and *the tip in advance*.

"Thanks, sugar," she says. And with a brilliant smile, she slinks off to find her next sugar daddy.

Alone at last, I suck on my drink and look at the dancers prancing around the main stage. The stage area in many clubs is called the "tip rail." It is not, as one stripper told me, "the sit-and-fucking-stare rail." So if you plant your ass by the stage, you're expected to tip. How much? While I received varying answers to this question, the common consensus among the girls I interviewed is that you should tip a dollar or two each time a girl passes by. But if a dancer performs some sort of Kama Sutra gymnastics trick that would snap a yoga instructor's spine in two, you should tip a little more. A fiver would be nice.

When it comes to passing out cash at the tip rail, different clubs have different rules. In some strip joints you have to place the money on the tip rail itself, sometimes in the girl's hand, while other establishments might let you slip it into her cleavage or under a garter or G-string. But whatever you do, don't use the tip delivery as an excuse to cop a quick feel. If you try sticking that dollar bill under the dancer's panties or into one of her bodily openings, you will probably spend quality face time with the asphalt in the parking lot. And here's another word of wisdom. If one of the girls onstage catches your eye and you'd like her to give you a lap dance or take you into a private booth, pass out a ten or twenty. You might as well send an engraved invitation. Conversely, if you don't want a girl to pay attention to you, then just tip her a buck and avoid looking at her. It sounds kind of brutal, but that's the way it is.

The worst kind of customer at the tip rail is the "beer nurser," the broke-ass clown who'll sip one beer for five hours, fill his eyeballs with pulchritude, and won't part with a dime. If you decide to be the strip club version of a *schnorer*, you run the risk of being verbally castigated by the DJ over the public address system, ignored by the dancers, and ejected from the club by some *really* big guys. The dancers onstage also have ways of making their displeasure with parsimonious customers evident. "I know one girl," a dancer told me, "who did a pole spin, and at the very end of her pole spin she kicked the guy's beer stein into his lap, making it look like an accident, saying, 'Oh, I'm so sorry, honey!'"

The tip rail is basically an audition area where men can survey the merchandise and decide which girl they want to receive lap dances from or take into the VIP room. While many of the women I interviewed were accomplished dancers who could put a Rockette to shame, quite a few of them *loathe* going onstage. Why? Strippers make the bulk of their money doing lap dances and in the Champagne Lounge. For them, time is money, and many dancers don't want to waste time onstage collecting singles when they could be hustling more lucrative clients on the floor. Most strip clubs have what are called house fees. Just as waiters and barbers were once forced to do, dancers have to pay a set amount of money for the privilege of working a shift. This is just another example of how employers skim off money from tip-earning employees. These fees can run from as low as $40 to as high as $200. The house fee at the Hippo on a night like tonight is $80. But if a dancer shells out an additional $50, she can be "offstage" and better utilize her time prowling the floor for fat wallets to pick.

As I sit on my couch glorying in my VIP status, one dancer after another relentlessly approaches me. After twenty minutes, two drinks, and four lap dances, my bankroll is thinning. I don't want to withdraw any money out of the two ATMs the Hippo thoughtfully provides. But if I stop spending money, I'll lose my big-baller status and get booted out. I decide to stop the money drain by leaving my coveted seat to take a walk around the club. Ben plants another high-roller into my seat before it gets cold.

As I bob and weave through the frenetic ocean of flesh, I can't believe how crowded the Hippo is—with women. With more than four hundred dancers working tonight, there are more strippers on the floor than patrons. What's even harder to believe is that strip club revenues are down almost 30 percent. There are a lot of guys in the Hippo, but like shoppers in a mall, a lot of them are looking but not buying. A dancer who commuted in from Utah once a month told me she used to make $10,000 in seven days. But after the economy took a nosedive, she said she'd be lucky if she made $7,000 in ten. "And the extra time away was taking a toll on my marriage," she said. Because of this dynamic, competition for customers can be cutthroat. Some girls will even tip the bouncers a little extra to guard their customers when they go take a powder. Why? Because it's not unheard of for dancers to steal their sisters-in-sequins' customers when their backs are turned.

Suddenly I hear a woman's shrill yelp, "That girl's not pretty. She shouldn't be here." When I turn toward the source of the voice, I see three bored women sipping fancy drinks near one of the smaller go-go stages. They're not strippers. They're female patrons. And since the Hippo mandates that female guests be escorted by a male customer, it's a good bet their boyfriends dragged them here. Strip clubs may be more mainstream now, but I think that taking your lady friend to a place like the Hippo is a bad idea. Many strippers told me that women are the worst tippers. Whether it's fair or not, historically women have always been viewed as bad tippers in general. If you ask a waiter if he or she would like to serve a table of four women or four men, he will almost always prefer the men. And according to most of the dancers I interviewed, women can be the worst customers to deal with.

"We've had lots of really bad female customers," Georgie, a fetching stripper from the UK, told me. "They feel that the rules don't apply to women. They want to be the ones onstage getting the attention. They get kind of jealous, especially if they're with their boyfriends. If I go up to a man with a girlfriend, I have to pay attention to both of them so the girl doesn't think I'm trying to hit on him. I'm like, 'You can keep him, hon. Honestly, I'm only trying to get money out of him.'"

"Do you think it's because they feel threatened?"

"Oh, yeah," Georgie said. "I've heard them comment very loudly about cellulite. 'That one's ugly.' 'That one's fat.' Stuff you'd keep to yourself if you think that. But some of them will say it out loud. They just don't know how to behave."

As I move away from the catty trio of women, a redhead in a skimpy country-and-western outfit comes up to me. "Hey, baby," she says. "Want a dance?"

"I'm okay for now," I reply. "Thanks."

The girl responds by grabbing my penis through my pants. "I'll get you real hard, sugar," she says, her speech rapid and pressured. "I'll get you *real* hard."

Normally a woman touching my johnson is cause for celebration. But as I look at the dancer, I notice her pupils are pinpricks and her body's slicked with a desperate sheen of perspiration. She's on something and probably trying to get more of that something. It takes every ounce of my self-control not to slap her hand away.

"No, thanks," I say, removing her hand from my privates. "Maybe another time."

"What are you?" the girl says shrilly. "Some kind of fag?"

"Go away *now*," I say sternly. The stripper gives me a furious look and storms off.

As I watch her go I think about what drives women to be strippers. We've all heard the stories of how drugs, broken homes, and less-than-adequate parenting skills lure women into a life of spinning around a pole. As the comedian Chris Rock observed, "If your daughter's a stripper, you fucked up!" Now, I'm talking to strippers about tipping, not their childhoods. But as I entered this world of fantasy and flesh, I began to realize you can't always judge a stripper by her G-string.

"The main attraction of being a stripper," Georgie also told me, "is money, freedom, flexibility, and the opportunity to do other things while you're working. Lots of girls are students."

In fact, several of the women I talked to prior to journeying to Vegas had advanced degrees. One had a master's degree in biochemistry from a university in Wisconsin, another had one in education, and yet another had earned a degree from the London School of Economics. Hell, *I* don't have a master's degree. Maybe there's something to the old joke that strippers are just girls working their way through medical school. I don't know about you, but I'd find it ironic to have an appointment with a doctor I once saw teetering nude on stripper's heels and then have her see *me* naked while giving me a proctology exam. "Just cough, baby. That'll be a dollar."

All the strippers I met said money was the overriding reason they started taking their clothes off for a living. "Women don't get into stripping because it's a minimum-wage job," said Avalon, a self-described "super stripper" who runs a website called Stripandgrowrich.com. According to her, the mind-sets of exotic dancers run the gamut. Some strippers are shrewd operators who treat their job as a business and "not a party." These women form LLCs, pay taxes, supply their own health insurance, keep their bodies in prime shape, and funnel the majority of their earnings into investment portfolios. Comparable to professional athletes, they take full advantage of their prime "earning years" and sock the money away until they can live off the interest from their money market funds. According to Avalon, these women are supremely skilled. "They make up ten percent of the strippers in a club, but they'll make ninety percent of the money." Avalon also noted that a good stripper will make 80 percent of her money from regular customers and 20 percent from walk-ins. In the world of tipped workers, that's not uncommon. Just talk to my barber. He makes all of his tips from customers he's known for years.

Other dancers treat the business just like a job but don't think past their life in stripper's heels. These performers end up leaving the life and taking work that pays a fraction of the income they made in their younger years. Some dancers are just students trying to get through school or women looking for parties, glamour, and excitement. Others are "subsistence strippers," who live from one score to the next. Usually head cases, they're the ones who'll go out and dance when the rent is due, when their car is in the shop, or when they need to feed a drug habit. I think my country-and-western girl was one of those. But I know it isn't *always* about money. Sometimes women become strippers for very personal reasons.

When I arrived in Vegas, I met a stripper named Nastia and her boyfriend at a sushi bar far off the Vegas Strip. Most of the strippers I'd interviewed had been in the business for years and were in their late twenties or early thirties. But Nastia was different. Having just turned twenty, she'd been stripping for only six months. In her skin-tight jeans and form-fitting top, it was obvious to the most casual observer that she had the physical chops to be a stripper. She was also breathtakingly lovely. Radiating the ferocious sexual aura of a much older woman, she possessed quick, intelligent eyes, a sharp wit, lustrous black hair, and high cheekbones that gave her a haughty, almost imperial beauty. When she told me that she was of Russian ancestry, I smiled to myself. A czarina in the desert.

"Why'd you get into stripping?" I asked, picking at my spicy tuna roll.

"To piss off my boyfriend," Nastia said. "He said he'd leave me if I did. So I did it."

"Any other reasons?"

"I was born and raised in Las Vegas," Nastia continues. "So lots of my childhood was spent on the Strip at night, passing those strip clubs and wondering what goes on. From growing up around it, it wasn't taboo anymore. It was another thing people do to make money." As we talk further, Nastia says that she's comfortable taking her clothes off in front of strange men.

"Does your mother know what you're doing?"

"No."

"Dad?"

"Dad knows. I think Mom knows, but she's in denial. She thinks I work in a grocery store at night."

Nastia's boyfriend suddenly interjects: "You gonna have to fess up to a little bit of your background, as to why you're so comfortable with this."

"My boyfriend's gonna prod information out of me," Nastia says, laughing. "What, pray tell, do you think is relevant, darling?"

"If I may," the boyfriend says to me. "The psychology of the girls who go into this business is very relevant. Because you'll find they all have a different story as to why they started. As to why they stayed with it and what they get out of it. Not all of the girls are strictly money driven. Not all of the girls are strictly excitement driven."

"So, what in your background makes you so comfortable with stripping?" I ask.

She tells me her father cheated on her mother, and as a result of that infidelity they got a divorce. Then, when Nastia was eleven years old, her mother remarried what Nastia described as a "hardcore asshole guy."

"So your mom married someone who wasn't the nicest person?" I say.

"Yeah, that would be one way of putting it." Then Nastia takes a deep breath and says, "When I was, um, eleven he saw fit to rape me."

I suddenly felt uncomfortable. My job was to talk about tipping, not to plunge into personal histories. But we'd gotten to this point and there was no going back.

"And rather than freak out and become one of these super-conservative, oh-my-God-rocking-back-and-forth people," she says, "I went, 'Okay, there's gotta be something that everybody sees in this. You know that was a really terrible experience but there's obviously a reason people are still doing it.' So I went in the completely opposite direction."

By "completely opposite direction," Nastia means she went out and explored "every facet of human sexuality." She told me that since the age of eleven she's dabbled in extreme BDSM, hit on friends' dads, had boyfriends, girlfriends, you name it. So by the time she got on a strip club stage at nineteen, her previous sexual adventurousness had largely removed the timidity most women feel about taking their clothes off in public. For Nastia, stripping was just another exploration of her sexuality. For her, it was *easy*. "It was like, why haven't I figured out how to do this before with a fake ID?" she said. In the back of my mind I remember something a therapist once told me: "Sometimes people try to master what they fear most." Maybe Nastia's doing that very thing.

Back at the Hippo, I wonder how many of the women working here have similar stories. Another dancer told me she'd always considered herself an "ugly duckling" and that she initially started stripping to prove to herself that she could be the object of men's desire. Maybe all the strippers cavorting around the Hippo started in the business because of one psychological reason or another. It gives new meaning to the phrase "There are a million stories in the naked city."

I circle back to the main stage and find Ben. It's time for me to go to into the VIP room. I ask for Caleigh.

"I'm sorry, sir," Ben says. "Caleigh's indisposed. But we have plenty of other girls here you might like."

"What do you have in mind?"

He snaps his fingers and a tall, slinky woman with a mountain of blond hair piled on top of her head appears. Her name is Roxy.

"Will she do?" Ben asks. Suddenly I feel like a farmer appraising a prize heifer. It's not a good feeling.

"Yeah," I say. "She'll be fine."

Roxy smiles, takes my hand, and leads me to the VIP lounge. I give my Amex card to the host/bouncer guarding the door. I know, I know. I'm going to get rolled on the fees, but I want to have the full experience. Besides, I'm going to write off this experience on my taxes as "research." Wait till my accountant gets a load of *that*.

Roxy and I aren't the only ones in the VIP room. Opposite us, a stripper's kneeling in front of a drunk middle-aged man bobbing her head up and down in his lap simulating oral sex. The guy looks like he's out of his mind.

Roxy ignores the other couple and quickly gets down to business. She climbs into my lap and draws my head to her breasts. "So, what brings you to Vegas, baby?" she asks.

When I tell her I'm a writer researching a book on tipping, her face registers genuine surprise. As I tell her about the project, she looks fascinated. Or maybe it's all part of her stripper hustle.

Before she has a chance to breathe her sweaty stories into my ear, trouble breaks out in the VIP pit. The guy across from us has tried slipping his hands under his dancer's panties. If there's one iron-clad rule in a strip club, it's never to touch a stripper's genitals. The stripper reacts by hooking her finger under the guy's nose and ramming his head into the wall with an audible crack. As the man groans, she gets up and runs away. Meanwhile, the bouncer rushes in, grabs the man, and, just like that, he's gone. Maybe they'll just toss him out the door. Maybe they'll lay a beating on him. A cold part of my brain doesn't care.

The kind of physical contact a patron may make with a dancer varies from club to club. In some places you can't touch the girls; only they can touch you. Other places will let you run your hands all over their bodies. "Vegas has the most sexualized kind of dancing I've ever seen," one stripper told me. "We call the amount of physical contact we get from customers 'mileage.'" At the Hippo, you can touch a dancer's body if she lets you. Personally, I'll be keeping my hands firmly planted on the sides of my chair. I have no desire to add to Roxy's "mileage."

"She should never have let him touch her like that in the first place," Roxy whispers in my ear. "That's asking for trouble."

"You're probably right," I say. Now it's official. I'm not having fun.

Guys, there's *no sex* in the Champagne Room. Oh, sure, there are strippers who wade into prostitution and quick sex, and the occasional blow job is not unheard of. But bad economy or not, strip clubs are in the business of making money. A prostitution sting will close them down. Trust me, they don't want that to happen, and the dancers know it. And while you may get turned on by a stripper's moves, the odds of her wanting to have sex with you are about the same as your being hit by an asteroid. Remember, it's all fantasy. "I don't become sexually aroused when I'm dancing," one stripper told me. "It's an act. It's an art, and we're entertainers."

While I sit back and let the stripper continue her ministrations, I think about some of the darker fantasies that get played out in strip clubs. I watch the shadows and light play on Roxy's undulating body and remember the story Nastia told me about her weirdest experience in a strip club.

"I'm in the VIP room in my club with a guy," Nastia said. "It was a half-hour room. I start to get undressed and the guy says, 'Only take off your top.' So I pulled off my top, and he goes, 'Now lie down on the couch.' 'Excuse me?' I said. He says, 'I'm not gonna touch you. I'm not going to do anything. Just lie down on the couch.' So I kind of lie down, and he kept giving me directions until I was like a rag doll on the couch. Then he goes 'Okay, close your eyes.'

"So I close my eyes. Okay, there are cameras watching, all will be well. And he knelt down next to my head and started petting my hair and said, 'Poor little dead stripper. I wonder what happened to you?' And for half an hour he sat there stroking my hair and my face."

"What did you do while all this was going on?" I asked.

"I just lay there and stayed as still as I could, because I didn't want to make any fast motions around someone like that. And as soon it was done, I collected my tip and promptly hid in the dressing room until he left."

"Did you tell anybody what had happened?"

"Oh, yeah. I told everybody."

"He didn't do anything out of line, though," Nastia's boyfriend said.

"Nothing," Nastia said.

"That's outta line!" I almost shouted. "I would've shot him! What are you talking about?"

"He was looking around the room for clues," Nastia's boyfriend said. "He was acting out this little CSI dead stripper thing."

"Yeah, seriously," Nastia said. "He was looking around the room for clues. He was, like, picking up my bra and looking at it. I was like, 'Oh, you're so weird.'"

Thinking back to what the workers at Passive Arts told me about the scary patrons they'd encountered, I realized Nastia might've had a very close call. Her customer sounded like a serial killer in training.

"So did Dead Stripper Guy tip you?" I asked.

"He tipped me very well," Nastia said. "It was a hundred-and-fifty-dollar room and he tipped me four hundred for my time."

I shook my head. When I was a waiter I had a customer who brought low-rent hookers to my restaurant and acted like a real asshole. Like Dead Stripper Guy, he used money to smooth over his deplorable behavior. Tips buy many things. They buy service, they buy gratitude, and in a city like Vegas they can buy insanity.

"What would you have done if he hadn't tipped you well?"

"If he'd only tipped twenty dollars for that, I'd have told the managers about him," Nastia said. "But you tip me four hundred, I forget all about you."

But it's obvious that Nastia's not forgotten about Dead Stripper Guy. And she probably never will.

Thinking of all this at the Hippo, I'm overcome with a feeling of desolation and loneliness. Nastia got to me. It's tough being in Vegas all alone. Sensing my distress, Roxy presses close to me and, in a ministry of kindness, plants a kiss on my cheek.

"You're a nice man," she says. "Thanks for the dance."

Then it's all business. The bouncer comes in with the credit card slip, and we settle the tab. I tip Roxy $50, because I know the Hippo will deduct 10 percent from her fee as a service charge. They get you coming and going. Then the bouncer makes me fingerprint my credit card slip to ensure that the club will get its money. I look at my watch. I've been in the Hippo an hour and a half and I've spent $600.

I exit the club and catch a cab. I've got one more stop to make before I go back to my hotel. I promised Nastia that I'd catch her act at the club where she works. I don't want to go, but I've promised.

Nastia's club is nothing like the Hippo. It's an all-nude place, and the clientele is much more downscale. Creepy is more like it. Sprawled out on their plush couches, a bunch of Goth guys with tattoos drink beer and try to look like vampire wannabes. As I look at their self-satisfied, lustful grins, I want to drive a stake through their hearts. Nastia is nowhere to be found.

"Nastia in?" I ask a bouncer, slipping him a twenty.

"Who's asking?" he says, snapping the money out of my hand.

"Just say her friend Steve's here. She's expecting me."

When Nastia emerges from the dressing room, my heart breaks. Wearing sweats and a T-shirt, with her makeup scrubbed off, she looks like a sixteen-year-old girl. She's also limping.

"Hey, there," she says.

"What happened to you?"

"I twisted my ankle," she says. "So I get to go home early. But, hey, I still made two hundred bucks."

I want to bundle her in my arms and get her away from the vampires. This isn't the place for her. She's just a little girl. It's in my genetic makeup to rescue damsels in distress, but that isn't my role here. I'm on a quest to become a tipping guru, not a white knight. Besides, dancers hate guys who want to rescue them. And as I've learned from bitter experience, you can never make anyone change her life until she's ready to change it.

"Sorry you didn't get to see me dance," Nastia says.

"Me, too," I reply. But I'm really glad I didn't see her naked. It would have been wrong.

"I've got to go, Nastia," I say. "Good luck to you."

"You, too."

When I get back to my hotel room I feel like I've been through an autopsy. I pour myself a stiff drink, fire up my computer, and start transcribing my notes. Stripping may be the business of fantasy, but after meeting Nastia, I realize in my gut that it's only that: a fantasy. Underneath the sexual bravado, glitter, and skimpy outfits, strippers are flesh and bone. These women are wives and mothers, sisters, daughters, lovers, and friends. Some work for tips to pay the bills, build a life, or throw their money to the wind. Some have their heads screwed on straight, and others are crazy. They can be happy. They can be sad. And, like all of us, they can be hurt.

As I type, I think of the pseudonym I'll give my desert czarina. I decide on "Nastia" because it's the diminutive of the Russian name Anastasia. If I ever have a daughter, that's what I'll name her. Why? Because Anastasia means *resurrection*. One day I hope Nastia experiences hers. Maybe the tips will help.

I told you it'd be a bumpy ride.

CHAPTER 11

Dignity and Shame
Shoeshine Men and Bathroom Attendants

I t is often said that when sizing up potential mates, a woman will look at a man's shoes. Yeah, yeah, I already know what you're thinking. Big feet equals big, uh . . . endowment. Well, guys, if you're wearing a size-eight loafer, take heart. In 2002, researchers at the University of London measured the foot size of 104 men and compared them to the length of their penises. When they analyzed the data, they concluded that "there is no scientific support of [the] relationship" between the size of your feet and the size of your nearest and dearest friend. Having big feet just means you need big shoes. For the record, though, I'm a size eleven.

Women look at men's shoes because they can tell a lot about the guy wearing them. And many women are cognoscenti when it comes to footwear. They can tell the difference between those kicks you picked up at Payless for $30 and a $1,830 pair of Berlutis. Good leather is good leather; cheap leather is just that: cheap. After tens of thousands of footfalls, a quality pair of shoes will maintain its good looks, while a cheap pair will fray at the edges. And, like it or not, the quality of your shoes usually indicates the size of your wallet. What you're wearing on your feet can say a lot about your personality and character. Wingtip lace-ups might indicate that you're a conservative Republican, while Birkenstocks scream you're a crunchy vegetarian lefty. Boat shoes with no socks? You went to Choate. A nice pair of Timberlands? You're an outdoorsy type, or like to pretend you are. High-priced sneakers? You like to keep things cool and casual. But don't ask me what wearing flip-flops means. If it were up to me, men wearing flip-flops would not be allowed to procreate.

Guys, the truth is most women look at our feet to see if our shoes are clean or dirty, well maintained or in disrepair. If you show up to a first date wearing a ratty pair of Nikes, she might think you don't respect her enough even to make the effort to look good. There's a saying: "Tasteful in small things, tasteful in all things." So even if your shoes aren't expensive, taking good care of them signals that you take pride in your appearance and pay attention to the little things. And if a guy can take care of these little things, some women reason, then he might be able to take care of *them*. Let's face it, the mating dance is a lot like going on a job interview, with the difference being that if you ace it, you won't get a cubicle and a dental plan; you'll get to see the other person naked. And like a good job interviewer, women are looking for signs that you've got your shit together. Is this guy's hair trimmed? Are his nails clean? Are his shoes shined?

Sadly, I don't heed that advice: most of the shoes littering the floor of my closet look pretty sad. It's a miracle I've ever gotten a date. But my luck is good in Vegas. One day while having coffee in a Starbucks I strike up a conversation with a lovely woman attending a convention, and we agree to meet for dinner in my hotel's restaurant. After I make the date, I realize the loafers I'm wearing look pretty awful. So I walk over to the stand in my hotel's lobby advertising shoeshines for seven bucks.

"Hey, man," I say to the vendor. "I need a shine."

"Hop on up," he says, pointing to a row of empty chairs. "I'm not busy."

I can count on the fingers of one hand how many times I've had my shoes professionally shined. To me, shoeshine stands are from a time when men wore fedoras and got barbershop shaves for two bits. And I have no idea what constitutes a good tip for such a service. Another opportunity to understand all things tipping has fallen into my lap.

As the man applies cordovan polish to my shoes, I tell him my name and what I'm doing in Vegas. He laughs when I mention the strippers, and graciously assents to be interviewed.

"My name's Byron," the shine man says. "I've only been doing this six months. Not a profession for me. I don't knock anyone else who does it."

"What's your busiest time of day?"

"Generally between ten o'clock and two o'clock."

"And how many customers do you get?"

"Feast or famine these days, buddy," Byron replies. "I mean, last week, a couple of times, I've done twenty-five, twenty-six customers in a day. This week I've had a day where I only got three."

When I was a waiter I had days like that. Sometimes I'd be crazy-busy, making money hand over fist. But on slow days I'd spend my time obsessively polishing the silverware to keep from screaming in frustration. I feel Byron's pain.

"Do you get compensated by the hotel?"

"No," Byron replies. "I'm an independent contractor." He goes on to tell me that an outside company runs the shine concession for the hotel and he works for them.

"So you get seven bucks for the shoe, right?"

To my shock, Byron tells me he gets to keep only a *dollar* for every pair of shoes he shines. He has to kick back six bucks from every customer to the company that owns the concession. He's paid no salary, and his income depends almost entirely on tips! When I hear this, a sick feeling erupts in the pit of my stomach. Like restaurant patrons who operate under the false assumption that waiters make a salary, I used to think shoeshine guys got paid at least minimum wage. So, in the past, whenever I got that rare shine, all I gave the guy was a dollar. Uh-oh. Bad karma.

"What do people normally tip you?"

"It works different," he says, massaging polish into my shoe. "I mean, it depends on the individual. The economy's kinda down a little bit now, so people's tips are kinda down. Occasionally we get some high-rollers here. Someone's had a couple of great days, you know, made some good money; they'll take care of you nice. Standardly, ten bucks is what most people tip. Not a ten-dollar tip—ten dollar on the deal."

"So it's seven bucks for the shine and a three-dollar tip for you," I say. "So you make four bucks on a shine?"

"That's what it is," he says. "At night I do occasionally get fifteen, twenties. I've had a fifty-dollar tip, a hundred-dollar tip doing this."

"But your income is all tips?"

"Tips is ninety, ninety-five percent of this."

"Do you think that most of your customers realize that?"

"Most of them probably don't," he says, sadly. "Most of them probably don't."

As Byron shines my shoes, I think about the day he had three customers. Assuming they all gave him a $3.00 tip, he pocketed just $12.00 working an eight-hour shift. That's $1.50 an hour. No one can live on that kind of money—not even close. When you factor in travel time and lunch, it'd have been cheaper if he had just stayed home.

As we talk, Byron tells me he's been in the service industry for thirty years. "Anything front of the house, back of the house," he says, "I've done." He's worked in hotels, restaurants, country clubs, and nightclubs. He's been a doorman, bellman, bell captain, banquet manager, and a bar manager. And because of his background, he's an excellent tipper.

"I'm probably one of the few people who tips at McDonald's or Burger King."

"You tip the people at McDonald's?"

"If I get that 'How ya doing, sir?'—yeah, I will. It blows them away. You have to remember, for over thirty years ninety percent of my income's been from tips." And now he's spending the tail end of that thirty years shining other men's shoes.

"What do you think of my shoes?" I ask fearfully. "I think I got them at Payless."

"You know," he says, shrugging, "I've shined more expensive ones and I've shined cheaper ones. As they say, I'm not one to judge a book by its cover. Anybody who comes and sits up here has a right to the same services as anyone else—whether you got these at Payless or these are some three-thousand-dollar Ferragamos."

As he finishes up, I suddenly feel uncomfortable having another man shine my shoes. Something's tickling the edge of my consciousness. An image. A memory. But like a name you can't remember, it remains tantalizingly out of reach. One thing is for sure: as I watch Byron kneeling at my feet, I know that some people would classify him as one of life's losers. Who else would polish another man's boots for pocket change? But as he tells me about his life, I realize he possesses a fierce sense of pride. He has a daughter he's crazy about and he sidelines as a singer. And even though shining shoes is not his first choice, he's proud to do it well. But part of me wonders if his sense of self-respect is artificially inflated as a defense mechanism to protect him from the sting of his social status and the insults he suffers at the hands of his customers. I slaved for tips all through my thirties, and people often treated me like shit. And if I'm completely honest, the sense of pride I took in my job was sometimes a buffer to shield me from my own feelings of inadequacy and career cluelessness. There were times I hated my job and myself. And as I watched my well-heeled customers wolfing down expensive food and wine, I often wished *I* was the one sitting down having a good time and a regular life. When people have nothing, they often make themselves out to be something more than they are. Sometimes your pride's all you've got left. And when you work for tips, for the sake of your sanity, you'll guard that pride ferociously.

When Byron finishes, it's obvious he's been shining shoes for only a short while. When I inspect his handiwork, I discover he's left a couple of dabs of polish on my pant cuffs. I pay him and tip handsomely anyway. There were times when restaurant patrons tipped me when we both knew I'd done a lousy job. I'm just paying karma back.

Later that evening my freshly shined shoes and I meet my date for dinner. After the first course is cleared, I excuse myself to go to the bathroom. There's a bathroom attendant on duty, and after I take my tinkle and wash my hands, the man hands me a towel.

"How's your night going?" I ask him.

"Okay, sir," he says, looking glum. "Kind of slow."

When I spy the man's empty tip jar, I realize the source of his unhappiness.

Let's be honest here. People get freaked out by bathroom attendants. When I asked a friend of mine about them he said, "The first thing I think is, 'I'm glad I'm not doing *that* job.'" And when I was in the men's room at the Peppermint Hippo, a drunk patron said to the attendant, "Why the fuck should I have to pay to go to the bathroom? Jesus Christ, the girls are sucking all the money out of my pocket as it is!" To his credit, the attendant just smiled and ignored the man. But I can relate to that customer's sense of discomfort. We Americans like to tell ourselves that we live in an egalitarian society. All people are created equal and have a chance to chase that American Dream. But when we encounter a human being who gets paid to take care of us after we have eliminated our bodily wastes, we realize on some level that that isn't always so. "Thank God I'm not that guy," I thought to myself.

But since a bathroom attendant launched my quest to become a tipping guru, they were among the first people I sought out. And when I interviewed a woman named Casey, a fifty-year-old bathroom attendant at a nightclub in the Pacific Northwest, I got the scoop on how people working these jobs see *us*.

"Many people are uncomfortable with bathroom attendants," Casey said. "They're prevalent in Europe but not here."

"Do you see a startled expression on people's faces when they walk in for the first time and see you there?"

"Oh, sometimes, yeah," she said. "I know I'm a weird thing that they come across that they didn't expect. But I think I do provide them a valuable service. When I first walk in the restroom on Friday and Saturday nights, I mean, these women can't even hit the receptacle to throw their paper napkins out. There are napkins all over the floor. There's water all over the place. There's no toilet paper in the holders. So I think I provide a good service, that they can come in and have a nice-looking, clean bathroom and have supplies ready."

Casey told me she is an administrative assistant by day and works at her club on Friday and Saturday nights. "I like to see all the young girls wearing the new fashions," she said. The owner of the club pays her a base salary of forty dollars for a shift that lasts from nine thirty at night until two thirty in the morning. On average, Casey pulls down thirty-five dollars in tips on Friday night and seventy-five on Saturday. So she makes roughly between fifteen and twenty-three dollars an hour. That's pretty good. But she is lucky.

Many bathroom attendants are illegal immigrants with substandard language skills or poor people who are exploited. In 2004, then–New York State attorney general Eliot Spitzer discovered that many of the bathroom attendants who toiled in some of the Big Apple's most exclusive restaurants, including Tavern on the Green, weren't receiving *any* wages and were forced to depend solely on tips—in clear violation of state labor laws. Spitzer also discovered that many employees working for Royal Flush Bathroom Attendants, a concession that supplied restroom services to many area restaurants, required their attendants to pay a "lease fee" for the privilege of working, and even forced them to kick back a chunk of the tips they received. They also misclassified the attendants as "independent contractors," so they could skirt the labor laws. The result? Some of these poor souls took home only five dollars an hour. Sometimes less than two! Employers often use independent contractor status to avoid paying benefits, and to employ a cheaper workforce. Heck, that dynamic exists in the white-collar world, too. How many "consultants" out there have no health insurance or 401(k)s?

As I plumbed the plight of bathroom attendants, I found more disturbing news. "In 2008," Albany's *Times Union* newspaper reported, "the New York State Department of Labor discovered that Portlock Maintenance Systems, a Pennsylvania-based company that had contracts with fairs in western New York, the Hudson Valley and Capital Region, was found to be employing restroom attendants and paying them no wages at all. Instead, the employees were paid only tips, and the company also required these workers to give back up to 50 percent of the tips they earned, both unlawful practices." When I read this, I thought about that old bathroom attendant I'd run into at the county fair in Pennsylvania. Was he working in those squalid conditions for pocket change? The odds are good that he, too, was being exploited.

As it says in Ecclesiastes, "There's nothing new under the sun." Companies have underpaid their employees and thrown their livelihoods to the mercy of the tipping public for ages. If an unscrupulous company can increase its bottom line by using tips as an excuse not to pay a living wage, they will. The Pullman Company used that ploy in the early twentieth century, and Portlock and Royal Flush used it in the twenty-first. The bathroom attendant scam is just an updated version of an old tactic.

Because of the New York State attorney general's actions,

Tavern on the Green agreed to pay $175,000 to compensate for minimum-wage underpayments stretching back five years. And whatever happened to Royal Flush? They had to fork over a $3 million judgment for misclassifying their workers as independent contractors and robbing them blind. They're now out of business. Royal Flush got flushed.

"So do bathroom attendants expect a tip every time a patron goes to the bathroom?" I asked Casey.

"Absolutely not," she replied. "But if I provide some sort of service or I give them something like the eye drops or antacids or a cigarette or something like that, yes, I expect them to give me a little something."

"And what's a good tip?"

"A dollar's fine."

To my amazement, I learn from her that most of those little items restroom attendants provide their customers—mouthwash, over-the-counter meds, combs, perfume, body lotions, body sprays—are purchased by the attendants themselves. And while her club owner provides some of the supplies, Casey supplements that inventory out of her own pocket, to offer the little niceties she's noticed her female guests like having around: lip gloss on hygienic applicators, tampons, Q-tips, hair clips, clear nail polish to fix pantyhose runs, and bobby pins and fasteners to help repair any "wardrobe malfunction" a young woman might encounter while moshing it out on the dance floor. She also likes to offer an assortment of mints and candies. I wish I had candy in my bathroom.

"Do you sell these items?"

"No," she said, explaining that the items are free of charge. "I have two signs out that say, 'Gratuities Are Greatly Appreciated.' But there are ladies who will help themselves to everything and *anything* and not leave me a tip. I had a nice little lollipop display, and there was this young lady who went, 'Oh, pops!' and she's grabbing them and handing them to all her friends. She had four in her hand, and I'm like, 'Excuse me, there's one per customer.' And she said, 'Oh, I didn't think there was any limit.' And I'm thinking, 'You're not dropping me any money. That's coming out of my pocket.'"

I guess there are *schnorers* everywhere—even in the can. Word to the wise: if you take an item from a bathroom attendant's display, leave a tip. Very often the cost of that item comes out of the attendant's pocket! Casey also told me that she never leaves her supplies behind when she goes to take a break. Why? "Because ladies tend to have sticky fingers."

"So, are the ladies good tippers?"

"Some are," she says. "But the guy working the men's room is pulling in a lot more than I am. I think that's just the nature between men and women."

"Are you saying women can be cheap?"

"You think?" she replied, laughing. "You bet your bottom dollar! I've had women hand me tens and twenties because they've been so appreciative I was able to do something for them. But for the most part, if I get a dollar I feel lucky." She goes on to explain that some women avoid tipping her by ignoring the towels she offers to dry their hands and getting their own towels. That's just wrong.

"Do ladies ever give you a hard time about being a bathroom attendant?"

"I've actually had a couple of people who were openly disdainful," she said. "Like what I'm doing is beneath the bottom of their feet. But I couldn't really give a shit, because I don't care what they think."

"But how does it make you feel sometimes when you run into those people? You're in such a confined space."

"I was surprised the first time it happened. Then I had to be amused, because I thought, 'How petty is that?' It really does not bother me. Because I figure any job worth doing is worthy of respect. It doesn't matter what you're doing. If it's work, it's work. And to those who look down their noses at you? I smile even bigger at them."

Back in the Vegas restaurant bathroom, I notice the dulled expression on the attendant's face and think about what Casey told me. Was she being honest when she told me how she felt about her job? Did she really feel that way? Or, as I suspected with Byron, was she just saying that to feel better about what she was doing? Not knowing the answer, I tip the attendant two bucks and head back out to my date.

But my date's a bust. "You're a nice man," the woman says, planting a peck on my cheek as we say good-bye. Funny, the stripper at the Peppermint Hippo said the same thing. I think I'm cursed with the Nice Guy Syndrome. Okay, okay. I know I'm being a bit of piglet here. But I was hoping for some "What happens in Vegas stays in Vegas" action. Maybe it *was* my shoes.

I don't quite believe Byron and Casey's assertions of feeling pride in what they do. There's a cold, cynical part of me that thinks they're kidding themselves. After all, I once kidded myself. There's nothing wrong with being a waiter, but part of me always thought the job beneath me. On some level I was always unhappy having to depend on the largesse of the tipping public. With all the nonsense that surrounds the underground economy of gratuities—the scams, the rip-offs, the cynical exploitation— is it possible to work for tips and keep your dignity? Did that man in the bathroom in Pennsylvania have his?

It wasn't until months later that I got my answer. Flash forward to the Port Authority in New York City on a cold November day. I'm on my way to do a photo shoot for a Russian magazine, to hawk my previous book. Since I'm having my picture taken, I've dressed carefully: designer jeans, cashmere sweater, and a full-length cashmere coat. But when I get off the bus from Jersey, I notice that my black clogs are dirty and scratched. I've got to do something about that. I don't want the women in Russia to think I'm a slob.

So I head over to Drago's Shoe Repair, where I meet Leonard, the shoeshine guy. Unbeknownst to him, he'll set my ass straight on tips and human dignity.

"How long have you been doing this, Leonard?" I ask as he gets started on my shoes.

"Forty years."

"Forty years!" I say, dumbfounded. "How'd you get started?"

He proceeds to tell me that when he was sixteen and his girlfriend was pregnant, he needed a job. Not doing much with his life other than hanging out, he stepped into a shoe repair shop on Eighty-eighth and Amsterdam to pick up some heels his girlfriend was having repaired. When the old man working there learned he needed a job, he told Leonard to head on down to Drago's and shine shoes.

"'But I don't know how to shine,'" Leonard said he told the guy. "So he gave me my first technique. I went out that following Monday. Never forget it. I did like he told me. I remember what he taught me. And I went to work. I got on the line. I was one of the youngest."

"So you've been working for this place a long time."

"I grew up with the family," he says, referring to the Dragos.

As we talk, I learn that Leonard has fathered twelve children. One of them died, and his mother helped take care of the rest. "What I couldn't do," he says, "she did." He tells me he didn't always live life on the straight and narrow. "I made so many stupid mistakes in my life. But life's been good to me. I got a second shot. Trying to enjoy it. Keep doing what I got to do. Ain't nobody gonna give you nuthin'. Gotta earn it. You don't earn it, you don't get it.

"All I ever did was shine my shoes," he says. "Shine my shoes. I mean, I tried other things before, but didn't work out. I'm comfortable with my shoes. My shoes don't talk back."

"The customers do, though, right?"

"I don't pay them no mind."

"Do customers usually want to chat with you, Leonard?"

"Sometimes," he says. "But most of my customers are not customers. They're friends."

"Regulars?"

"No," he says. "One more time. Most of my customers, after the first meeting, we usually wind up being friends. Because they say it's my attitude. That's the way I am. They appreciate it."

Seeing an opportunity, I ask, "Why don't you tell me what your philosophy on shoeshine and tipping is?"

"Tips?" he says. "You've got to look at it this way. It's the way people appreciate what I do. I work. It's how people . . . it's how people *feel*. I get people who look at me and they look at their shoes and they go, 'Wow. It's gorgeous.' I got a lady who comes in here, and she don't usually curse when she comes in here, she says, 'You know what, Lenny? You're a fucking artist. I love it.' She came straight at me, and she's a pretty good damn customer of mine."

Leonard tells me the cost of a shine at Drago's is four bucks. That fee goes directly to the shop. And while he's paid a small salary, the bulk of his income is from tips.

"What would you say the minimum tip on a shoeshine is?"

"A real nice shine? Three or four dollars. But I'm going for the extreme. Sometimes I look for more, or hope for more. It's part of living. If I can do better than what I'm doing, I'm not going to turn it down. Best tip I ever got was some years back. Guy gave me a hundred-dollar tip. Then I had the one for two or three hundred for doing a couple of pairs of shoes. That's more of a tribute, if you know what I mean."

"But the normal day-in, day-out tip is?"

"Three to five," he says. "Sometimes ten. My favorite is when I get my twenties."

"Who's the most famous person whose shoes you've shined?"

"You might love this answer," he says, smiling slyly.

"I'm all for it."

"Me," he says, pointing to a Plexiglas frame on the seat next to me.

When I look, I see that he has framed a *New York Times* article that was written about him. I grin to myself. Another writer has beaten me to it.

"I can see you've already been immortalized, Leonard."

"Never been able to get excited about famous people," he says, shrugging. "No man is my idol. I might favor him, but he can't be my idol. You know why? Because I always felt I got the same thing another man got. He can get up there and sing and make the girls scream. All right. But if I get up there and I start screaming, they're gonna treat me the same way. Why should I pay tribute to him? I pay tribute to *myself*."

But the cynical ex-waiter in me is suspicious of what Leonard's saying. Maybe he's just another tipped worker trying to protect his ego. On some level, he picks up on my thoughts.

"I don't want to sound like a ham," he says. "I mean, you know it's there or it's not there. You deal with it. I'm a hustler. I'm an honest hustler. Doing what I can do to make ends meet. Like they say, you can't get in on every ride, baby. You can't go down on every shift. But you can have a little bit of understanding with yourself. It's like I said: respect goes a long way. If you can respect yourself, you can respect the things you do."

As Leonard talks, the memory that tickled my brain while sitting in the chair of the shoeshiner Byron bursts fully formed into my mind. When I was in the seminary on retreat, I assisted the celebrant during the Holy Thursday liturgy when he washed the feet of twelve of my classmates—reenacting the moment Jesus got down on his knees and washed the feet of his twelve disciples. Now, feet back in Jesus's day were nasty things. People walked though the dusty, dung-covered streets in the ancient equivalent of Birkenstocks. God knows what they got on their tootsies. So feet were considered offensive. Don't believe me? In some Middle Eastern countries today, if you show a person the bottom of your shoes, that's seen as a sign of disrespect. So back in zero A.D., washing someone's feet was considered an act of incredible humility. And the twelve disciples were none too happy with Jesus's idea. They considered it beneath him. It went down like this.

"Lord," Simon Peter said, "are you going to wash my feet?"

Jesus replied, "You do not realize now what I am doing, but later you will understand."

"No," said Simon Peter, "you shall never wash my feet."

Jesus answered, "Unless I wash you, you have no part of me."

"Then, Lord," Simon Peter replied, "not just my feet but my hands and head as well."

Then, when Jesus wrapped up his ablutions, he said, "I have set you an example that you should do as I have done for you. I tell you the truth, no servant is greater than his master, nor is a messenger greater than the one who sent him."

You don't have to be a Christian or even to believe in God to understand the power of those words. Long before the age of Enlightenment and the Declaration of Independence, in a time when people were hemmed in by a brutal class system of nationality, race, religion, and wealth, someone figured out that all human beings are *equal*. So, no matter what job you do, whether you're a banker, a bathroom attendant, or a shoeshine man, your work is noble. Why? Because it's performed by a human being. I remember Casey's words: "I figure any job worth doing is worthy of respect." So when companies cynically exploit tipped workers by failing to pay wages or by stealing tips, they're playing with karmic fire. They're disrespecting the human dignity of their workers, and eventually, one way or another, they'll get their comeuppance.

My flashback to Holy Thursday explains my unease about getting a shoeshine or seeing a bathroom attendant. When I was a waiter, I got sick of being a servant. I wanted to be the master. But my lack of pride probably had less to do with being a waiter than with the lack of respect I had for myself. It wasn't the job that was beneath me; it was how I was looking at it. When I was a kid, my dad told me he'd love me if I became president of the United States or a garbage man. "As long as you're a good person, that's all that matters," he said. It's not the job you have, it's the person you are. "No servant is greater than his master." While this realization sinks in, I watch Leonard work. But my shoes are working for him, not the other way around. As he shuffles his feet in a well-practiced rhythm, his hands a blur of polish and rags, I think back to what my high school teacher Mr. Binkowski taught me about the Greek word *arete*. On the surface the word translates into "excellence," but it means so much more. *Arete* is living up to one's full potential, having courage in the face of adversity—becoming what you were meant to be. Leonard is a living example of that word. He's been through the ringer and he's emerged as one of the finest shoeshine guys in New York City. And as I look at my worn clogs being burnished into glowing resurrection by the man now kneeling in front of me, I realize I'm watching a master at work.

"There you go," Leonard says, slapping the rag against his thigh. "All done. Don't kick nobody."

I look at my shoes in shock. When I walked in they looked tired and old. Now they look brand new. I feel the same way. *But later you will understand.*

"Leonard," I exclaim. "You're a motherfucking artist."

"Hell, yes," he says. Needless to say, Leonard gets his twenty. It's a tribute.

Oddly rejuvenated, I walk out of the shop with a light heart and a new spring in my step. And as I watch my newly shined size elevens gleam under the Port Authority lights, I smile to myself.

CHAPTER 12

Pillar of Fire
Taxi and Limousine Drivers

When I was a waiter we always used to joke about gratuities being influenced by unseen "table gods" and karma. But in Las Vegas, tipping is an energy force flowing through millions of cell phones and furtive whispers. Feeding on opportunism and greed, it shits money and turns the brains of tipped workers into its own collective neural net. In Vegas, tipping is not only alive, it has achieved godlike *sentience*. Hovering over the city's neon lights, it watches and waits, rewards and punishes, creates and destroys. And like all deities, it enslaves legions of fanatical devotees to do its bidding. So how did I come to this theistic conclusion? Simple. I got into a Vegas taxicab.

Before flying into McCarran airport, I discovered a cab driver's blog called Las Vegas Cabbie Chronicles. I liked the blogger's writing so much that I contacted him and asked if he'd like to be interviewed. To my surprise he did me one better and invited me to do a "ride-along" in his cab. So here I am in Vegas waiting for him to pick me up at six o'clock. With a few hours to kill, I decide to head over to the Paris Hotel and Casino and do the tourist thing. I figure I'll have a late lunch, do a little gambling, and look at the famed fountains at the Bellagio.

I pop into a cab. "You wanna go to a strip club?" the driver asks before I can even sit down.

"That's okay, my man," I say. "Just take me to the Paris Hotel."

"Sapphire's the place to go," the cabbie says, not knowing when to quit. "They have beautiful girls there. Best in town. I take you there."

"I'm strip-clubbed out, my friend. Just the Paris for now."

The driver shrugs, and swings the cab onto Las Vegas Boulevard. As the crow flies, the Paris isn't far from my hotel. But Vegas's streets are laid out in such a way that being a pedestrian is a risky undertaking. "The biggest gamble in Las Vegas," a lifelong resident wryly told me, "is trying to walk across the Strip."

When the cab pulls up to the Paris, I ask, "Just out of curiosity, what's the fare from my hotel to the airport?"

"Forty bucks," the cabbie says, handing me his card. "When you ready to go home, just call me." When I'd asked the doorman at my hotel what the going rate was, he said the trip should cost only fifteen bucks.

"Sure thing," I say, taking the cabbie's card. "And by the way, the fare's only fifteen bucks."

"What?"

"Thanks for giving me your card, asshole," I say, anger heating my voice. "Maybe I'll rat you out to the Taxi Authority."

"I make mistake," the driver stutters, "I—" But I slam the door shut on his voice and walk away. I won't report the cabbie. Letting him stew in anxiety is the best revenge.

After dropping $300 at the blackjack tables, I exit the Paris and am recognized on the street by someone who saw me on *Oprah*—the first and only time that has happened. After making polite small talk about my quest, I walk over to the half-scale replica of the Eiffel Tower to view the Bellagio's fountains across the street. During the day there's a choreographed water-and-music display every half hour. As I wait for the show to start, several Latino men and women wearing T-shirts proclaiming "Hot Ass Escorts" and "Girls Direct to You in Twenty Minutes," are cruising the sidewalk handing out picture cards of naked women to the tourists gawking at the tower behind me. In order to gain attention, the hucksters quickly slap a single card against the thick pack they're holding in the opposite hand—creating an annoying clicking sound that makes you want to grab them so they'll cut it out. The locals call these people "porn slappers."

As I watch the porn slappers do their job, I notice that different passersby elicit different numbers of clicks. If an elderly person walks by, they're lucky if they get one click. Married couples and middle-aged guys get several clicks, while two girls in short skirts walking arm in arm get ten or twelve, accompanied by a wolf whistle. But when a herd of drunken male twenty-somethings stumble by, the clicking takes on the masturbatory ferocity of a nymphomaniacal hummingbird.

As the porn slappers ply their trade, I notice one of them doing the clicking thing differently. Holding a card between his thumb and index finger, he rapidly flicks it with his middle digit while fluttering the card near the noses of unsuspecting pedestrians. As I walk up to him, he maneuvers the card near my face, and I snap it out of his hand with such ferocity that he steps back, alarmed. I look at the picture on the card. It's of a busty white girl named Simone. She's all mine if I call the number on the card.

"The girl in the picture," I ask the guy. "She really look like this?"

"*No habla ingles*," the man says.

"*La chica se parece a este?*" I ask in mangled Spanish.

The guy looks at me sharply. "What do you think, mister?"

"I didn't think so."

The man walks away and I put the card in my pocket. If I called that number, some poor Central American girl would probably get sent up to my room. I shake my head. Sex is for sale everywhere in this town. Even now, high above the street, a giant billboard featuring the perfectly formed derrière of a Vegas showgirl looms over me. But after seeing so much naked flesh last night it doesn't titillate me in the least.

As I watch the tourists milling about and furiously snapping pictures, I sigh deeply. I'm getting sick of Sin City. For five days there's been no respite from the noise, smoke, pulchritude, and bipolar desperados that inhabit this town. When I had breakfast this morning, I sat next to a couple arguing about how much money they'd lost and whether they'd be able to scrape up the cash for bus tickets home. Tears welled up in my eyes, and I felt an overwhelming sense of homesickness. I feel isolated and untethered from the reality of regular life. I want to go home. Vegas's corrosive atmosphere is wearing down my soul.

According to sociologists, life in Vegas can exact a terrible price. Clark County's residents are as much as 62 percent more likely to commit suicide than people elsewhere in the country. And people visiting Sin City are *twice* as likely to kill themselves than if they'd stayed home. According to a 1997 study, one in every twenty-five visitor deaths in Vegas is a suicide. "There's a reason the hotel windows in this town don't open," a social worker I met at a bar told me. "Someone kills themselves in Vegas every day."

Finally the water show at the Bellagio starts and dispels my melancholic thoughts. The display is mildly entertaining, but when the music reaches its crescendo and the fountain spurts a geyser of water 430 feet into the air, an association forms inside my brain. Smiling, I look at the faux Eiffel Tower behind me and shake my head. How fucking apropos.

I catch another cab back to my hotel and prepare for the evening ahead. Since the desert nights get chilly, I grab my leather coat and stuff a pen, pad, and tape recorder inside the pockets. But since being a cabdriver is one of the most dangerous jobs in America, I also clip a razor-sharp pocketknife to my belt. Sure, I'm being a bit paranoid, but the readiness is all.

At six o'clock, I walk out of my hotel and scan the cab line for my tour guide. I have no idea what he looks like, but just then a voice calls out, "Hey, Steve! Over here!" My blogging cabbie's name is Luther. Six foot two and 250 pounds, he looks like a defensive tackle. But despite his size, he has a wide-open, friendly Midwestern face framed by a set of wire-framed glasses.

"So here's the deal," Luther says. "I've cleared everything with my boss. But if a passenger asks why you're with me, the cover story is that you're a trainee."

"Got it."

"So, you ready?"

"Ready as I'll ever be."

After I climb into the front passenger seat, Luther drives the yellow Dodge Charger out of the hotel lot and swings onto a highway running parallel to the Strip. As the dispatch radio squawks unintelligible codes, I look through my grit-blasted window and watch the sun drop behind the Spring Mountains and plunge Sin City into night.

As we head downtown, I ask Luther why he became a cab-driver. He tells me he had a falling-out with his family back in Kansas and moved to Las Vegas ten years ago to take musical education courses at UNLV. "I knew right away I was gonna stay here. I didn't want to go home."

"Kansas, huh? I thought you looked like a farmer."

"Yeah, I get that a lot," he says. "But I needed a change from Kansas. A new beginning. Vegas is more my kind of town. I like the faster pace, the twenty-four-hour lifestyle. I like the fact I get off work at four in the morning and I can still get a beer. I like the variety more than anything. Different kinds of people, different kinds of backgrounds. Everybody here's from somewhere else. Vegas is a giant melting pot."

"How can you stay down on the farm once you've seen gay Pierre?"

"Something like that."

After dropping out of school, Luther tried his hand at the

corporate world. But like Jake in Ohio, he soon got tired of being bossed around and he turned to driving a hack to reclaim his autonomy. "I wanted something that offered a little more freedom," he says. "Where I could tell my customers to fuck off when I wanted to."

"How's that working for you?" I ask, watching the street-lights slip by.

"This cab is *my* domain," he says. "The law says I have certain rights of refusal. If a customer doesn't have money, is drunk or disorderly, I don't have to take them. But if you just look sketchy, I won't pick you up either. This is my home, and if I don't feel like letting you into my home, I ain't gonna."

I ask Luther if he engages in racial profiling. In New York City it's not unusual for cabbies to avoid African Americans, in part because of the perception that they're bad tippers.

"I know black drivers who won't pick up black customers," Luther says. "But it's been my experience that Canadians are bad tippers." Ah, those pesky Canucks. I knew we should've invaded them when we had the chance. Oh, wait—we did, and they handed our asses to us.

"So how do people in Kansas tip?"

"They suck," Luther says. "And Minnesotans and Iowans aren't better either. But when it comes to who's a good tipper, it's been my experience that it's not necessarily where you're from but more what you do. I've said a million times, a bartender is going to tip way better than a CEO. I'd much rather take someone who works for tips. Most drivers will tell you when the bar and nightclub convention's out here, that's the best time to work."

He tells me a story that ties his philosophy all together. A few years ago he caught a charter to drive a young black woman named Keisha to drop her kids off at school and then take her to the grocery store. The reason Keisha didn't have a car was because it had gotten destroyed along with her house by Hurricane Katrina. She had been a server at Delmonico's in New

Orleans, and had gotten a transfer to the restaurant's Vegas out-post and started her life all over again.

"I gave her really good service," Luther says. "I helped bring her groceries into her house and I enjoyed talking to her. She told me about how she stayed at the Superdome for two nights, watching people die and looking for their kids. But she was very positive. There wasn't any of this 'Life's got me down, I need a bailout' bullshit. She played the hand she was dealt and was doing whatever it took to keep her family moving forward."

"That's one tough waitress."

"And she gave me an eighty-dollar tip on an eighty-dollar fare," he says. "I was just blown away. No one tips better than people who work for tips—nobody. If you run into a server named Keisha, you take care of her. I hope she does well. I hope her life works out." I smile to myself. If Keisha can maintain her sense of generosity in the face of such adversity, she has what it takes not only to survive, but to thrive.

Most people are in the dark when it comes to how cabdriv-ers make their money. In the vast majority of cases cabbies don't work for themselves. They work for taxicab fleets. And the rea-son they work for fleets is because it's very expensive for a pro-spective hack to go into business for himself. In New York City you have to shell out $572,000 for the medallion that allows you to work as an independent owner/operator. And corporate-licensed medallions, the ones the taxi fleets have to buy, cost a whopping $766,000. Now, different cities have different sys-tems and rates, but the vast majority of cabbies lease their cabs from fleet owners. And because of that lease system, cabbies are dependent on tips.

"If the average American knew about leasing and cabs," a cabbie in Cleveland told me, "there'd be an outcry in this coun-try. It's a losing proposition."

The reason driving a cab can be a losing proposition is be-cause the lease rates cabbies pay are often usurious. In New York City it's not uncommon for a cabbie to spend $800 a week leasing a cab. As one Manhattan hack told me, "Say I take in three hundred dollars during a twelve-hour shift. That sounds good until you realize my lease is a hundred and fifty a day and I have to pay for my own gas. So at the end of the shift, I'm lucky to break a hundred. And on a bad day I can make just thirty bucks."

"So tips are important."

"Pal," the cabbie told me, "you have no idea."

In Vegas the system works a little differently. All the cabbies drive for a company and get a percentage of the meter. That percentage varies from company to company and is influenced by seniority. Luther's company lets him keep half the meter plus his tips—but he has to pay for 50 percent of his gas. Other outfits might let their guys keep only 39 percent of the meter but don't make them pay for gas. So it's basically a wash.

"But there's another variable called trip charges," Luther says. "Every time I do a pickup and turn the meter on, it costs me sixty-five cents to the company out of my pocket. You do twenty rides, that's thirteen bucks—another way for the company to screw you." So no matter whom you work for in Vegas, you'll keep about a third of the money you make on the meter.

One thing that makes life easier for Luther but harder for the tourists, however, is that Vegas cab fares are among the highest in the country. In New York City the initial charge when you enter a cab is $2.50 and $2.00 a mile. And you'll pay $0.40 for every fifty seconds you're stuck in traffic. That sounds pretty pricey, until you find out Vegas cabs charge $3.30 the moment the meter gets switched on, an additional $2.40 a mile, and $0.50 a minute, or $30 an hour, waiting time. So if a Vegas cabbie's taking you to McCarran airport via the congested Strip at the height of rush hour, the odds are good he's long-hauling you—cabbie terminology for ripping you off. Since I've been in Vegas, I've spent $300 on cabs. My advice? When you come here, rent a car. The parking is almost always free.

When Luther and I get to the Fremont District we pick up

our first fare of the night, a shifty-looking Russian guy just off the bus from L.A.

"Take me to the Wynn," he barks.

"Yes, sir," Luther says.

I look at our fare in the rearview mirror and things just don't add up. He is scruffy and unshaven, wearing old clothes and carrying a ratty duffel bag, and he took the conveyance of the poor to Vegas: a bus. But he's going to the Wynn, which is a very expensive hotel. I've read way too many crime novels, and now my head's spinning. Maybe our fare is a courier with drugs, guns, dirty money, or a human head stuffed in his bag. But the odds are good he's just a degenerate gambler trying to have a last hurrah. Vegas is full of people like that. That's one reason why the suicide rate is so high.

When we drop off our shady passenger at the Wynn, he stiffs Luther on the tip.

"What an asshole," I say.

Luther shrugs. "I've always been on a very even keel regarding tipping. I don't get that upset when it's not going my way and I don't get that excited when it is. You can't live and die with every good and bad tip."

"What do you consider a good tip?"

"The expected tip is fifteen percent of the fare," he says. "But there's a big difference between a good tip and an *expected* tip. If it's a ten-dollar cab ride and you've given me a dollar-fifty, that's not a good tip; it's the expected tip. But if you tip five dollars on a ten-dollar ride—now, that's a good tip."

According to Luther, tips have a tendency to decrease in direct proportion to the length of the ride—large fares yield lower tips and smaller fares produce greater ones. "You'll do a six-dollar ride and a guy'll give you ten bucks," Luther explains. "That's more than a sixty percent tip. But you'll do a fifty-dollar ride and get a flat fifteen percent tip of seven-fifty. So I prefer to do thirty short rides instead of fifteen long hauls. The tips are better."

He is describing a simple phenomenon I encountered while
working in the restaurant world. People almost always tip a
higher percentage when eating a cheap meal in a diner than a
more expensive meal in a fancy place. When you go to a diner
and order three dollars' worth of scrambled eggs, how often do
you just pay with a five and say, "Keep the change"? You've just
tipped that diner waitress nearly 70 percent! A good waiter in
a busy diner can pull down just as much money as a server in a
white tablecloth restaurant—but it's pure hell on your feet.

As we wait in the cab line at the Wynn, Luther explains how
being a cabbie in Vegas is different from driving a hack in other
cities. "People are here to have a good time," he says. "They're
on vacation. So you have to keep the conversation light and
friendly. People don't want their cabbies bringing them down."

"Does chatting up your customers increase your tips?"

"Oh, yeah. If you can build a relationship, even for a couple
of minutes, that can do wonders for your gratuity."

Relationships. There's that word again. Liam told me the
same thing while delivering furniture in the Bronx. "It's all about
the relationship you make with the customer," he said. "It's kind
of like a microscopic relationship—and how you handle that relationship in the brief amount of time you have makes all the difference." As I sit in Luther's cab, the half-formed idea that's been
rattling inside my preconscious mind starts to emerge from the
shadows. I'm on to something here. It's almost within my grasp.

But before I can connect all the dots, a trio of young men
wearing the Vegas clubbing uniform—tight open-neck silk
shirts and dark slacks—jump into our cab.

"Where to, gentlemen?" Luther asks.

The men laugh drunkenly. "Where you guys wanna go
now?" one of them says to the others.

"What kind of scene you looking for?" Luther asks.

"Ah, we're looking for women," the leader of the pack slurs.
"Late twenties, early thirties. You know, sluts."

"Give us the best of the lounges and the best of the nightclubs," the least inebriated member of the group asks. "Some-place cool."

"I can see you guys at the Ghost Bar at the Palms," Luther says. "Or maybe the Playboy Club would be a good spot to hang out."

"Is that place cool?" the Alpha Male asks. "I can see us going to the Playboy Club and seeing hot waitresses, and mil-lions of dudes hitting on hot waitresses. And I'd kind of like the ratio to be somewhat . . ."

"Go to the Ghost Bar," Luther says. "It'll have good music, but it won't be a straight-up nightclub scene. It'll be more lounge and table talk."

"Insurgents?" Alpha Male asks. "Will we see insurgents there?" He's not talking about keffiyeh-wearing Al Qaeda op-eratives wielding RPGs. He means gay guys. Alpha seems to be a bit of a homophobe. Oh, well, the fear is the wish.

"Actually, a spot you guys should check out," Luther says, ignoring the question, "is the Peppermill. It's right by the Riv-iera. It's a great place for late-night food, and there's a cool lounge in the back a lot of locals hang out at."

The slut seekers accept Luther's recommendation and we drop them off at the Peppermill. "Thanks, man," Alpha says, handing Luther a sheaf of bills. "Appreciate your help."

"Be cool," Luther says. As we count the money, it turns out the party guys tipped heavy. *It's all about relationships.*

Before the cab's backseat has a chance to cool, three very attractive girls wearing miniskirts and high heels tumble inside. Exposing lots of cleavage and thigh, they're tittering about the three "cute guys" who just exited the cab.

"Where to, ladies?" Luther asks, flipping on the meter.

"We're going to the Foundation Room," says a blonde wear-ing way too much mascara.

"Oooh, look at you guys," Luther says. "Who do you guys know?"

"Tony Clemente."

The Foundation Room is a private club on the top floor of the Mandalay Bay. On Monday it is open to the public, but during the rest of the week it's for members and their guests only.

"You're not going to ask us if we want to go to a strip club, are you?" one of the other girls asks. "Every time we get into a cab in this town we get asked if we want to go to a strip club."

"No, miss," Luther says. "But we've got the Men of Sapphire if you're into giant penises."

The girls burst out laughing. "What's a good strip club in this town?"

"The Peppermint Hippo's a good place. I know it's one of Steve's favorites."

"That right, Steve?" Mascara Girl asks. "Did you like the girls there? Were they hot?"

"Not as hot as you three," I say gallantly.

"Oh, you're sweet," Mascara says. "Do you have any other favorite places?"

"Well, there's the Glitter Gulch in the Fremont District," I say. "That's where old strippers go to die."

"Don't listen to this guy," Luther says, while the girls laugh. "He's just a fucking trainee."

After we drop the girls at the Mandalay Bay, Luther points out the huge line of people waiting for cabs. "You see that mess?" he says. "That's an example of a Vegas scam. There are plenty of cabs, but the doormen are purposely creating a line by only letting people into one cab at a time."

"Why are they doing that?"

"Because the doormen are in league with the limo drivers," Luther says. "Artificially increasing the wait time causes people to get frustrated, and that's when the doormen swoop in and say, 'Hey, if you don't want to wait, I'll get you a limo.' And since these people are tired and cranky, they fall for it. Then, at the end of the night, the limo drivers kick back a portion of the fare to the doormen." I smile to myself. It's the old "buying the door" scam writ large.

"That's why taxi drivers hate the scumbag doormen in this town," Luther says. "They're stealing our business." To be fair, I tried interviewing Vegas doormen, but all but one declined to talk to me. The one I did manage to interview worked days and said he made $60,000 a year with benefits. "The guys at night might pull that shit, but not me. You can get fired for that kind of stuff. It's not worth losing my job," he said.

Luther doesn't want to waste time and money waiting in the Mandalay's cab line, so we hit the streets in search of fares.

"So, why is it," I ask, "that every cabdriver in this town asks if you want to go to a strip club?"

"Ah," Luther says. "You've just touched on one of the biggest moneymakers in Vegas."

He explains that since there are so many strip clubs in Vegas, they're in ferocious competition with one another. So much so that they'll pay a cab or limo driver fifty dollars a head for every patron they bring to their club. "So if you pile five guys into your cab," Luther says, "you can make two hundred and fifty free and clear."

"Holy shit," I say. "That's huge."

"That's why the cabbies are always fighting over who gets the minivans at the yard. You can stick more strip club guys inside a van than in a car."

"So, if you get four guys who want to go to a strip club, I'm getting out?"

"You better believe it. But don't worry. I'll come back to get you."

"Just don't dump me in the ghetto."

"I wouldn't worry about it," he says. "Those strip club rides are few and far between. The doormen at the hotels intercept most of those fares and toss them into their buddies' limos. That way they get half the take. That's another reason we hate them."

"Why don't the strip clubs just stop paying bounties? That'd put an end to it."

"They tried a couple of times," he says. "They banded together and for three whole months there weren't any payouts. But all it took was one club to break the truce and it was back to the good old days." No wonder the Peppermint Hippo was so happy to send me a limo. That saved them fifty bucks.

We cruise back to the Fremont District and pick up a fare by the Plaza—a young, thin black man wearing gangbanger duds. I tense up the minute he gets in the cab. Before you accuse me of racial profiling, the reason I'm skittish is not because of his race or ensemble. I'm skittish because the guy *stinks*.

"Where to, my man?" Luther asks, rolling down the windows. The guy mumbles an address located in what's called the Commercial Center. As we drive off, we try to engage the young man in conversation.

"You from L.A., man?" Luther asks.

"Yeah," the guy whispers, "from Compton." But that's the only thing we get out of him. As we head toward our destination, I try to keep from coughing. From my time working in mental hospitals, I'm familiar with the sour stink coming off this guy. It's the smell of someone who hasn't taken a bath in a week.

"Here we are, man," Luther says, pulling up in front of a nondescript building with a large line of people queued outside the front door. "That'll be ten bucks." The man pays, leaves no gratuity, and walks out.

"What the fuck was up with that guy?" I ask.

"The Commercial Center's got a lot of gay bathhouses, swingers clubs, glory holes, shit like that," Luther says. "Guy probably came in from L.A. just to get laid." If that young man was gay, it might explain his reticence. Being a gay black man in the 'hood can be a risky proposition. No wonder he took a bus all the way to Vegas. But if he's hoping for some action, I hope he takes a shower first.

As we pull out of the parking lot we spot a transvestite teetering on a set of high heels. "Hey, look," Luther says. "A tranny."

"An ugly tranny. That guy hasn't shaved in three days."

"Be fun to give him a ride. Something for you to write about."

"My book's about tipping," I say. "Not *Taxi Cab Confessions*."

As Luther guides his Charger down Sahara, he points out several pawnshops and massage parlors lining the avenue. And there, incongruous amid the hock shops and rub-and-tug joints, is a Starbucks.

"Oh, look," I say. "You can get a latte after your happy ending."

"Sex is for sale in this town," Luther says. "No doubt about it."

I think back to the connection I made outside the Paris Hotel. "Luther," I say, "have you ever noticed that the fountains at the Bellagio look like one gigantic cum shot?"

"That's fucking brilliant," he hoots.

"It's like, 'Look at me! Pow! In your face.'"

"That should be our new tourism slogan," he says. "Forget 'What happens in Vegas stays in Vegas.'"

I ask Luther if he's hooked into the Vegas sex trade. He knows a few call girls and is not above "making arrangements" for his customers in exchange for part of the hookers' fee.

"I've got ten girls' numbers on my phone," he says. "But I've gotten screwed so many times. Some whores are penny-wise and pound-foolish. They'll do the customer but not pay me my cut." He explains that when a working girl stiffs a cabbie one too many times, it's not unheard of for a driver to make the call and get her arrested. The tipping god is a wrathful god.

Of course there are legal houses of prostitution outside Clark County. But it's often a three-hundred-dollar round-trip ride to reach these houses of ill repute. "When I take a guy to one of those places, I'll waive the fare because I'll get [kick backed] around eight hundred bucks—almost as much as the girl gets. That's one reason why those legal places are so expensive. But I've only gone out there twice in five years."

He tells me there's another scam that some unscrupulous

brothels and cabbies pull. Let's say you're in the mood for some erotic fun and have a cabbie drive you to a legal bordello. Then let's say you don't find a girl you fancy or are overcome with remorse and want to leave. Well, you better have three hundred bucks in cash to pay the cabbie or you'll find yourself walking home—in the desert. And sorry, no credit cards accepted. Faced with this dilemma, unwilling johns are often forced to pay for a girl's services, even if they don't make use of them.

"So this town runs on tipping and bribery," I say. "Doesn't it?"

"Check this out," Luther says, keying his radio mike. "I'll find us a tattoo parlor that kicks back. Zero-six-eight. Over," he says into the radio.

"Go ahead, Zero-six-eight," the dispatcher says.

"Any friendly tattoo parlors out there?"

For a moment there's silence. In the background I hear the electronic chatter of cabdrivers rise and fall as they crisscross the city.

"Can anybody help us out?" the dispatcher asks.

"There's a place called the Precious Slut Tattoo Parlor," a male voice crackles over the radio. "On Charleston and Tenth." Luther and I burst out laughing.

"Can you repeat the name again?" Luther asks.

"The Precious Slut. Charleston and Tenth."

"That's a check. Thank you, sir."

Back when I was talking to hotel concierges, I was amazed at all the "arrangements" they set up to augment their income. But compared to the action in Vegas, they might as well have been running lemonade stands. Tipping is a god in Vegas, and everybody here tithes part of their income to appease the god's insatiable appetite. Everybody scratches everybody's back with a nod and a wink, and if you hold out like those cheap hookers who don't pay off their cabbies for a referral you can find yourself stranded and alone in the desert. Just like organized religions the world over, tipping in Vegas is both a social network and an economic engine. Using his radio, Luther can hook you up with massage parlors, brothels, strip clubs, tattoo shops, dentists, doctors, lawyers, veterinarians, wedding chapels, restaurants, nightclubs, and even a golf shop—all in exchange for a little taste of green. And in Vegas, everybody throws business people's way in exchange for a cut.

"I had a regular customer who needed a ride to L.A.," Luther says. "But I was off that day and needed to spend time with my girlfriend. So I threw the charter to a friend of mine. That's a thousand-dollar ride, man. And when he gets back he'll give me part of it. On the flip side, I had a cabbie friend who was off and threw me some strip club business. I made two hundred bucks. So when I met up with him, I gave him half. And why not? It was the easiest hundred I ever made."

Some people might take umbrage at this kind of wheeling and dealing, but let's face it, tipping exposes how the world really works. Just look at how doctors refer patients, at insider trading on Wall Street, and at political horse trading in Washington. The only difference between Vegas and the rest of the country is that the dynamic is more overt here.

"You hungry, man?" Luther asks. "We can get something to eat at the airport and catch a fare."

"Sounds good," I say, looking at my watch. "I haven't eaten in hours."

After getting sandwiches from a cart at McCarran that the cabbies lovingly call the roach coach, we pick up a young couple in from Sacramento for a weekend of fun.

"So who are you?" the young woman asks as I hold the door open for her. She's very cute and all of twenty-two years old.

"I'm a trainee," I say. "Tonight you get two drivers for the price of one."

The couple is going to the Wynn, and judging by their body language, they're a recent item. This is probably the first trip they've ever taken together, and the girl looks nervous.

"So, what made you want to be a cabdriver?" she asks me, breaking the tense silence.

"I got divorced and my wife got custody of the kids," I lie. "So I came out here to start over."

"Oh, that's so sad," the girl says. "Where you from?"

"Chicago."

"That's a great town."

"Sure is," I say, automatically slipping into a Chicago accent. "Ever been there?"

"Oh, lots of times. Where did you live?"

"Near Dunbar Park. Not far from Comiskey."

For the rest of the night I lied about who I was to every passenger. I told people I was an actor, a divorced father of three, a washed-out cop, an ex–Special Forces operator, a *New York Times* reporter, a cigar salesman down on his luck, a degenerate gambler, and, my favorite, a private eye who'd lost his license. There was something amazingly liberating about the whole thing. In Vegas for a night, I could be anybody I wanted.

At two in the morning, Luther's got another two hours left on his shift, but I'm crashing. "Getting late, man," he says. "Want me to take you back to the hotel?"

"One more fare," I say wearily.

As we head back to Fremont, he and I talk about his future. He's got a girlfriend he's crazy about and, like another blogger I once knew, he has dreams of becoming a writer. He picks my brains about the publishing world, which, honestly, I know little about. But I give him my take on it and make him a promise: "When I get back to New York I'll talk to my agent about you. You're a good writer."

"You'd really do that? Tell your agent about me?"

"I can't promise anything will come of it," I say. "But yeah, I will." A smile crosses his face, and for a moment, he looks like a Kansas farm boy dreaming of the big leagues.

We cruise down Fremont, but the pickings are slim and Luther starts getting impatient. But just as we're about to leave the area, two scraggly kids stumble out of the Gold Spike and flag us down.

"Where ya going?" Luther asks, eyeing them suspiciously.

"We got to go to a friend's house on Third and Gass and then a motel on Charleston," one of the boys says.

Luther looks them over and makes a quick risk assessment. Cabbies everywhere have good reason to be cautious. Robbery and homicide stalk hacks like the Grim Reaper. A few years ago a guy got into a Vegas cab with a bottle of Snapple and told the driver to give him all his money. Not seeing a weapon, the driver told him to fuck off. Well, the robber did have a weapon. The Snapple bottle was full of gasoline, and he set the driver on fire. The cabbie did not survive.

"Do you have any money?" Luther asks.

"Ten bucks."

"That's enough. Get in."

As we drive I look at the kids in the rearview mirror. They might be in their early twenties, but they look like a couple of prematurely aged Dust Bowl Okies you'd find in those photographs from the Great Depression. Judging by their gaunt faces, hollowed-out eyes, and lack of sartorial splendor, they look like strung-out druggies. Crystal meth is my instant assessment. I also notice the girl is crying.

"We'll work it out," she says softly to her boyfriend. "Don't worry."

As we drive, I wonder if they're discussing a conundrum many street addicts face: whether to use their money for drugs or a place to stay.

After a few minutes we pull up to an address in a bad neighborhood. The girl and her boyfriend exit the car, say they'll be right back, and walk up to a dilapidated frame house with an unpainted plywood door. There are no lights on inside the house, and when the door opens it looks like a shadow hole leading to a world of utter nothingness. Somewhere a dog barks. The kids disappear inside.

"They're probably scoring right now," Luther says.

After a minute the two emerge from the house and get back

into the cab. Whatever they were doing, they did it quick. "Okay," the boy says. "Now we can go to the motel." I look at the meter. So far this ride's cost six bucks. They've got only four left.

After we travel about a mile the couple starts murmuring to each other. "Yeah," the girl says. "We have to. It's only right."

"Hey, man," the boy says to Luther. "Pull over."

"We're not at the motel yet."

"Yeah," the boy says. "But we've only got ten bucks. There's eight on the meter and we've got to tip you."

"That's okay, guys," Luther says, his demeanor softening. "Don't worry about it. I'll get you guys to the motel. Even if the meter runs over."

"No, man," the boy says, handing over a crumpled ten. "Keep the change."

When the girl and boy get out of the cab I look at Luther. He's dumbfounded. "Holy shit," he says. "That was a twenty-five percent tip, and they couldn't even afford it."

There's a story from the Gospel of Mark that's one of my favorites. After Jesus gets through teaching his disciples what a bunch of hypocritical scumbags the Pharisees were, they sit around and watch the people in the Temple put their offerings in the collection box. Some of the rich people make a big show about their generosity, but it isn't really a big deal, since they are all loaded anyway. But when Jesus watches a poor widow putting her last nickel into the box, he says, "For they all gave out of their abundance, but she, out of her poverty, gave all that she had to live on." My old sociology professor once told me a value isn't a value until you've suffered for it. Well, in Jesus's day, being a widow was a raw deal. A dead husband meant a woman was without support and vulnerable. So when that lady gave up her money, she suffered. She gave *until it hurt.* How many of us are willing to do that for anything or anyone?

That's what the druggie couple did—and they put the rich and powerful of Vegas to shame. They tithed to the tipping god out of their poverty, and their reward in heaven shall be great.

"I'll bet they used to work in the service industry," Luther says, shaking his head. "Just like I said about Keisha, they're the best tippers in the world."

"Considering all the people you've had in your cab, that was your best tip of the night."

We both decide to call it quits, and Luther drives me back to my hotel. Since I sat in the front seat all night, he was unable to take a couple of fares. I promised to make up whatever he'd lost.

"Well, my book's two-fifty," he says. "Normally I'd have made three hundred."

I hand him a hundred-dollar bill.

"Hey, man," he says, looking at the money. "You sure?"

"I'm sure. And I'll call my agent the day I get home. A promise is a promise."

"Thanks, man."

As I watch him drive away, I sigh. Working in this town has damaged part of him. As a cabbie he's participated in things he's not proud of. But the tipping god can be a cruel bastard, and he's wounded me as well. Luther and I are fellow travelers. And through that kinship I can tell he is a good, decent man. I say a silent prayer that he will write his book one day. But I also send up a prayer of thanksgiving. In this town of isolation and human disconnect, I made a friend. And if I ever come back to Vegas, Luther's will be the only cab I ride in.

When I get up to my hotel room I take off my coat and pull three miniature bottles of scotch out of the minibar. Emptying them into a water glass, I light up a cigar and pull a chair up to the window of my palatial living room. The traffic on the Strip thirty stories below murmurs like a gentle brook, and the Boulevard looks like a ribbon of white and red light. As I drink, I think long and hard about that druggie couple. Why did they tip when people with more money did not? I think about Leonard the shoeshine man, Nancy and her crew of baristas at Ristretto, the bathroom attendant, my amazing moments with

Manny, the girls at the dungeon, and all the people I've interviewed. I think about my life as a waiter, and all the people I've
loved and lost. "It's all about the relationship," I hear Liam say.
"It's all about the relationship."

Shifting my gaze, I look at the gigantic beam of light shoot-
ing from the top of the Luxor Hotel. The Luxor is shaped like
a large Egyptian pyramid. The last time I read about Egyptians
and beams of light in the desert was in the Old Testament—
when Moses and the Israelites were fleeing Pharaoh's armies.
"And the Lord went before them by day in a pillar of a cloud, to
lead them the way; and by night in a pillar of fire, to give them
light." And it's then that I feel the connections I've made start
spiderwebbing inside my mind. An epiphany is coming, I can
feel it. I take a long pull on my cigar and let the images twirl
through my mind like the curlicues of smoke streaming from my
cigar. "Wait for it," I tell myself. "Wait for it."

And it is then, illuminated by the pillar of fire, that the god
of tipping comes down from his neon heights and reveals his
face to me. When he whispers in my ear, I suddenly understand
why some people tip and others don't. Like Simeon of the Stylites, I had to suffer in the desert to find my answer. I take a long
pull on my drink and smile. At last I have reached the end of
my quest.

I have become the guru of tipping.

CHAPTER 13

Only Connect
Guru of the Gratuity

t's Thursday night at the Cigar Emporium in Lyndhurst, New
Jersey. Tonight is the owner's birthday, so there's enough cake,
cannoli, sfogliatelle, custard zeppoli, and beer to take care of
any cholesterol deficiency we might have. The crowded shop is
thick with cigar smoke, a basketball game is on television, men
are playing dominos, and a friendly poker game is about to get
under way.

"Happy Birthday, Teflon," I say to the owner.

"Thanks," he replies.

"So how'd the wife like the tattoo?" The day before yester-
day Teflon had a large, patriotic screaming eagle tat inked on
his right shoulder.

"She's pissed."

"You didn't tell her you were getting a tattoo?"

"I did," he says. "But she didn't know it was going to be this
large."

"Hey, Professor!" an ex-cop nicknamed Sammy shouts from
the domino table. "So, when you gonna write about my life?"

"When you have something interesting to tell me."

All the regular patrons at the cigar shop have nicknames:

Terminator, Doc, Maestro, Shoes, Ragu, Tuna, and Castro. Of course, as with all nicknames, you never get to pick your own moniker. I got stuck with Professor because I often bring in my laptop to write. When they gave me that handle, I said, "So where the hell's my Mary-Anne?" I know. After all my lusting after redheads you'd think I'd be the Ginger type. But there was just something about Dawn Wells in her cropped red gingham shirt and short shorts that made me all gooey inside. But overall, I'm happy with the nickname. It could've been much, much worse.

The Cigar Emporium welcomes female clientele. But once ladies get a whiff of this man cave's tobacco-and-testosterone atmosphere, they usually don't stay long. And something tells me most of the patrons here wouldn't have it any other way.

I grab a beer out of the fridge and go around the room to say hello to everybody. The cigar shop's got an interesting unwritten rule: you have to shake the hand of every man in the place. Sometimes, when it's too crowded, you can just yell, "Hey, guys," but no matter what, you have to acknowledge everyone. The shop's clientele is a mixed bag of plumbers, county workers, restaurant employees, lawyers, doctors, cops, union guys, truckers, electricians, the unemployed, a writer, cantankerous retirees, and even the conductor of a symphony. But when you walk through that door, you leave whatever status you have in society out on the sidewalk. In here, everyone's equal, and the handshake ritual reinforces that fact. Every once in a while a guy who thinks he's a big deal will walk through the door, but when he realizes no one gives a shit, he'll turn around and leave. For some people the cigar shop's social-leveling effect is too much for their fragile egos. But the Emporium is a welcoming, nonthreatening place. The only other rules are that you keep your word and don't act like an asshole.

The Emporium is a quintessentially blue-collar Jersey place. Guys come dressed in sweats and wife beaters, leather coats and jeans, biker duds or Carhartt jackets with well-worn work boots.

And as we carouse and smoke, we complain about our state's perennially screwed-up government, bitch about taxes, discuss where to get the best cannoli (Rispoli's in Palisades Park), talk about the Nets and the Devils, make impromptu evaluations of the big-haired Jersey babes sauntering past the large picture window, and, when the topic of our neighbors across the Hudson comes up, we say, "Fuck New York!"

After returning from Vegas, walking into the Emporium is like wrapping myself up in the Garden State's yellow flag. Yeah, the Turnpike sucks, and occasionally our state smells, but it's home. And no matter where I end up in life I'll always be a Jersey boy at heart. So why am I ending my gratuity pilgrimage in a cigar shop? *Because these guys get tipping.*

"So, what'd that tattoo run you?" I ask Teflon.

"Six hundred bucks."

"Did you tip him?"

He smiles. He knew I'd ask that question. Lately we've had many conversations about tipping, because I wrote the bulk of this book in his shop. I guess you can say the smokers here have been my little own Talmudic council on gratuities. They've been my sounding board and advisors, helped me hash out ideas, provided me reality checks, and given me leads for interviews.

"I gave him a hundred," Teflon says. Then he explains that because the tattoo artist is so talented, regular patrons often have to wait months for an appointment. But because Teflon tips him so well, the artist said he'd come to his house to ink him up.

"So, did you write about tipping on cruise ships?" Teflon asks.

"Not this book," I say. "Maybe in the sequel."

"Well, you should," he says. "I went on a cruise and we gave our cabin steward two hundred bucks the moment we boarded the ship."

"And what'd that get you?"

"We're party animals," he says. "We'd sleep in late, so we'd always miss breakfast. So every morning our steward brought us an assortment of everything they were serving, a pot of coffee, and a pot of orange juice. No muss, no fuss. Shit, if I asked that guy to blow me, he would." The cabin steward might have a different opinion about fellating Teflon, but the cigar shop owner and his patrons have a firm grasp about what tipping's about.

"You can't get something for nothing," Doc, a chiropractor who favors Rocky Patel cigars, told me. "You wanna be treated special, you got to pay up. When I go to the Acapulco, I tip heavy at my resort. And when I come back from my fishing trips they'll cook up whatever I caught and I let them keep the rest for themselves. They know me, I know them, and they treat me like a king."

"What I can't understand," Sammy once told me, "is how can people not tip? What the fuck's wrong with these people? Don't they know this is how people make their living? I not only believe in tipping; I believe in *overtipping*."

What Doc, Teflon, and Sammy know—in fact, what almost all the guys in the cigar shop know—is that tipping is a lubricant that helps make the world run smoothly. But they also understand that gratuities are so much more than a way to get what you want; they're a way to establish *relationships*. Through tipping, Teflon established a rapport with his tattoo artist and Doc with the staff at his resort. They understand how to connect with other people and how passing a little green around makes that happen. And that was the nugget of wisdom the tipping god whispered in my ear that night in Vegas. *Tipping is all about relationships*.

Thinking about it, I see that it makes perfect sense. Tipping, at first glance, follows no rhyme or reason. As Professor Lynn pointed out, "Service has no more effect on the tip than how sunny it is outside." And waiters and other service personnel have always been mystified by who tips and who doesn't. While they've come up with numerous theories to explain why teachers or women or fat nurses are poor tippers, those explanations merely use specific examples to make a general conclusion. It's bad logic, and it doesn't explain a thing. I was a waiter for almost nine years, and in that time I was generously tipped and stiffed by everyone: blue bloods and working-class Joes, Jews and Gentiles, people fat and slim. Figuring out how and why people tip based on their profession, looks, gender, education, or income level is a dead end. But when you look at tips as an indicator of how people deal with *relationships*, then everything falls into place.

To adopt a phrase from the late politician Tip O'Neill, "All economics is social." Tipping is both an economic and a social activity—it is something that occurs between *people*. Liam said that service workers form microscopic relationships with their customers, but I think he really meant it's a *microcosmic* one. And if people have problems with relationships in the larger world, those issues will get played out in the microcosmic social world of the tip.

We've all had problems with relationships. We've all suffered from failed loves, broken marriages, and business partnerships gone awry. I myself have spent so much time on the psychoanalyst's couch that I can categorize every speck of the lint in my navel. Lord knows I've hurt people in my time. We all have. But there are quite a few individuals out there who have no idea how their "disconnect" hurts other people, especially service workers. So to prove my point about how relationship issues adversely affect tipping, I'm going to examine the characteristics of a personality disorder that makes it almost impossible for people to have meaningful relationships at all: narcissistic personality disorder, or NPD. No, I'm not getting all psychobabbly on you.

A personality disorder is a psychiatric condition that grossly interferes with a person's daily life and is usually marked by considerable personal and social turbulence. According to the *Diagnostic and Statistical Manual of Mental Disorders*, NPD is classified as "a pervasive pattern of grandiosity, need for admiration, and a lack of empathy." Hmm . . . sounds like a bad tipper to me. So let's look at the symptoms of NPD and see how they dovetail with people who leave lousy gratuities.

HAS A GRANDIOSE SENSE OF SELF-IMPORTANCE (E.G., EXAGGERATES ACHIEVEMENTS AND TALENTS, EXPECTS TO BE RECOGNIZED AS SUPERIOR WITHOUT COMMENSURATE ACHIEVEMENTS)

Remember how strippers call big-spending customers "big ballers"? I call them "wannabe rock stars." Anyone who's ever waited tables has run into these people: They're the customers who say, "I know the owner" and who demand the best table in the house without a reservation. They're the hotel guests who expect to be waited on hand and foot but who leave the maid a shitty tip.

REQUIRES EXCESSIVE ADMIRATION

Oddly enough, a narcissist will sometimes leave a big tip not because he recognizes the service being provided, but to feed his insatiable need for admiration. But a narcissist can be like the two-faced Roman god Janus, a Jekyll-and-Hyde type. Once he has received the admiration he craves, he will quickly devalue the very person giving him that admiration. These are the people who will leave you a big tip but still treat you like crap. Once you've accepted his money, he thinks you owe him something and he treats you like you're something he found on his shoe. I once had a customer who tipped me lavishly—I'm talking hundreds of bucks—but whose behavior was so beyond the pale that I eventually had to toss him out on his ass. His response? "I spend a lot of money here!" Sorry, pal, your money doesn't mean you can treat me like a doormat. Since these nut jobs pass out cash, they're somewhat easier to take.

HAS A SENSE OF ENTITLEMENT (I.E., UNREASONABLE EXPECTATIONS OF ESPECIALLY FAVORABLE TREATMENT OR AUTOMATIC COMPLIANCE WITH HIS OR HER EXPECTATIONS)

Ah yes, the Lexus people. Remember what Adriana the car valet from California said about people trying to get their cars ahead of other people? "You'll get people trying to jump the line, yelling, 'I want my car and I want it now!' but not offering you any money. Do you think I'm going to bend over backward for you?" Or how about people at the car wash who expect a "thirteen-dollar miracle" but who refuse to tip? These are the people the VIP host Rick hated, the quarter-slot gamblers who expected to get comp'd dinner or a free room. These are the *schnorers* of the world.

IS INTERPERSONALLY EXPLOITATIVE, (I.E., TAKES ADVANTAGE OF OTHERS TO ACHIEVE HIS OR HER OWN ENDS)

I talked to an Upper East Side doorman named Philo whose residents routinely asked him to give up his hard-won parking space on the street so they could have it for themselves. And when his union went on strike, it was those kinds of tenants who were the first ones to turn against him. "But I treat you right at Christmas," they'd holler. "Why are you doing this to me?" These are the kind of people who use tips, no matter how paltry, to guilt-trip people into bending to their will.

SHOWS ARROGANT, HAUGHTY BEHAVIORS OR ATTITUDES

Oh my God, that describes 20 percent of all the restaurant customers in America.

LACKS EMPATHY: IS UNWILLING TO RECOGNIZE OR IDENTIFY WITH THE FEELINGS AND NEEDS OF OTHERS

This symptom is the most important. These are people unable to identify with or care about the plight of workers—even if they're workers themselves. These are the people who'll stiff Lenny the shine man on a tip. These are the people who'll say, "If the waiter doesn't like what I left him then maybe he should get another job." These are the people who don't give the bathroom attendant a dollar but who help themselves to the mints and goodies the attendant provides. Not getting a tip hurts—whether you're a waiter, a car wash attendant, or a parking valet. But in Las Vegas, a strung-out druggie couple, despite their multitude of problems, cared enough about Luther the cabdriver to give him a gratuity they could barely afford. Within that microcosmic relationship, they formed an empathetic bond with him. If the druggies could leave a tip out of their penury, what's other people's excuse?

Ironically, according to a recent article in *Psychology Today*, we like narcissists "at first sight" and often describe them as "having a 'charismatic air': attractiveness, competence, interpersonal warmth, and humor." We've all met people like this. Witty and seductive, they can make you feel like the center of the universe—but only to get what they want. Narcissists are admiration addicts who crave constant affirmation of their attractiveness, specialness, and self-worth. World-class show-offs, once they've gotten their admiration "fix" from a lover, workmate, or friend, they'll cast that person aside in search of a new sugar daddy, not realizing the damage they've left in their wake. And because they're always on a quest for new people and adventures to buck up their self-esteem, it's impossible for them to build long-lasting relationships with other people. Therefore, narcissists usually have numerous acquaintances but no real friends. They need constant ego stroking, so they usually flip out when someone criticizes them. If you tell them that they're bad tippers? Watch out! And since they're often described as being "disappointing gift givers," it's no wonder their gratuities suck. On the surface these individuals seem okay, but once you see the anguish and emptiness in the center of their souls you'd be wise to run away. As that concierge in Napa Valley said, "They're nice people, just not decent people."

Look, all of us can be self-centered and act like jerks at times. But I wanted to describe an extreme case of dysfunction like narcissism to prove my point: people who have trouble relating to other human beings will have problems giving out tips. And I'll bet that if psychologists administered personality tests to *chronically* bad tippers they'd find that these people had some sort of pathology that made it difficult for them to establish meaningful relationships of any kind.

And this dynamic applies to service providers as well. If a person working for gratuities has problems with relationships, he won't do well in the social give-and-take that constitutes tipping either. Let's face it, do we really feel like tipping that antisocial bartender, surly bellhop, or rude waiter? Truth be told, during my last days waiting tables I was a complete asshole to my customers, and my tips suffered as a result, not because I provided them with poor service, mind you—I was always professional—but because I lost the spark every waiter needs to make a customer feel special. Remember, friendliness was found to be one of the few factors that caused customers to slightly increase their tips. I was no longer able to build relationships with my customers. And if you aren't good with people, you shouldn't be in the service profession. The ups and downs of waitering finally burned out my patience. I got out just in time.

The reasons I give in earlier chapters as to why people tip—

reducing server envy, maintaining social norms, being generous, feeling guilty, gaining approval—are all very *human* motivations. And those motivations transcend tipping. When we get a big promotion at work or have a spectacular success, don't we try to reduce our friends' envy through self-deprecating humor and modesty? When we've hurt someone and feel guilty about it, don't we do something nice for her? Buy her flowers or her favorite bottle of wine? Don't we try to impress potential mates with displays of generosity and grace? And when someone is suffering, don't we try to empathize with that person's pain? These responses have everything to do with building and maintaining relationships. So it should come as no surprise that tipping is an economic and relationship skill. And that's why we all go bananas when we don't know how to tip in certain situations. Gratuities make us uncomfortable because relationships can make us feel uncomfortable.

Of course having a relational screw loose is not the only reason we stumble with gratuities. Ignorance is a large part of it. Before I went on this pilgrimage, I had no idea that card dealers should be tipped. I didn't know how to tip a shoeshine guy until I asked. I had no idea that bathroom attendants often pay for the sundries they provide, that brewing espresso was an art form worthy of a tip, or that bartenders are looking for 20 percent. So here's another lesson that I, Stephen Dublanica, Guru of the Gratuity and the Grand Poobah of the Tip, have learned: if you don't know what to tip, just ask. Trust me, people will be happy to tell you.

Some people get their panties in a bunch because of the age-old argument "But I've already paid for a service! Why should I have to pay a tip on top of it?" Man, that sounds like a flea or *schnorer* if ever I've heard one. Okay, let's mix this up a bit. Say you work on Wall Street and bring down $250,000 a year. Not bad. Now let's say that the higher-ups decide not to give out bonuses. Wouldn't you be pissed? Well, why should you? The company's already paid you for your work! Why should you be paid more on top of it? "But a bonus is not like a tip," you counter. "It's performance-based!" Oh, give me a break. Look at all the executives who ran their banks and our nation's economy into the ground and still got bonuses. Citigroup suffered $27 billion in losses in 2008 but paid out an estimated $5.33 billion in bonuses that year. How's that for rewarding bad performance? Despite all the bullshit reasons the banks used to justify such outlandish payments, their core reasoning only reinforces my premise. Banks paid out bonuses to retain talent. They used bonuses to strengthen their top earners' relationship to the company and secure their loyalty. So a bonus is very much like a tip.

These are the ramblings of a man who lived on tips for almost nine years and has journeyed into the heart of the American tipping monster. Do I claim to know everything about tipping? No way. There are many tipped professions I was unable to cover in this book because the subject is so vast. Gurus deal in *mystery*, and like God, tipping will never be totally understood. But I think my pilgrimage has shed some light on this great and contentious subject.

Some people have philosophical objections to tipping. They would like to see businesses pay their workers a living wage and jettison tipping altogether. That was the goal of William Rufus Scott back in 1916 and, as we've seen, the attitude of many people today. Does that mean those people are soulless human beings? No. There's nothing wrong with holding that position. I would like to see a world where everyone is paid his or her worth and tipping becomes a quaint anachronism. But we live in the *real* world. Tipping will probably never go away because it's so tightly interwoven into the economic life of America. And a sign of emotional intelligence, a sign that you know how to relate to other people, is the ability to live in an ambiguous world of gray. It's the ability to hold two opposite beliefs in your head. You may love your spouse deeply but hate how he snores at night. You may dislike some of your girlfriend's gal pals but put up with them because you love her. You may not agree with everything your fellow town councilmen believe, but you try to hammer out a compromise. Samuel Gompers, the great labor leader, once wrote, "While, of course, I have followed the usual custom of giving tips, yet I have maintained the principle of tipping to be unwise and that it tends to lessen the self-respect of a man who accepts a tip." Gompers hated tipping, but he had enough empathy to leave a gratuity, because not to do so would have damaged the very workers he had spent a lifetime protecting. Gompers could live in a world of gray. He knew how the world worked. But many people today cannot. So you have a decision to make. Will you go through life being a flea, a *schnorer*, or a George? Will you be a nice person or a decent one?

Back at the cigar shop, Shoes walks in the door smoking a stogie and shakes everyone's hand. Tipping is a lot like that handshake. It's a way of saying we're all in this together. No matter what you do or where you are in life, we respect one another as human beings. And you know what? That *is* the spirit of America. When William Rufus Scott wrote *The Itching Palm*, he may have thought tipping was antithetical to the egalitarian spirit this country was founded on. But now that idea has been turned on its head. A tip is a payment, a bribe, and a thank-you—but it's also a sign of your ability to relate to other people, that you can treat them as *equals*. The great English novelist E. M. Forster once wrote, "Only connect! . . . Only connect the prose and the passion, and both will be exalted, and human love will be seen at its height. *Live in fragments no longer.*" Tipping helps you connect with people, if only for a short while.

On some deep level I've always known this. That's why the idea was swirling for so long just below the surface of my conscious mind. I've always grasped that tipping tells us a lot about ourselves. It reflects our ideas about class and money, the status of the American Dream, our sense of generosity and, most important, how we relate to people as a whole. And as I sit back in my leather swivel chair and light up my Maduro, I look at the men in the cigar shop. Like Rick, Luther, Liam, and that druggie couple in Vegas, these guys know the most valuable thing in life are the connections they make. Remember what Lenny said? "Most of my customers are not customers. They're *friends*."

"Hey, Professor," Sammy says. "We're playing poker. Wanna get in on the action?"

"Deal me in."

Before long, chips are flying around the table; straight flushes are beating full houses; men are laughing, swilling beer, and telling stories; and I'm losing my shirt. I take a long pull from my cigar, listen to their tall tales, and smile. The nickname they gave me means I'm now connected to this merry band. "Only connect," I think to myself. "Live in fragments no longer." That's tipping. And that's life.

Acknowledgments

There is a saying that an author's second book is the hardest to write. I used to think that axiom was balderdash, but I have discovered that it's very true. Writing is like getting into a knife fight with yourself in a phone booth. And since I've emerged victorious, I have a lot of people to thank.

First off, I'm grateful to my editor, Matt Weiland at Ecco, for his deft touch with words, his commitment, and his sense of humor. I'm also deeply thankful to my publisher, Dan Halpern, for his patience and faith, and to Emily Takoudes and Virginia Smith for their help bringing this book to fruition. And no thanks would be complete if I didn't acknowledge Rachel Elinsky and the rest of the team at Ecco for all the hard work they've done over the years.

I owe a *huge* debt of gratitude to Kerry Segrave. Almost everything I know about the history of tipping came from his excellent book *Tipping: An American History of Gratuities* (McFarland and Company). I'm also grateful to Dr. Ofer Azar of the Ben Gurion University of the Negev for his scholarship, and I'm indebted to Dr. Michael Lynn of the Cornell University School of Hotel Administration for his invaluable assistance and guidance. I was never good at statistics, Mike.

To Avalon Vigglioti, who helped guide me through the world of strippers, and to all the dancers who agreed to be interviewed for this book, thanks for the wild ride. Kudos to "Rick," who helped teach me how Las Vegas works; to Denis Grady and Las Vegas Cabbie for guiding me through the bright lights of Sin City. Write that book, man!

I'm also grateful to Mia Saling, Rebecca Gaffney, and Amanda Sowards for the hospitality they afforded me in California, and to the owners and employees of Passive Arts in Los Angeles for teaching me about a world I knew nothing about. I'd also like to acknowledge Richard Schave and Kim Cooper of Esotouric, who helped me chase Raymond Chandler's ghost through the streets of L.A. and discover one hell of a coincidence. And to Manny, Panama, and all the staff at Musso and Frank Grill on Hollywood Boulevard. You guys are the real deal.

To Nancy Rommelmann, her husband, Din, and the gang at Ristretto Roasters in Portland, Oregon—thank you for your warm welcome and teaching me how to "pull a shot." Sorry about all the coffee I wasted. And to Jeff Johnson: I enjoyed the Jameson with water backs and your insights into tattoos, writing, and life. Because of you guys and the wonderful staff at the Ace Hotel, Portland will always be a magical city for me.

Of course I'd be remiss if I didn't thank my parents, family, friends, the "Dog Park Crew," and the guys at the cigar shop for putting up with me as I blabbed incessantly about tipping. Thanks are also due to Launa Kliever, Greg Mortimer, Liong, Pete Schessler, Leonard C. Johnson, Buster, Charles Pivirotto, Charlene Barnes, David Weintraub L.M.T, Nick Harris, Richard, Tina, Marilyn, Joe, and to all my neighbors for their enthusiasm and support. (You see? I really was doing something sitting on that porch! And thanks for digging out my car, Phil!) Thanks also to John Amatucci for his law enforcement experience and to Don for his sunny disposition and the clean clothes. I'd also like to acknowledge Lou Pechman,

Judith Karfiol, and James W. Versocki, Esquires, for all their help navigating the law.

To all the people I interviewed for this book, I'm deeply grateful for the gift of your time. This book would not have been possible without you. I'd also like to extend my condolences to the family of "Mona," who died a few months after I talked to her. And to all the faithful readers of my blog, Waiter Rant, you guys are the reason I'm a writer today. Thank you.

Finally, what can I say to Farley Chase of the Waxman Literary Agency? "[W]e climbed up, he first and I second, so far that I saw some of the beautiful things that heaven bears, through a round opening; and thence we came forth to see again the stars."

Appendix A

What to Tip at the Holidays

Ah, the holiday season. A time for family and friends, presents under the tree, kissing beneath the mistletoe, lighting the menorah, office party binge drinking, gladiator-pit shopping malls, snarled traffic, atheists bitching over religious symbols in front of City Hall, familial guilt, credit card debt, and, most of all, blistering anxiety over what to tip the people who served you so faithfully during the year. Pass the eggnog and benzodiazepines! When it comes to gratuities, it's that special time of year.

You might get a slight case of agita when you encounter that tip jar at Starbucks during other times of the year, but stressing out over what to tip during the winter solstice is enough to induce a coronary. A lot of this stress stems from the fact that tips don't always fall into the neat categories that Dr. Azar outlines. More often than not, the boundaries between the types of tipping get blurred and produce gratuity hybrids. Here's a perfect example. When I was a waiter, I had a lovely patron named Clarice who ate in my restaurant once a week and always tipped me 30 percent. To say I adored this woman would be an understatement. Not only was Clarice kind, gracious, and decent, but her tips covered my monthly car payment. And every Christmas she would pull me aside, slip me $300, and say, "This is for *you*. Happy holidays." When her company transferred her to China, I was almost suicidal.

By definition, a holiday tip is something you give people you ordinarily don't tip during the year—residential doormen being a perfect example. It's a lump sum payment that covers all those little extra services for which you didn't give a gratuity. Normally we don't tip postal workers, but at the end of the year, we might give them a little something to say we appreciate their not snickering when they deliver our dildos and bondage DVDs. (Despite the plain brown wrappers, they know what's in there. Trust me.) Technically, postal workers are not allowed to accept money. And any gifts they do receive must not exceed a cash value of twenty dollars. My mom used to give our postman McDonald's gift certificates every year. She's a sweet lady. I'd *like* to tip my postman, but since I have a different one every day, and my bills get delivered to my neighbor's house, I'm not that sweet. But if I did have a regular postman who remembered my address, I'd tip him in booze.

During the holidays, tipping causes people to go haywire. Just what are we tipping for? My wonderful customer Clarice *reward-tipped* me throughout the year, allowing me to drive something better than a rusted-out Chevy Nova. And because she was so generous, reservations for her were optional—she never waited for a table and always got the best seat in the house. So her weekly tips were also like bribe tipping and tipping in advance combined. And her big holiday tip? That was a combo of all three, with the holiday and gift tip mixed in for good measure. Because Clarice was such a class act during the course of the year, it wasn't necessary for her to give me a holiday tip. If she hadn't slipped me that $300 I wouldn't have cared. But I'm glad she did.

Because waiters make their living off the reward tips they collect all year, you might think they shouldn't receive a little Yuletide jingle. And many customers do indeed think this way.

But when they hear about patrons doling out holiday cheer they can get all confused. Should I be doing that, too? Should a person who gets tipped all the time get a holiday payoff? And what about those people we tip only at Christmas? What's the protocol? How much should I give? And if we're cheap, what's going to happen to us? Will the worker be resentful and treat us like crap the rest of the year? Tipping may be a social norm, but during the holidays it's anything but normal. And this lack of clarity drives people insane.

My first experience with holiday tipping was when I was an eleven-year-old paperboy in Clifton, New Jersey. Because the news carrier Mafia in my town made Tony Soprano and his crew look like choirboys, I was given a very tiny piece of the action—twenty-five customers within a five-block radius of my house. Despite my small territory, when Christmas arrived, visions of money-stuffed envelopes danced in my head: thank-yous rendered in legal tender for all the times I'd delivered local hack journalism to their homes in the heat, cold, snow, and rain. Ah, to be so young and naïve again!

The customers on my route were octogenarian shut-ins, alcoholics with daily liquor deliveries, crazed families with delinquent kids, paranoiacs who pushed the subscription payment under the door, two fat hippies sleeping on a bare mattress in their living room, and one creepy middle-aged guy who probably had several dead bodies producing methane in his backyard. Half my customers were behind in their payments, didn't tip at all, or acted like they were handing me emeralds when slipping me a thin dime. But as I toddled along my route on the collection day before Christmas, I knew that day would be different. *That day* people would do the right thing. Back then, the normal holiday tip was double the price of a weekly subscription: about five bucks. If everyone tipped the expected amount, I'd take home $125—a princely sum to a little kid. With that money, I could buy the Huffy dirt bike I had my eye on, or a model rocket set.

As it turned out: no Huffy dirt bike, no model rocket set. One nice lady and her daughter gave me a hearty tip, and my parents kicked in some, but overall I got screwed. On that day the words *cheap* and *motherfucker* might have come out of my innocent mouth for the very first time. Working that paper route was my first experience being on the receiving end of cheap people. And it wouldn't be the last. So, foreshadowing the waiter I would become nineteen years later, I started indulging in a little payback. Papers got thrown into bushes, left sodden and exposed to the elements, or not delivered at all. I also got more aggressive collecting from my deadbeats. I became like that psychotic paperboy from the movie *Better Off Dead*. "I want my two dollars!" Even the serial killer on my route feared me. And by the time I finally gave up my paper route at the embarrassing age of sixteen, I had increased my territory and the holiday tips were rolling in. Persistence had paid off. (And my parents had bought me that Huffy, so don't get all weepy.)

Tipping during the holidays is a sticky wicket, but I follow a simple rule that I think covers most situations—tip out the amount of the service you've received. My barber, Spiro, charges me twenty-five dollars for a haircut, and I reward-tip him five dollars every time I visit the shop. But when Christmas rolls around, I give him a twenty-five dollar tip—the cost of the service. Many people have personal trainers who normally don't get tipped over the course of the year. But if they charge you eighty dollars a session trying to whip your ass into buns of steel, then you should give them eighty bucks at Christmas. If you don't, you might leave the gym walking funny for a week. Babysitters aren't usually tipped, but when the holidays roll around you should tip yours the amount you pay her to watch your children for an evening. Have a nanny? One week's pay is a good holiday tip. Employ a live-in nanny who is exposed to your familial insanity six days a week? A month's pay, if you've got the scratch. (And if you have a live-in nanny, you've got the scratch.) One au pair told me that her employers gave her an all-expenses-paid trip to the Bahamas as a thank-you. Another told me she got only a cheesy card and twenty bucks. That's a good way to get your children's pictures on the back of a milk carton. Dog groomer? Same as a barber: tip the cost of one visit. Dog walker? One week's pay. More if Fido bites.

What about the hunky UPS guy or the FedEx worker? Delivery companies often prohibit employees from accepting cash tips. When in doubt, give them alcohol. But if you've actually taken the time to talk to your delivery person and have learned about his hobbies, then give him something to help him follow his bliss. Is your UPS guy a fly fisherman? A hand-tied lure will do just fine. A wannabe gourmet? A nice cookbook. A movie buff? A gift certificate to the cinema.

Since we're on the subject of packages, it's time to discuss the holiday tip that drives people, especially Manhattanites, up the freaking wall. What to tip the doorman?

Why am I segueing from package delivery to doormen? Because New Yorkers who live in doorman buildings have a *royal hard-on* for packages. I don't, because I live in a house in New Jersey. When my UPS guy drops off a package he usually leaves it on my front stoop, unless it's something extremely dangerous, like rifle ammunition. But when you live in a busy urban area, leaving packages on the stoop is just not an option. Of course, since you're working seventy hours a week to afford that five-hundred-square-foot Upper West Side pad, you're never home when your packages arrive. And if your building doesn't have a doorman, your stuff goes back on the truck. And if you miss a delivery one too many times, you have to pick the package up at a regional depot or it goes back to Sharper Image or Inflate-a-Mate. Some people avoid this problem by having their packages delivered at work. But sometimes you don't want your coworkers knowing about your fetish for ladies' underwear or the cheap antipsychotic medications you get shipped in from Canada. Let's face it, some packages are just not work-appropriate.

"So, what's the biggest perk of living in a doorman building?" I ask Glenn, a finance lawyer living in a beautiful apartment building overlooking Columbus Circle. "The package thing," he says. "When you get packages delivered, they go down to a central location. They used to call you [when a package arrived], but now they send you an email." Ah, the impersonal touch of the Internet. Glenn also told me food deliveries are a big deal in New York, saying, "We're proud of the fact you can get anything delivered [in this city]." But one of the scams tenants in doorman buildings pull is to have the delivery guy leave the food at the front desk, wait for him to leave on his bike, and then come down to collect the food. That way the tenant can avoid giving him a tip.

"Jesus," says Sal, a swarthy Lower East Side doorman/super. "Those friggin' packages! At my building, we doormen do the mail. We're what's called 'a drop house.' We sort the mail, and that's like two or three hours' work. Then, at the peak time between five and seven o'clock, we've got people coming home, UPS guys coming in and out, the buzzer's buzzing, the phone's ringing. It's crazy. People are like, 'Where's my packages? Where's my dry cleaning?' I went to the seven-to-three shift because I was going to have a heart attack."

Now, many people who live in doorman buildings love the convenience of having their packages delivered to a secure location. But sometimes they're ambivalent about the very workers who watch over their stuff. In fact, many people despise having doormen in their building, "Especially," one wag commented on the website Gothamist, "when sixty dollars would buy a keypad lock that would replace him permanently." But, as another commenter wryly rebutted, "A keypad lock ain't gonna sign for your FedEx package." Touché.

For years the *New York Times* and other newspapers have shed thousands of gallons of ink prognosticating over what to "render unto the doorman." To get the real skinny about what tenants should tip during the holidays I went straight to the source: the doormen and building supers of the Big Apple.

"If you live in a one-bedroom," says Philo, a lanky, white-haired doorman on the Upper East Side, "you should tip [each doorman] between seventy-five and a hundred bucks. If you've got a two-bedroom? Between one hundred and one-fifty."

Now, the units in Philo's building run from $800,000 for a studio to $3,000,000 for a four-bedroom unit. "So, what if you've got a tenant living in some macked-out apartment?" I ask. "What should they tip?"

"Between four and five hundred. *Each.*" Jesus. That's a lot of money.

After several months talking to New York doormen on what they think their residents should tip, I came up with these convenient guidelines.

BUILDING SUPERINTENDENT: $100 minimum

DOORMAN: Between $75 and $100. Half of this if they're only part time; more if you live in a larger apartment

HEAD PORTER: Anywhere from $75 to $100

ASSISTANT PORTERS: $50

HANDYMAN: $100. His assistants? About $50; more if you're feeling generous

BOILER ROOM OPERATOR: $75. You like heat, don't you?

And all of these amounts are for *each* worker in the building. When you add up the amount of holiday tips you're expected to shell out, the numbers can be staggering. Glenn tells me he lives in a building where there are at least *twenty-six workers* on staff. If he tipped everyone, that'd be thousands of dollars! But he also tells me he's a renter, not an owner. If he owned his apartment, he opines, he'd be inclined to tip more because, in a sense, all those workers would be his employees.

So, what happens if you're a good egg and tip your doorman throughout the year, slipping him or her a fiver every time he unloads your car or does you a small favor? Should you still leave a holiday tip? "Oh, yeah," Philo says. "It doesn't matter. At the end of the year you still tip." But not all doormen feel that way. Sal told me if a tenant gives him tips during the year, he's not expecting a heavy holiday tip. "But a fifty-dollar token of your esteem would be nice," he says. "Hey, everyone likes to get something at Christmas."

Many of us can't afford to shell out holiday tips to the people who serve us all year. As Sal said, "You got it, you got it. If you don't, you don't." Now don't get me wrong, workers still want that Christmas and Hanukkah cash. But if you can't give what the *New York Times*, Emily Post, or I say you should give, give them *something*, because something's always better than nothing. And no matter what you tip them, be sure to treat those workers who do for you all year like human beings. "Do unto others as you would want them to do unto you."

And that's what the holiday spirit's all about.

Who Gets Tipped What at a Wedding

A wedding is one of the most expensive productions people will probably ever put on in their lives. And even though it's the bride's special day, a wedding is also partly a business transaction—so, you guessed it, somebody somewhere has got to get tipped. So just how do you dole out the gratuities at a wedding? After talking to Mia Saling and Rebecca Gaffney of Red Letter Events, a wedding planning outfit in San Diego, I can offer you some helpful hints about how to get through one of the happiest and most stressful days in your life with your tipping integrity intact.

Now, you're probably thinking, "Weddings cost a shitload of money as it is! I have to tip people, too?" Yes, but don't panic. You don't have to slavishly follow the 15–20 percent rule. For example, if your DJ costs $2,000, you don't need to tip him or her $400. In fact, no single worker at a wedding should be tipped more than $150. And check your contracts closely. Many wedding service providers slap on an automatic gratuity to the bill, so there's no need to double-tip. And please note, it is usually the best man's job to dole out the tips on behalf of the couple. But if the guy is uncomfortable with that role, blasted out of his mind, or too busy trying to score with the bridesmaids, then the bride and groom should designate an alternate person to hand out the cash. And yes, all the tips should be in folding money.

So who has to be tipped?

THE OFFICIANT: Somebody's got to marry you, and they need to get paid. Now, most priests, ministers, rabbis, and imams will have a "suggested" donation at their respective houses of worship, ranging from $50 to $500. Well, it's not just "suggested"—you actually do have to cough up that money. And if you stiff the officiant, that's some seriously bad nuptial karma. Trust me, I knew priests who laid bets on how long the marriage would last as soon as the limo pulled away from the church. Besides, this is not a tip—it's a fee. So just hand them that envelope at the end of the service and be on your merry way. But if you want to give a little extra, I know clergymen are fond of booze.

ALTAR BOYS: You should tip the acolytes ten to fifteen dollars each. My brother used to live for these tips when he was an altar boy. And you know what? The same tip is appropriate for funerals. Coincidence? I think not.

LIMOUSINE DRIVERS: They get you to the church on time. If a gratuity is not built into their bill, tip them 10–15 percent of the limo bill at the end of the night.

MAKEUP ARTIST: They're making the bride look beautiful and have to put up with her pre-wedding jitters and psychotic breaks to boot. Whether you go to a salon or they come to you, the standard tip is 15–20 percent of the bill.

WAITERS: These are the people who'll be working the hardest while you're dancing the night away. Normally a caterer will add an automatic gratuity to the bill and pay the servers an hourly rate out of that money. However, if you feel that the waiters did incredible jobs, give them all twenty bucks at the end of the night. And if you're a wedding guest, leave a couple of bucks on the table before you stagger home.

BARTENDERS: Sometimes the gratuity is built into the liquor bill. But if it isn't, the best way the bride and groom can handle this situation is to leave the bartenders 10–15 percent of the bill at the end of the night. That way the bartenders won't need to put out a brandy snifter marked "Tips," and your guests can get bombed without having to think about gratuities. If you're a wedding guest, however, and that tip jar's out there, slip each bartender a five or ten for the whole night. Remember, you're drinking for free.

VALETS: Wedding guests are horrible when it comes to tipping car valets. I once saw couples parking their cars several blocks away from a wedding venue in the California desert and trudging through 103-degree heat just to save a dollar. That's crazy. If you're a guest, tip. And if you're the bride and groom and a tip is not built into the valet contract, give each of the valets a dollar for every parked car.

THE DJ: Just like at a strip club, a DJ can make or break a girl's evening. If the DJ owns the company, you aren't obligated to tip, but most of them like to see a little green. That's up to you. If the DJ is an employee of the company, fifty bucks will suffice. If there's an MC and a DJ, a hundred bucks between the two of them will do. But if the DJ was like the dolt at my brother's wedding—he butchered our family name despite numerous corrections and forgot half the music—then tip him nothing. (That guy really pissed me off.)

COAT CHECK GIRLS: If the guests don't tip, give these ladies a dollar for every coat checked.

CHURCH ORGANIST: They usually have a set fee, but if not, tip them anywhere from twenty-five to forty dollars. The music from "Here Comes the Bride" is actually from a pagan song, and some churches refuse to play it! So if you want that tune going down the aisle, cough up. Everyone can be bribed, even in the Lord's House.

Then there are the service providers who don't have to be tipped but who love it when you do. As noted, you're spending oodles of money anyway, and no one has to be tipped over $150.

WEDDING PLANNER: After seeing Mia and Rebecca in action, I think you're nuts not to hire a professional wedding planner to make sure your day runs smoothly. They're the ones who deal with the snafus, who wrangle drunken groomsmen, who hound the photographer to wrap up on time, and who argue with the caterers so you can focus on having a good time. You can also designate them to hand out the tips at the end of the celebration. Wedding planners are professionals and do not expect tips. But if you feel that they went above and beyond, tipping 10 percent of their fee is a wonderful gesture. Mia and Rebecca told me that a nice bottle of wine or a gift certificate to their favorite restaurant is a great tip.

FLORIST: You do not have to tip the florist, but tipping the people who deliver and set up the flowers five to ten dollars each is nice.

PHOTOGRAPHER/VIDEOGRAPHER: These guys cost a mint, and if the photographer owns the company you don't have to tip him. But if he has assistants, fifty dollars for them to share is a nice gesture.

MUSICIANS: If you're so inclined, five to ten dollars a person is good. And if you can hire a band, you can probably afford it.

Besides, these guys will probably be suicidal after playing "The Funky Chicken" for the thousandth time.

THE MAÎTRE D': Very often these guys get a cut of the auto-grat the catering hall tacks on to your bill. But if your maître d' hustled your shitfaced uncle into a cab, kept the bridesmaids from crashing someone else's reception, or prevented your new father-in-law from busting up the joint, a fifty-dollar bill's a good idea. And if the wedding hall's contract calls for the maître d' to get an outlandish tip—fight it.

BANQUET OR CATERING MANAGER: They don't need to be tipped. But if they cut you a deal, then $100 is appropriate.

BAKER: Just tip the guy who delivers the wedding cake ten bucks. If he drops the cake, then forget about it.

That's it, folks. And if you tip well at your wedding you're guaranteed seven years of great sex. (Okay, I just made that up.)

Appendix C

How to Start a Conversation about Tipping and Race

Tipping is a powerful light. It not only illuminates our inner psyches and attitudes about money, class, and the American dream, but it also forces us to examine one of the most explosive issues in our country today: race. We may live in the age of Obama, but let's be real: it's difficult to have an honest discussion about race in this country without it devolving into name-calling, finger-pointing, political opportunism, and character assassination. And that's when you want to have a constructive dialogue! But since I've become the guru of all things tipping, let me confront this issue head-on.

"Black people don't tip," my training waiter told me on my first day serving tables. "I don't mean to sound racist or nothing. It's just true."

"I guess you can kiss that NAACP Waiter of the Year award good-bye," I said.

"Stick around," my trainer said. "You'll see it's true. And women? Ugh. They're almost as bad." Then he proceeded to rattle through a list of populations he perceived as bad tippers: Jews, Mexicans, Indians, Canadians, tourists, doctors, rich people, schoolteachers, nurses, old people, teenagers, clergymen, and everyone from the continent of Europe.

"But gay guys?" he said, smiling wistfully. "They're the best tippers in the world."

Right now you're probably thinking this guy was an anti-Semitic, racist, euthanasia-loving, misogynistic card-carrying member of the Ku Klux Klan, and a Communist to boot. Actually, he was one of the nicest people I've ever met, and he counted numerous individuals from the groups he mentioned in his bitter diatribe as friends. But he was a waiter. And waiters hate anyone who fucks with their tips.

In 2009, I asked my blog readers to list who they thought were bad tippers. The list ran the gamut: black people, rich people, Indians, Jews, in-laws, teenagers, Europeans, "unsophisticated Southerners," teachers, Asians, tourists, doctors, lawyers, women in general, country club members, college students, people who say, "You're the best waiter I've ever had," early-bird-special enthusiasts, salesmen, IT professionals, academics, sexual harassers, professional basketball players, dairy farmers, artists, old people, Red Hatters (sorry, Mom!), Jehovah's Witnesses, Mexicans, political officials, people who have a PBS tote bag or who listen to NPR, real estate agents, Republicans, Polish people, lesbians, sexually frustrated men, accountants, white trash, anyone with a coupon, pig farmers, drunks, patrons who come in five minutes before closing, nonsmokers, Democrats, Amish people, Gypsies, Arabs, patrons with black Amex cards, and, almost edging out African Americans, the Sunday after-church crowd. According to my readers, if you love Jesus you're a bad tipper.

None of this surprised me. My readers didn't mention anything I hadn't heard when I was a waiter. (Well, okay, the pig farmer one threw me.) But if you can get anyone who's ever waited tables to give you an honest answer, most will tell you that African Americans are the worst tippers. I've heard liberal white waiters say it, I've heard cracker racist waiters say it, and

I've even heard black waiters say it. "Do you think black people are good tippers?" I once asked an African American colleague. "Hell, no!" he replied.

The issue of how African Americans tip is so filled with tension, fear, anger, and ignorance that waiters and restaurant owners will only whisper about it among themselves in hushed, embarrassed tones. Frankly, it's one of the industry's dirty little secrets.

Now, I will never say that I'm completely free of prejudice. I'm a middle-aged white guy living in the United States and I'm certainly not perfect. But when I was a waiter I was very resistant to the idea that African Americans could be lumped together as bad tippers. I prided myself on the fact I was more open-minded than my prejudiced counterparts. I thought that thinking that way was racist and an example of faulty logic. But as time went by and I talked to servers of all races, I began to have a sneaking suspicion that the stereotype was true. Since I no longer wait tables, though, I thought it'd be a good idea to interview African American servers and get their candid take.

"Have you heard it said that black people don't tip?" I asked Anton, a waiter in a New Orleans hotel.

"Actually, that's the truth," he said. "And I've experienced it as well. . . . I worked a convention, a Christian Conference [where African Americans made up the bulk of the attendees]. Worked from sunup to sundown, and left barely making fifty dollars at the end of the day." He went on to add that he felt that many African Americans just didn't know how to tip.

"Black people don't tip?" remarked Cecil, a waiter at a high-end eatery in Manhattan. "I think that's a fair assessment, but it saddens me. . . . Black people, for the most part, because they really don't go out to fine dining establishments, they don't understand the professionalism behind the service industry and equate the restaurant business as almost like being a slave in a way. They don't understand this is a great job." He went on to add, "You get a professional black guy paying the bill, for the most part you're going to be fine. But for the average black person who really doesn't go out that often, or doesn't go out to high-end restaurants, it kind of throws them off. They don't know what to do. It's a shame, but it happens."

Anton and Cecil have suggested that one of the reasons African Americans tip less than whites is because they don't patronize sit-down restaurants as often as whites. They may not be far off the mark. Statistics show that blacks are less likely than whites to eat at sit-down restaurants. "That doesn't mean they don't spend money eating out," Dr. Michael Lynn stated in a 2003 NPR interview. "In fact, blacks are more likely than other groups to get carryout. This pattern in part reflects the poor service blacks get because they're perceived as poor tippers."

"Tipping behavior has to be looked at in its totality," Gerry Fernandez of the Multicultural Foodservice and Hospitality Alliance, said in the same NPR interview. "We have to look at it for its cultural elements, for the institutionalized racism that exists in this industry, and then education. How do people learn about tipping? If you don't go, you don't know. . . . If that is not learned behavior at home, then how can you expect any particular group to understand what the norm is around tipping?"

One of the theories posited for African Americans tending to tip less is that they have not had the opportunity to be inculcated into the social norm of tipping. In Dr. Lynn's 2003 study "Ethnic Differences in Tipping," he states that 63 percent of African Americans and 30 percent of whites in the United States are unaware that the standard tip in a restaurant is between 15 and 20 percent. According to that study, the average black person would tip 13 percent of the bill while the average tip a white person would leave was 16.5 percent. When I called Dr. Lynn in 2010 to review these numbers, he said, "I don't know if it's exactly thirteen percent and sixteen and a half percent today. That was an accurate description for *that* study. But I can tell you I'm pretty consistently finding blacks tip about three percent of the bill less than whites do." Dr. Lynn, who is white, was a waiter and bartender before he became an academic. Over the years he has also studied the tipping difference between Asians and whites and Hispanics and whites. But when he studied how black and white people tip, he found the disparity between the two groups to be more "robust."

Let me tell you, I was pretty uncomfortable reading Dr. Lynn's study. Part of that discomfort stemmed from the fact that I knew some people would cite his work out of context to validate their own racial prejudices. But what I found most disturbing was that Lynn's study found that blacks' tipping less than whites isn't urban legend or a racist stereotype, but a mathematically quantifiable reality. I didn't want to believe Lynn's conclusions.

"Not every black person is a bad tipper," Dr. Lynn stressed. But *on average*, he found there's a three-percentage-point difference between black and white restaurant patrons. "But the exact size of that average difference is going to vary depending on where you are in the country."

We all have to learn about tipping from somewhere. And since about 24 percent of African Americans live below the poverty line, that they're not eating out as much as whites didn't surprise me. But as I talked with Dr. Lynn further, I was surprised to discover that my kneejerk socioeconomic analysis was somewhat off the mark.

"Yes, there are race differences in income and education, and more educated and wealthier people do tip more," Lynn told me. "So, part of the race differences in tipping is because of the socioeconomic status differences between whites and blacks." But Lynn also said, "[That's] part of the story but only a little bit of the story." His 2003 study showed there was a marginally significant interaction between race and patronage frequency—that is, the more frequently people went out to restaurants, the smaller the race difference became. But he found that those results were "not quite statistically significant." A few years later he performed an Internet survey on a large sample of blacks and whites, some college educated, some not, and examined how much they tipped. He saw that dining frequency has only a tiny effect on African Americans' tipping habits. "[In] the previous study where I found a marginally significant interaction," he said, "that I couldn't replicate it with a much bigger, better sample suggests it [the finding from the 2003 study] was probably just a chance effect. So I have no reason to believe that going out to restaurants more frequently would eliminate the black/white difference in tipping." So, according to Lynn, education, income level, and frequency of patronage have only a small effect on African Americans' tipping habits.

"So, there is truth in what waiters, black and white, say?" I asked. "Black people don't tip?"

"Oh, absolutely," Lynn said, adding, "I'm very comfortable saying blacks tip less than whites. There's enough data that I can defend that."

You may not agree with Dr. Lynn's findings. But whether it's a fact or a stereotype, the perception that African Americans tip less than whites has profound effects on waiters and the restaurant industry as a whole. Whenever black customers walked into my restaurant, some of the waiters would groan, "Oh, no. I don't want that table." And then arguments would break out over who caught it. "No!" some waiters would say. "I got the black table the last time. It's your turn!" And this sentiment isn't solely the provenance of white waiters. "We [African Americans] already have a bad stigma when we walk into a place," Anton told me. "And even with me, when I'd get a black person in my section, I'm like, 'Oh, no. Here we go.'" Cecil added, "A table of black people will walk into your buddies' station and you laugh at him. 'Ha Ha! Best of luck!' It's sad, but it happens."

So, right off the bat, African American customers are at a disadvantage when they walk into a restaurant. Now, some people have said that this sets up a self-fulfilling prophecy. If a black customer walks into a restaurant expecting bad service, and the server already thinks he or she's going to get a bad tip, bad things will happen. In 1999 a Japanese restaurant owner in Miami tacked a 15 percent tip onto a black couple's bill. When the couple compared notes with the white diners sitting next to them and discovered a tip had not been automatically added to their bill, they asked the owner why they had been singled out for this treatment. "You black people don't tip well!" the owner replied. Well, karma's a beautiful thing. The black couple complained, and the State of Florida sued the restaurant owner $15,000 for deceptive and unfair trade practices. So I guess it makes sense that African Americans would order takeout more often than going out to restaurants. Who wants to put up with that shit?

Before you conclude that blacks tip less and don't frequent restaurants because of prejudiced bad service, hold on. It's part of the story, but not all of it. When Dr. Lynn sampled customers of all races coming out of restaurants, asking them about the quality of service, the bill size, and the tips they left, he discovered that African Americans tended to rate the service slightly higher than whites but still tipped less. There are no easy answers here, folks!

So if socioeconomic factors and dining explain only a small part of why African Americans tip less, is education the answer? Back in 2003, Dr. Lynn suggested that restaurants begin a campaign to educate customers of all races as to what the standard tip in a restaurant is. He suggested printing tipping guidelines on the menu, putting out pamphlets—even having a game where people who tipped at least 15 percent would be eligible to win a prize. But would these efforts have an impact on the tipping habits of African Americans? Would they tip more? Dr. Lynn did a study recently to find out. The results were very interesting.

"If we eliminated black/white differences in the awareness of the tipping norm," he said, "and ff we made blacks as aware of the tipping norm as whites are, only about a third of the black/white difference in tipping would disappear." (That is a significant result.)

"So why did two thirds of the tipping difference remain?" I asked. "Why didn't blacks who were aware of the norm tip like whites?"

"I don't know," Dr. Lynn said. "I don't know how to explain it or eliminate it. Income and education is part of the story, but a very tiny portion. The bulk of the story I have yet to figure out." When pressed, he wouldn't even hazard a guess.

That two thirds really interested me. So I asked my African American server friends what they thought was going on.

"Some of it I think is ignorance," Anton told me. "Ignorance to a point where it becomes stubbornness."

"Well, I think at the end of the day it's a behavioral thing," Cecil said. "You know? That two thirds? I don't know. It's tough. Is it because there's a cheap gene in us?" he said, laughing. "I don't know. But in their [black people's] minds, you're the waiter; you're beneath me in a way. 'Cause it's sort of like slavery. Black people used to be slaves and they served people and 'How dare you take this job? Clearing people's dirty dishes?' They don't see the integrity and the professionalism behind the job."

When I asked if the experience and history of being black in America might be the reason why African Americans tipped less, Cecil replied, "For a lot of black people there's a chip on their shoulder. Everyone's out to get you. Especially for older black people who grew up in the sixties and had to go through what they went through. They have a different mind-set than younger black folks who have come up in a more integrated world. . . . Imagine now your mother's taking you out to dinner for a graduation party or something and you're going out to this fancy restaurant . . . How does she feel as an older black woman knowing that when she was growing up she could not be allowed in this kind of establishment? So there's a lot of psychological issues that are not being addressed, that need to be brought out."

There's a tongue-in-cheek video on YouTube by an African American male who goes by the handle "Mr. Offensive." "Psych!" he screams. "What the hell do you think been going on? Why do you think we don't tip? We've been giving your ass free food for four hundred years. . . . That's why we ain't tipping! What the hell do you think is going on? We built this country! And ya'll gonna talk about giving you all a tip? *You all still want money?* You all ain't getting it, baby . . . We ain't tipping nobody!" While this video was meant to be humorously provocative, it raises a valid point.

African Americans were once slaves. And tipping got a leg up in this country in part by the Pullman Car Company's exploitation of black men. In the 1950s, African Americans weren't allowed to eat in many of the same restaurants as whites. And even today, despite the fact that an African American holds the launch keys to our nation's nuclear arsenal, racism is still alive and well in America. Many African Americans live below the poverty line and are denied opportunities because of the color of their skin, and a wildly disproportionate number of black men are incarcerated in our prisons. As one guy told me, "It's tough being black in America." Can anger over past mistreatment be one of the reasons why African Americans tip less than whites?

When I shared this hypothesis with Dr. Lynn, he said he had no idea if this was the case. But he brought up an interesting point: African Americans tip a lower percentage than whites to *both* white and black servers.

"Does being a black waiter make it easier to deal with black customers?" I asked Cecil.

"Oh, it totally does."

"But does it change your tip compared to that of a white waiter?"

"No," he replied. So maybe anger is part of the story.

According to Dr. Lynn's study, the only thing we can say about African American customers is that they're twice as likely as whites to be unaware that the tipping norm is 15–20 percent, and that they tip 3 percent less than whites even when they perceive the quality of service to be the same and that one third of that difference disappears when their awareness of the tipping norm is the same as that of Caucasians. Unlike a waiter who sees a slice of life in one or two restaurants, Dr. Lynn has high confidence in his results after years of studying and sampling large populations. And the reasons many blacks don't tip, no matter how familiar they are with tipping norms? Well, that's a mystery. We can only speculate. Any other appellation applied to African American diners is probably the result of faulty logic or racist thinking.

Cecil told me that when he started out as a waiter he used to say, "Okay. Great. I got the black table." But as the years went by, he evolved beyond that mode of thinking. Now he knows that no matter what preconceptions he may have about a customer, they deserve his best. "You can never judge a book by its cover," he told me. "And people have surprised me."

As he mentioned, despite the tips, being a black server helps him wait on African American customers. "If you're a professional, you'll do what's expected of you. And the older waiters who've been in the business long enough understand that. What I usually do for my black tables is I go above and beyond; to explain and articulate the menu for them, give them that experience that this is something special. And hopefully that transcends into the tip. A lot of times it doesn't. But for the most part, I know I've done my job. I've educated them." Then he added, laughing, "Someone's got to do it."

"As hard as it may be," Anton said, "we have to grin and bear it and just make the experience the best, period. Even if they [black people] don't tip well this time, maybe this will stay in the back of their minds somewhere and next time somebody might be a beneficiary of a bigger tip."

Back in 1985, when I was seventeen years old, I used my dad's credit card to take a lovely young woman to dinner at the Brasserie in Baltimore. Nervous as hell, I didn't know which knife and fork to use, and the menu was in French and incomprehensible to me. Luckily for me, my waiter was a gem. He gallantly complimented my date, guided me through the menu, and made sure I didn't make an ass out of myself. And it was at the Brasserie, sitting by the front window as the rain fell outside, that I felt like an adult for the first time. I remember my date's red hair, the feel of her hand in mine, how she leaned across the table and planted a kiss on my lips. It's one of my happiest memories. But I'm fairly sure that, in my ignorance, I didn't tip that waiter. I wonder how he felt getting stiffed. Maybe he was angry. Or maybe, like Cecil and Anton, he chalked it up to fate and prayed I would know better the next time. So years later, when it was my karmic turn at the wheel as a server, I always had a soft spot for customers who seemed out of their element. Whether they were kids, poor folks who'd scrimped and saved enough to have a special night, black, white, Hispanic, gay or straight, I always tried to make their experience special. And did I get stiffed? You bet I did. But as Cecil said, I know I did my job. I educated them.

Waiters teach Americans of all colors, creeds, and persuasions how to tip. It's an awesome responsibility, when you think about it. No matter what the studies say, no matter what the stereotypes are, waiters should attend to all their customers, irrespective of race, with the same professionalism and care they would want in return. "Do unto others as you would want others to do unto you." If we all lived by those ancient words, racism and bigotry would be a thing of the past.

In a 2001 radio interview, Tavis Smiley, the African American talk show host, discussed black people and tipping. "I hate generalizations, but God knows it's true," he said. During the interview, Smiley said his mother was "one of the world's worst tippers," and she occasionally embarrassed him.

"This is reality, I think," he said. "Again, I hate to generalize, [but] I think it's true. The problem is that people don't want to discuss it because, if they discuss it, then we're going to accuse them of being racists. So this morning, rather than have the white folk tell us we're horrible tippers, let us have a conversation, shall we?"

So let's take this topic out of the darkness and move it into the light. Let's no longer talk about it in hushed, embarrassed tones. Like a family in therapy, healing can occur only when issues are brought out into the open. And we are one family, the *American* family.

Let's have a conversation, shall we?